EAST OF ISLINGTON

Sam Taylor

GIBSON SQUARE

London

This UK edition first published in 2010 by

Gibson Square

| UK | Tel: | +44 (0)20 7096 1100 |
| | Fax: | +44 (0)20 7993 2214 |

| US | Tel: | +1 646 216 9813 |
| | Fax: | +1 646 216 9488 |

| Eire | Tel: | +353 (0)1 657 1057 |

info@gibsonsquare.com
www.gibsonsquare.com

ISBN 978-1903933695

Contents

4. Religious Quarter / 91

Rite on Rev. Knocking on Heaven's Door. Last Supper Book Club. Dana International Relations. Book of Revelation. Loveable Mop-Heads. Twin Souls. Do-do L Ron-Ron. Make Mine a Monk. Scottish Assembly. Highland Fling.

5. Lovers Lane / 120

Seasonal Cheatings. Never-Never Land. Enchanted. Greek Goddess. Greek Gifts. Greek Ruins. www love.com. Shop Till You're Dropped. Current Affairs. Three Minute Wonder. 50 Ways to Leave Your Lover...

6. Kennel Club / 150

Babe Magnets. Guinea Foul. Obi Wan Kenobi. On the Buses. Hamster Reels. The Stud. Hedge Rows. Beggar's Belief. Single Mum. Who's the Daddy. Dangerous Dog Act. Snip. Willy's Last Stand. Bit Hairy...Foxed. Mad Dogs and Englishmen.

7. Parenting Classes / 191

Les Mums. New Car Cruelty. Chippy. The Anti-Climax. Southern Comfort. Brett the Bionic Maori. Head Girl. Boy George. Liam Neeson is Missing.

Dedicated to Mark
and in memory of two furry old friends,
Poppy and Willy.

1

Neighbourhood Watch

In the Beginning
It was cheap. And it had a garden, or a least half a garden. For a girl with no money and a dog it was the perfect flat. By the time I took my first official steps over the pile of discarded mail in the communal hallway, it was too late to worry what the neighbours might be like. But the estate agent's reaction should have given me some clue. 'The area is supposed to be up-and-coming,' he said, as he handed over the keys. 'Although I wouldn't bank on it.'

But what did I care? It was the beginning of a whole new chapter: new home, new friends, new life. I didn't need a smart postcode. Besides, how bad could it be? The screaming started about an hour later.

Tuneless and disturbing, it sounded like a man being systematically tortured somewhere towards the back of the building, precariously close to my newly purchased patch of shrubs. Emboldened by two glasses of celebratory wine and a recently acquired proprietorial air, I pushed my way out the back door, past the overgrown ivy and onto the cracked patio. Handily, although this was not necessarily one of the flat's unique selling points, I could now see quite clearly that the so-called sleepy synagogue next door was very much open for business and fitted with 24-hour Nasa-grade neon lighting. In fact, it was pumping out enough wattage to illuminate the whole neighbourhood. The other revelation was the newly erected scaffolding that bore the sign of a roof replacement company – a small detail the previous owner had omitted to mention in the hand-over notes.

As I approached the tubular structure, the tuneless screeching grew louder and louder, occasionally giving way to a kind of slapping sound, intermittently broken by the noise of someone shouting the word: 'Cheeky!' I stood there for a while, clasping my glass of Jacob's Creek and wondering if perhaps I might be better off calling the police. But as I'd only just moved in, and announcing my arrival with a flashing blue light might have seemed a bit showy, I went for being bold instead.

'Hello,' I called out tentatively. 'Is everything all right up there?' Silence fell, quickly followed by a sudden out-burst of raucous laughter. Looking up, I spotted a man clad as a pirate, straddling a plank and handcuffed to one of the scaffold poles two storeys up. Behind him was a slightly larger man decked out as Nelson who appeared to be waving what looked like a lurid-pink rubber glove attached to a small broom handle. I had just met the neighbours, or at least two of them.

'Hello darleeng,' the one dressed as Nelson boomed down at me. 'Welcome to our humble home,' he said, waving the lurid-pink implement. 'We wondered who we were going to get.'

He was in the arts, an opera singer to be exact, and they had just returned from giving their very best during a rendition of *The Pirates Of Penzance*, the populist version. Hence the Nelson outfit and the rubber-on-broom-handle thing, a prop apparently, something he called his 'Mr Whippy'. 'Very popular with that section of the audience who like things a little bit more panto,' he said. 'Needs must, darleeng.'

Apparently singing just wasn't enough these days. The captive pirate was his partner, a dancer, Dazzling Darren to his friends, his lycra-clad legs much in demand with the fee-paying public. 'We like to give them a bit more of a show...' the opera singer continued, by way of explanation. He could see that things might look a bit odd from where I was standing but the scaffold planks were perfect for practising pirate manoeuvres and the handcuffs were only there for added security. And authenticity, of course. 'After all, he is a naughty pirate, darleeng'.

They wondered if I wanted to have a drink. I could just shin up the scaffold and join them. 'Like Catwoman,' Dazzling Darren suggested. 'We might even have a costume somewhere,' they both chimed, warming to their new theme. I thanked them but said that I thought I'd had enough excitement for one day and was going to go and get my head down. 'Lucky you,' they squealed, and with that the slap-and-tickle of populist opera resumed as I hurried back inside to check my lease.

The following morning the door-bell rang. On the

doorstep was the roofing contractor with a pair of hand-cuffs and the 'Mr Whippy' prop in his hand. 'Hello, babe,' he said. 'Please tell me these are yours.'

The Course of True Love

Unlike my other male neighbours, it seemed Piano Pete was not a confirmed bachelor. He was simply a man who couldn't get a girl. 'Do you know any available women?' he asked when we first met on the front steps. He wasn't too picky, but he did have quite specific needs. The lucky girl had to be able to get married, quickly, and then pro-duce a bountiful crop of children, in rapid succession. And she had to be younger than him, although from first impressions, that would appear to include most of the city.

Apparently it was a problem that had been bothering him ever since his father, the Air Commodore, had announced that he was going to bequeath his entire estate to those of his offspring considerate enough to give him grandchildren. His two siblings were already delivering and Piano Pete was growing increasingly nerv-ous.

It wasn't easy, he explained over his kitchen table. He was a white, middle-class, almost middle-aged man with no real visible means of support. And he was straight. In this neighbourhood that wasn't hugely helpful. The tra-ditional avenues of entrapment were just not working for him so he had decided to seek expert help. He had consulted Dr Chuck, an American relationship guru who came from Florida and sported an orange tan. Apparently Dr Chuck worked, or 'concentrated on his technique' as he preferred to put it, for only three months of the year. 'Any longer, and my powers would diminish,' he had explained on his website.

The cost of a two-day course was £375. 'But what price do you put on loving success?' challenged the accompanying literature. From Piano Pete's point of view, it was a small investment that he had hoped would yield a much larger return.

In a smart London hotel suite, he had joined several other hopefuls desperate to find out where they were going wrong. 'Don't blame yourselves,' Dr Chuck had assured them over complimentary coffee. 'There are simple reasons why love eludes you and I am here to explain them,' he continued. Over the course of the morning, these simple reasons were slowly revealed.

There was the man from Birmingham who kept seven Afghan hounds in his two-bedroom flat without a garden. There was the 43-year-old geography teacher from Luton with an Antonio Banderas fixation that extended to a 6ftx8ft poster above her bed. There was the couple from Harlow who hated each other and were hoping to find someone interested in a swap. Then there was the man who only bathed once a month who was forced to sit a long way from the five women looking for millionaires.

'I can help you all,' Dr Chuck had assured them. 'It might take more than one course, though,' he added, pointing out that recidivists qualified for reduced rates. Piano Pete positioned himself at the back of the room, scanning for a woman who might fit his bill. 'Have your love radar on,' Dr Chuck had encouraged them. It was a line that Piano Pete was taking literally.

In the lunch break, those searching for love mingled

over the triangular-cut sandwiches. After a while, an attractive young woman approached Piano Pete. 'Hi,' she said. 'My name is Valerie.' She was a 29-year-old lapsed Catholic who worked for a third world charity and was in the market for a husband who would give her children.

Piano Pete grabbed her arm. 'Me too,' he said swiftly, as he saw the Afghan fancier approaching. 'I mean, I'm in the market for a wife. And fast.' Strangely, she seemed undeterred by his desperation and they exchanged knowing glances right through Dr Chuck's afternoon session, called 'Say What You Want'.

On the second day they were asked to work in twos. So, not wanting to miss any opportunities, Piano Pete quickly sidled up to Valerie. 'Shall we?' he asked, pointing to two chairs paired together away from the throng. The session was called 'State Your Desires', and Pete wasted no time in explaining that he really wanted a wife, badly, and at least two children, preferably sons. None of this seemed to be a problem for Valerie. Her own desires, however, were marginally more complicated.

'I would need my husband to give up alcohol,' she told him. 'He would also have to be circumcised and we would have to become Muslims on our wedding day.' Valerie believed that the world's problems would be cured if we diluted the Islamic issue by undertaking mass conversion.

'After all,' she explained cheerily, 'If everyone in the world was fat, no one would think it was a problem.' Even Piano Pete could see that perhaps Valerie was a problem. But on other hand, she was attractive and clearly willing. He just wasn't sure how this paradigm shift would go down at home. In short, would he still get the money?

He asked her to excuse him for a moment, as he had to make an important phone call. The Air Commodore answered swiftly and Piano Pete explained that he had met a girl who was attractive, but demanding. His father welcomed him to the real world.

Piano Pete then casually recounted her bizarre list of relationship prerequisites and wondered if his father had any objections. There was a long pause before the old man replied. 'I don't mind you getting your todger cut off,' he said. 'But I draw the line at having a teetotaller in the house.'

Lying Doggo

Weirdie Woman was the owner of the other half of the garden – in as much as it had been billed as a shared garden – except sharing wasn't her specialist subject. Her moniker, tough but, I later realised, quite fair, had been handed to me by the previous owner on a post-it note taped to my back door. *'Beware Weirdie Woman,'* it had said, with an arrow pointing upwards.

Her flat, sandwiched between the costume-loving Gay Opera Singer upstairs and my basement below, was something of a social no-go zone I later came to realise. Not that she took very long in coming down and introducing herself. Far from it: 48 hours after moving in, she was loudly banging on the door, an act designed purely to make Poppy my Westie run through her entire barking repertoire – as a dog, it was really her only job and she loved doing it. I opened the door. 'Oh, I didn't know you had a dog ...' Weirdie Woman said, lying.

'It's my Dad's ...' I replied, also lying. (Why do we always blame our parents?) I explained that the dog was just staying with me while he got better.

'I wonder if we could talk about the garden,' she said, unmoved. 'And which part of it you think is yours.'

It was 8am on a Saturday morning. I had a raging hangover. She wasn't there to talk 'garden', she was there to talk 'dog'. Dogs were a murky area in the lease and she had read hers, thoroughly. Still, we both pretended it was about garden carve-up and we fought our way out there. Poppy trotted dutifully behind. Once on the turf, Poppy acted like she'd never seen a lawn before, like I had never taken her to Dog Poo Park and proceeded to make full use of this expansive new bathroom. Weirdie Woman was agog. All the evidence of dog danger she needed pooped out before her.

Desperate, I said that the poor animal had been very badly affected by my father's affliction. 'What's wrong with your father then?' she asked.

'He's a manic-depressive alcoholic and he's gone into a rehabilitation centre for treatment. That's why I've got the dog.' I said.

As far as my father was aware he was playing golf in Bushey, but in a parallel universe, who knew? This really had her stumped. 'And the dog is his only friend.' (They'd met once.)

'So you see I have to look after her in the hope that he'll pull through.' (With his handicap he had a good chance.)

Weirdie Woman backed away from me like I was a bad case history from Jerry Springer. She said that under the circumstances the dog could stay as long as necessary, that she realised that all families face problems, and while she was not a pet lover, she could understand that they might fulfil some kind of strange role. However, I was not to let the dog anywhere near what she described as the 'rose bed' and there were to be no barbecues. I assured her that the latter shouldn't be a problem; Poppy struggled to answer her own name so I felt certain that marinating chicken legs might be beyond her.

That afternoon I broke the news of my father's illness to my father. He didn't take it too badly and even suggested running stark bollock naked around the disputed territory for the price of a bottle of Scotch. In truth, the story hadn't been too much of an exaggeration. Later I replayed the moving tableau to the Gay Opera Singer and Dazzling Darren, who in turn filled in Matt Boomy, their lodger, a man who lost everything in the Eighties except his Stonyhurst accent.

It was perceived as a victory, a first even. I was applauded. Apparently the previous owner wasn't allowed to even stand on the patio for the last two years of his occupation. So, result.

Some days later, Weirdie Woman caught me taking the bins out.

'Is your father out of the clinic yet?' she asked, staring down at the bothersome animal by my heel. I couldn't quite remember where I was up to with the lie that allowed Poppy to stay in the basement I had paid a fair sum of money for, so I decided to continue improvising. I could have decided to challenge her on the lease but that really did seem like hard work. Easier to stick with the Jerry Springer script. 'They let him out for Christmas but sadly it didn't go too well,' I explained, patting the dog. 'And now he's taking drugs.' Weirde Woman looked fairly startled at this latest revelation. 'What kind of drugs...?' she asked. I panicked, trying to imagine what kind of recreational drugs a 67-year-old retired engineer would be into, but there was no going back. If I said he was okay, the dog would have to go.

'Glue,' I said, finally. 'He sniffs glue. It's all the rage amongst confused old people.'

Before this absurd narrative could develop any further, Cambridge arrived and immediately twigged that we were in the middle of a drama – he had been in Footlights, which always comes in handy. After we had safely closed the door behind us, he said he thought that perhaps I had gone too far, but maybe not far enough, with the glue-sniffing. Clearly, he said, I was facing a classic script impasse. You don't really want to kill the character, he explained, but they can never appear on screen again. Or if they do, they have to come back as somebody else.

So what do I do with my dad, I asked him. 'Simple,' he said. 'Tell her he's been kidnapped by aliens and you are negotiating for his release. That the government are helping but they are being very slow. That should get her off your back for a bit.' It might even earn her the right to hand over the Weirdie Woman mantle.

Good Catch?

Every girl needs a boy, and Poppy was no exception. She had been allowing Willy, a frisky border terrier, to regularly shower her with unconditional love and attention for some time now. Willy's Walker and I had therefore spent quite some hours strolling through the local park, each attached to the leads of our respective pooches when he finally made his move.

'I wondered,' he mumbled, 'if perhaps you might like to come to France, for a holiday?' True, we had consumed several dinners together, and on occasion had even indulged in an overnight trip to the seaside, for the sake of the dogs of course. But a holiday. In France. This was uncharted territory.

'Will we be completely alone?' I asked. There was a long pause. 'Actually, no,' he replied. It turned out there would be around eleven other people, although they wouldn't be there all the time and we would only have to see them during the day. In fact, I wouldn't have to see them at all if I didn't feel like it. He would quite understand.

Apparently it was some kind of specialist group outing. Not really the sort of thing that he would go on usually, but the rate had been good and he thought the idea of a tour through Bordeaux and Samur might appeal. 'We wouldn't be taking the dogs,' he added. 'So in that sense we would be on our own.'

Eventually I decided to go. After all, my summer holiday alternatives were limited. And anyway, what had I got to lose?

Things started to go wrong at Dover. The boot was popped in a routine customs search and the false bottom lifted. Willy's Walker had been less than truthful with me. His newly cleaned, smart, sporty German automobile was full of the contraband designed to send most sensitive women into hysterical paralysis – cricket gear.

Not wishing to make a scene, I refrained from

screaming until we were firmly locked inside *Le Shuttle*.
'What,' I screeched, 'are all those bats and balls doing
there?'

But I knew what it meant. I was a woman on a cricket tour. Women on cricket tours get to sit on the side-
lines. They get to lay out the crockery and cutlery for tea.
They get to clap and mutter words of congratulation and
condolence when something happens on the great green
yonder.

Nothing, but nothing, happens at a cricket match that
can be deemed of any interest to any woman who still
has a firm grasp of her faculties. Occasionally, a middle-
aged man gets injured attempting the kind of flying
manoeuvre that forced Nadia Comaneci to retire from
international gymnastics, while the other players stand
around muttering something about silly legs. But mostly
nothing happens. And then they have tea.

In Bordeaux they had tea. In Samur they had tea. In
fact, wherever we went they had tea and mumbled to
each other about the position and condition of their silly
legs. But mostly they drank tea, for their country. At the
end of the games they awarded each other cups – the
French hosts heartily thanking the British visitors for
travelling all that way to take tea with them and the
British visitors roundly applauding the size and magni-
tude of the teas provided, and so it went on, all over
France.

On the last night of our romantic holiday à *deux*
(with eleven other people), Willy's Walker took me to an
incredibly expensive, chic, romantic restaurant. I sensed
that he had been itching to ask me something all day.
Perhaps this was it. Perhaps the French air had got to

him and he was about to pop the question. Perhaps this is why he had brought me on this romantic holiday *à deux* (with eleven other people).

I was suddenly in a blind panic. How would it affect Poppy? Should I say 'yes' or 'no'? Unable to contain himself any longer, Willy's Walker leant over the candlelit table, lowered his eyes and spoke: 'Darling?' he said. 'Yes?' I smiled back nervously. 'Can I ask you something?' he continued. 'Please do,' I urged. 'I don't suppose that you noticed that I took the best catch of my life this afternoon did you?' The answer was definitely 'no'.

Parking Lottery

Sultan, the garagista on the opposite side of the road, rarely spoke to us. It wasn't that he was unfriendly; it was just that he rarely spoke. Or if he did, it was in Turkish, so then we rarely replied.

Nobody in our house had much in the way of cars. I drove an ageing red 2CV, when it felt like starting, but that didn't really do it for Sultan. No, often the lack of communication was simply a matter of motoring ergonomics. Sultan spent most of his waking hours with his head rammed inside the bonnets of broken-down cars; ageing BMWs usually, but he wasn't fussy.

His welding torch constantly whirring above the din of Radio One, occasionally he would surface, smile, and wave a greasy palm in our direction, but mostly he was focused on a quest to fill the street with yet more crushed and rusting carcasses.

It was never clear why Sultan arrived, nor why he stayed. After all, no one ever saw any of his customers drive away their vehicles. In fact, his preferred means of completing a job seemed to be the scrap yard truck, but still desperate owners continued to come, and once a year he would have a bargain clear-out sale.

The assorted innards of various engines would be strewn over the pavement and a collection of anoraks would descend on the street in search of the impossible dream: a clutch fitting for a 1974 Ford Capri, for instance.

Otherwise, things were pretty much mundane. As I said, he rarely spoke. But recently, life had taken a dramatic turn and Sultan had become extremely vocal. It had coincided with a notification from the council that we were to be given the dubious gift of a controlled parking zone.

For the price of a cheap flight to Barcelona, residents East of Islington would be allowed to do what they had always done, i.e. park their cars outside their houses. Or at least outside someone else's house if that person had foolishly decided to take their car out for a spin and failed to place their dustbin in its place.

True, it had never been easy. The ratio of cars to parking spaces had always been a confusing equation, especially in our street, particularly the end opposite Sultan's emporium, but we had managed.

Mostly, any disagreements were resolved with a half-hearted exchange of expletives and a stand-off.

For Sultan, with upwards of 20 cars scattered along the street, parking rage was all in a day's work. Besides, he had his 'boy' on permanent look-out for any openings. As soon as a glimmer of the black stuff became visible, he filled it, immediately.

For a small fee, and as long as it didn't inconvenience

Sultan, the 'boy' would also 'reserve' a spot for a local. In return, we rarely complained about his illegal Sunday opening hours.

However, the council officials were not interested in such parochial bargaining. They wanted hard cash, and they wanted it now. The new traffic wardens had been fitted for their uniforms and the finance department had already budgeted for the added revenue flow.

Most of us faced the inevitable and coughed up. Some made a principled stand against what they saw as yet more bureaucratic control. Petitions were raised, councillors lobbied, rabbis consulted, but it was a losing battle. It wasn't so much their gains they were looking forward to, as our losses.

For Sultan, it spelt penury. Within two days of the new regulations, he had incurred £600 in parking fines. None of it made any sense to him, not least because they were all written in English.

Then, pretty soon, things started to get very complicated. Not content with collecting a mere £50 each time they issued a ticket, and £100 if you didn't pay immediately, the council upped the ante. They brought in a tow truck. For Sultan, it was the final straw.

He watched, confused, as the neon-jacketed attendants craned a customer's exhausted Nissan Micra onto the rear of their new vehicle. A cursory look down the street suggested that they would be back for his remaining 17 cars.

'Why do you do this?' he asked them, bewildered. It was an existential question really, to which there seemed to be no answer. The neon jacketed parking attendants, however, gave it a go. 'You're in the zone now, mate,' they replied, firmly. But for Sultan, and the rest of us, it continued to make no sense.

Would they, he wondered, be bringing the car back later? '£250 and it's yours again,' they said. Sultan looked at them, incredulous, before bursting into hysterical laughter. 'No, thank you,' he replied courteously. 'I'd have to pay £50 to have it taken away.' And at that moment it finally made sense to us all. As far as the parking restrictions went, it was the twilight zone.

Lebensraum

The doorbell rang. Outside were two smiling faces from the local police station. 'Hello, madam, we're from the Community Section,' they whispered. 'We understand there has been some trouble with the neighbours?'

It wasn't exactly trouble with the neighbours; rather, trouble with the neighbours' letterbox. The trouble had started off as a kind of whimper, but very quickly there was no mistaking it. There was a 'Help me, help me!' noise emanating from the front door at number 32.

A quick straw poll of assorted residents revealed that nothing much was really known about the people at number 32, except that they were German, and, possibly due to the synagogue at the top of the street, they usually kept a low profile. But the low-profile vow seemed to be off that morning, as they were positively hollering through the letterbox while simultaneously rattling a toothbrush from side to side through the opening.

Mrs Eisenhower had been the first to hear it. 'Hello, hello, can you come over here, please?' the normally reticent Germans had implored. Unfortunately, they had picked the wrong person. Mrs Eisenhower, ever on the lookout for the Communist invasion, immediately demanded the authorities be called. Willy's Walker, who was trying his best to exit the street without getting involved in the letterbox saga, eventually agreed to call Plod while Mrs Eisenhower kept a lookout for what she described as 'any unexpected manoeuvres'.

By the time the police arrived, Willy's Walker was nowhere to be seen. Having already suffering the indignity of phoning 999 and describing the ludicrous scene, he felt he had performed his civic duty. So I faced Plod alone.

They wanted us to get them out of there, I explained. We thought about calling a locksmith, but we weren't sure. What if they were burglars, or worse? Plod immediately seized on this theory. Our fantastical little scene had suddenly turned into a potentially violent life-threatening situation, one for which they would surely have to call for back-up – a helicopter and several squad cars at the very least.

'You're quite right, madam,' they concurred. 'They might have robbed the place and got stuck inside. They've probably done it before. Did they ask anyone if they had a spare key?' It's true, they had asked Mrs Eisenhower if she had a spare key, but I thought that this was simply an act of common sense. She was, after all, the next-door neighbour. 'Aha,' they smiled. 'We could have a right pair of con artists here, madam.'

The voices coming from the letterbox had now reached auditorium proportions. From our vantage point at the bottom of the steps, we watched as the younger of the two community policemen knelt before the letterbox and proceeded to remove his peaked cap before gently coaxing the toothbrush out of their hands and carefully placing it in a plastic bag for evidence. It took a little time – they had been calling for assistance for over two hours now – but finally the toothbrush duo gave up their story. They had been staying with the Germans and had said farewell to their college chums at around 8am. With their train not leaving till lunchtime, they had decided against leaving the house with their hosts, instead opting for catching a few more minutes of English culture by watching the end of breakfast television. They now realised this was a big mistake, in more ways than one.

Packed and ready to go, they had entered the tiny communal hallway and closed the flat door behind them, before being hit with the terrifying truth. The street door was double-locked, and they had no key. They were trapped in a tiny vestibule, hundreds of miles from their home in Baden Baden. It had been mounting hysteria and a lack of any other implement that had forced them to shove the toothbrush through the letterbox. They weren't incompetent burglars, or members of some bizarre cult hell-bent on attacking the world through the letterbox at number 32: They were just tourists desperate to leave East of Islington. And who could blame them?

To help make them more comfortable until someone with a key arrived, Gay Opera Singer bought them a can of Coca-Cola and two straws so they could sip through the letterbox. 'Oh, darleengs,' he purred. 'It's just like Cavaradossi's prison scene in *Tosca*.' Two sets of eyes stared out at him, blankly, through the rectangular gap. 'We just want to go home,' they whimpered. 'Oh no, really,' he continued. 'You must think of this as your home.' It took a whole box of man-size to stem the flow of their tears.

Gay Grass

Gay Opera Singer didn't like to think of himself as a supergrass. Super maybe, 'grass' certainly not. But every man has his limits. He had been walking the tightrope of neighbourly relations for many years and something had finally snapped.

It wasn't that he didn't like the Hassidic rabbis who occupied the synagogue next door. With their Volvos, elaborate silverware, ceremonial candles and stunning fur hats for Saturday best, as the 'chief rabbi' was fond of saying, 'What's not to like?'

In short, as style gurus went, Gay Opera Singer felt they were in a league of their own. But devoutly religious as the group may have been, they did seem to be lacking a spirit level. Or not one that they had ever felt compelled to employ during their many sorties into 'home expansion' market.

To date, the Rabbis had added an underground car park that was without proper foundation and on a 30-degree angle, so that collisions were unavoidable. Hence the Volvos. They had also created two side-access gateways, neither of which opened, and a front-porch extension that forced visitors to scramble up a ziggurat of milk crates in order to enter the building. On many levels, not only the spirit one, Gay Opera Singer felt it just wasn't kosher.

The week before the builders had returned, accompanied by a hardcore pneumatic digger and a swiftly erected tarpaulin tent. Night and day they dug under their makeshift cover, skip after skip filled to the brim with London's finest clay, until finally Gay Opera Singer snapped and called the planning department. It was a number that he knew off by heart. He was almost on the Christmas card list.

Farouk at Planning said it was nice to hear from him again, it had been a while, and they were wondering how he was getting on. Gay Opera Singer thanked him and said that things had been fine. He'd had lots of work and his Pinkerton had been very well received, but unfortunately his creative impulses had now been rudely interrupted. Farouk sighed. It was the same MO every phone call.

He would listen attentively, as Gay Opera Singer detailed the latest transgression. Farouk would go through the motions of checking whether planning permission had been applied for. It had not. Then he would ask whether Gay Opera Singer might consider making a written complaint. He would not. Farouk would then sigh again. No written complaint, no way of sending round a member of the 'enforcement team'. No visit from the enforcement team, no halt to the bad building design.

However, there was now a third way. In a bid to encourage neighbours to tell tales on each other, the council had decided to make the written complaints procedure anonymous. Gay Opera Singer said he was keen. Farouk said great, he would email over a complaints form. Gay Opera Singer asked how anonymous was that? After all, Farouk would have his personal email address and Gay Opera Singer was anxious not to be labelled a 'grass'.

Farouk said not to worry, his secret would be safe with them.

Within minutes, the form had arrived and Gay Opera Singer had completed it in some detail, confidently ticking the box guaranteeing anonymity before sending it back.

Later that afternoon, he was staring out of his sitting room window when he saw two men pull up, one of whom was holding a clipboard. The 'enforcement team' had arrived. The builders, who were just packing up for the day, walked over to greet them. The newly formed group chatted for several minutes before the shorter of the officials took a photograph of the inside of the tent. Gay Opera Singer was ecstatic – it was surely a good sign.

Then the short official turned and pointed directly at his house. This was undoubtedly a bad sign. Gay Opera Singer ducked, but it was too late. They had seen him and were approaching, watched intently by the builders. Two minutes later, the men from the council were knocking at his door, and Gay Opera Singer was frantically dialling Farouk's number.

'You said I wouldn't be identified,' he screamed down the phone, having explained that he now had two council officials outside his front door. 'Oh, they just want to say hi,' Farouk replied. 'And thank you for your community spirit. Apparently the builders were very grateful.'

Gay Opera Singer said he found that difficult to believe and looked out the window at the workmen. In any other circumstances he might have felt that two men mooning at him had a certain charm. However, in this instance, the word GRASS fibre-tipped on their abutting buttocks did little to raise his expectations. But he asked the council official if he could borrow their camera anyway.

Can't Drive for Toffee

It had started off innocently enough. A trip to the garden centre, accompanied by the Sixties Starlet, who was the closest thing to Norma Desmond that East of Islington had to offer. The dogs, Poppy and Willy, had come along for the ride. The weather was still warm, the car was running smoothly, and there was a special offer on winter-flowering pansies. So, all in all, it was a perfectly charming, almost normal, early autumn outing.

And then the Sixties Starlet spotted the toffees on the dashboard. 'Ooh, toffees,' she purred in her mockney accent. 'I 'aven't 'ad a toffee in years. Do you mind?' It was a mixed bag, flavoured, with four choices – rum, Brazil nut, cream and brandy. Not exactly what you would call upmarket, but they did the job.

I chose cream, although I knew from experience they all tasted the same. The Sixties Starlet chose rum. 'Luverly,' were her last words before speaking became a momentary impossibility. For a good few seconds we crawled along in the traffic, our mouths working hard to flatten the tough sugary substance clinging to our jaws. The dogs whined pitifully for the chance to chew the empty wrappers. Radio Two buzzed in and out of reception.

Then, without warning, our sweet little scene suddenly turned very sour. With no announcement, the Sixties

Starlet stopped chewing, wound down her window and lobbed her toffee out of the moving car. 'Taken my bloody filling out,' she moaned. 'I knew there was a reason why I hadn't had a toffee in years.' Discreetly, I quickly swallowed my own half-macerated lump and apologised profusely, vowing only to stock soft centres in future.

We continued to crawl along while the Sixties Starlet used her tongue to perform a reconnaissance search of the inside of her mouth. The report back was not good. 'Christ, the toffee's taken two teeth with it,' she said, her tongue sunk into a cavernous hole in her rear-molar section.

'You'll have to get out and get it,' I said, 'before it gets run over.' I applied the brakes, stopped the car and waited. All around irate motorists started beeping their horns as the Sixties Starlet retraced our route up the road.

Knees bent, back hunched, eyes on the ground, and rising occasionally to make European hand signals at the screeching drivers, Sixties Starlet, by some miracle, found the abandoned toffee lying by the kerb six cars back, the missing teeth sticking out of it like a bizarre mini-sculpture. Relieved, she returned to the car and proudly held up the startling concoction.

The toffee itself was very flat; she had done an excellent job on the chewing. And the teeth looked, well, like teeth really. Through shock, I suppose, she tried fixing them back into her jaw with the toffee still attached. It wasn't a good look.

'I don't think that's going to work,' I said sympathetically. 'Perhaps we should go to the dentist.' Sixties

Starlet had been going to the same dentist since, well, the Sixties. It was uptown and private. The waiting room was half-full of other Sixties survivors, all wearing dark glasses and features they hadn't been born with. We sat, quietly, in the corner, with the teeth/toffee combo held aloft, delicately balanced on its original wrapper.

It seemed inconceivable to me that something could be done with it, but Sixties Starlet was adamant. 'He's seen everything, babe,' she said. 'Road-kill toffee-teeth are nuthin'.' Quite what went on in the Sixties has never been properly explained to me, but apparently this dentist had been there through it all, building bridges over troubled waters.

His nurse came outside and ushered us in. The dentist looked like living death, but with a suntan. He took the half-mauled sweetie with its attached two teeth and dropped them into a bowl of specially-prepared toffee-melting fluid. While we waited for the chemical separation to occur, Sixties Starlet recounted her story. 'Wow,' he said, at the end of it. 'What a trip, man.' He wasn't wrong there.

Deluged with Acclaim

Gay Opera singer and Dazzling Darren had been planning an operatic soirée upstairs for several months. The great and the good of the artistic community were (hopefully) going to be there. With split-second timing, they had rehearsed every move of the proceedings. There were to be no mishaps and definitely no ad-libbing. The placement settled, the musical accompaniment softly playing, the champagne cooling in the fridge, everything was ready for the arrival of the first guest. By the end of it all, Gay Opera Singer and Dazzling Darren expected nothing less than a standing ovation and several hefty investment cheques for their little company's forthcoming season.

And, should anyone be less than generous with the cheque-book the couple felt sure that the new costumes for *Rigoletto* should swing things. 'Who can resist thigh-length leather boots, darleeng?' Gay Opera Singer had cooed, while stroking the specially liveried items.

And then, just as they were putting the final touches to their already word-perfect presentation, the doorbell went. Nobody who was anybody was quite that fashionably early. So the shrill sound emanating from the buzzer could only mean one thing – a change to the evening's programme.

There, standing on the doorstep, was Mr Singh-Singh, the normally quiet and retiring next-door neighbour, a look of alarm set firmly on his face. He was terribly sorry to intrude, he explained, but there was an emergency. There seemed to be a flood in their garden, and the water was more than three feet high. Mrs Singh-Singh was extremely worried. 'She has seen the shed, floating,' he whispered. 'And it's not one of her visions.'

Barely able to contain his irritation, but not wanting to appear rude, Gay Opera Singer followed him over to the drawing room window. A cursory look downwards revealed all. Three feet of water, and rising, was indeed lapping around the adjoining houses. The esteemed guests might have to swim for their supper.

'There is nothing in the script about a moat,' Dazzling Darren sobbed. 'And it's too late to write one in now,' he added petulantly. There was no alternative. Someone was going to have to plunge in and relieve the obstruction that appeared to be blocking the main drain.

Mr Singh-Singh objected on religious grounds, and Dyno Rod were going to take too long (while Willy's Walker and I were out for the evening, mercifully), and so, as they had the most to lose, the task fell to Gay Opera Singer and Dazzling Darren.

As the only access was over Mr Singh-Singh's garden wall, he kindly offered the services of his ladder, although he had little in the way of tools. Thankfully they had the props cupboard.

Armed with two papier-mâché swords, one plastic breastplate, and with Dazzling Darren clad in the thigh-length *Rigoletto* crowd-pleasers, the unlikely DIY duo headed for the garden. 'Show it the sword, darleeng,' Gay Opera Singer bellowed as Dazzling Darren waded around in the muddy water. 'Swash and buckle, sweetie, swash and buckle,' he enthused.

But, thrash as he might in the muddy waters, the obstruction was refusing to budge. By now there was quite a crowd. Even Mr Eisenhower had taken a seat centre-stage. 'Poke it, boy, poke it,' he shouted, with no sense of irony.

Eventually there was only one option open to him. Dazzling Darren was forced to strip off, save for the boots, and plunge, headfirst into the murky depths. Like Jacques Cousteau in a watery panto, he bobbed up and down alongside what had once been the Singh-Singhs' decking, searching for salvation.

Finally, he emerged, triumphant, his sword held aloft, the unspeakable and unidentifiable contents of the drain skewered by its papier-mâché tip. 'My hero,' squealed

Gay Opera Singer. In his elation, he too stripped off, and plunged into the now-subsiding lake.

The triumphant water-warriors preened themselves, lapping up each new encore from the assembled neighbours with renewed gusto. But then, as they rose from yet another bow, it hit them. Their guests had arrived, and it was fair to say that the pair had been caught with their breeches down.

Startled by the scene that greeted them, the artistic community's great and the good simply stood and stared. Gay Opera Singer, however, didn't miss a beat. 'It's *Rigoletto Riverdance*, darleengs,' he called out to them. 'The crowds will love it,' he added. And, as if on cue, the grateful neighbours screamed for a further encore.

For the great and the good, it was a tricky moment. Only a moment, though. 'Populism, luvvies,' one of them whispered to the others discreetly. 'Bums on seats.' It was all the direction the rest of the party needed. 'Love it,' they shouted back, their cheque-books spontaneously performing a Mexican wave.

Fungus Gets Married

It came as a something of shock to his friends that someone had agreed to marry my friend Fungus, a man who claimed to be supernaturally attuned to female *parfum* of any kind, yet doused himself in athlete's-foot powder every day.

And it was an even greater shock that this deluded creature was a stunning beauty, a member of the Scottish aristocracy, with a long list of letters before and after her name. In fact, there were some for whom the potential injustice about to be served was just too much to bear. As the unsuspecting bride glided gracefully down the aisle there were audible murmurs of 'Run! Run!' from Fungus's female friends, who were unable to contain their better instincts.

Her relatives sat expectantly on the right-hand side of the church. There wasn't a cheap hat or threadbare sporran among them: they had come down from the Highlands in all their finery to see their girl handed over to a member of London's conservative elite. In reality they were greeted by the sight of Fungus attired in a nine-piece, orange-check suit complemented by patent spats and a fob watch embellished with a cameo portrait of himself.

As anyone who knew him was fully aware, there was nothing Fungus liked more than gazing at his own image, a hobby that came as quite a shock to the official photographer, who was eventually reduced to physically abusing the groom in order to squeeze the new bride into the rose-tinted photographs.

Her hand-woven, ivory, silk-organza gown looked priceless, a fact not wasted on her new husband; by the end of the reception behind her back he was busy taking orders for cheap copies for delivery by his trusty Taiwanese tailor. The more business he could generate, the greater the reduction in his own annual couture bill, a not inconsiderable sum of money.

Meanwhile, no expense had been spared by the bride's proud parents. The reception was a lavish affair. A Raj-style banquet was laid on and champagne of the highest quality was quaffed by the bucket-load. The man conscripted to video the event for posterity was notably diligent here, but he was ably abetted by several other characters from Fungus's nefarious past. On more than one occasion, a former lap dancer had to be dragged out from under the top table, where she was boldly attempting to reveal a Scotsman's secret. A feat he found neither appetising nor original.

The bride's father's heart-warming speech had obviously been prepared for the day his daughter married an upstanding member of the community. This, clearly, had not happened. But gallantly, he attempted to ignore the disintegrating scene, and deliver the speech anyway – protocol was protocol. There wasn't a dry eye on their side of the room. 'How much worse can it get?' the increasingly distraught Scots sobbed.

Unfortunately, many of their number had no idea that Fungus had insisted on organising the entertainment himself, with the result that he, personally, was going to sing, for a full 40 minutes, at his own wedding. Despite a petition signed by more than 50 people, including the bride.

But first there was to be the best man's speech, given by Mr Engel, a leading member of London's haut literati, a normally easy-going fellow who had agreed to speak against his own better judgement, and that of his agents. 'I have known the groom for a long time,' he started. 'But only because he still owes me money.'

Mr Engel settled into his flow. 'I'd like to thank the bride's father for his hospitality, and to applaud his liberal attitude. It's not every father who wants his girl to marry a man who dyes his eyebrows and likes wearing strange leather garments under his nine-piece suits.' There was silence, save for the uncontrollable bouts of hysteria emanating from Fungus's more knowing side of the room.

As Fungus readied his vocal chords for his forthcoming solo performance, a contingent of Scots elders hurriedly convened a meeting in the gentlemen's convenience. Stunned and shell-shocked, the men in kilts wanted answers. What had gone wrong? How could this have happened? As their fury rose, so did their complaints – the cost, the shame, the embarrassment. At that moment Mr Engel entered. 'Who is that nancy?' they shouted at him. 'We were told he was a captain of industry.' Mr Engel sighed. 'Umm,' he said. 'And you're about to be told he can sing as well.'

2

On the Town

Life is Cheap

'The ambulance is coming, love. Have another sip of shandy, you'll be all right.' The girl in the purple spandex trousers was comforting her friend. She'd managed to drag her to one side of the dance floor, so she didn't get crushed during *The Birdie Song*. But nevertheless, things didn't look good.

'Do you think that girl is going to be okay?' Spooky shouted above the din. There was no way of knowing, but it did rather depend on the paramedics' ability to line-dance. Desperate not to go home after a Saturday night in the local Indian, Spooky, myself, Gay Opera Singer, Matt Boomy (the man who lost everything in the Eighties except his Stonyhurst accent), Sweet Phil, Cambridge and Professor Lolly had picked the only pub still open – The Butchers, a sticky-carpeted hell hole with a £5 entrance fee.

It was 1.30 am and nearly 40 people were wedged onto a 10-foot square patch of lino in the corner of the

pub specially set aside for gyrating. The publican had
hung flashing Christmas lights and a plastic tree from the
ceiling, even though it was March.

His brother-in-law Kevin was playing the records.
'I'm Kevin and you're so in heaven,' he screeched over
the records, to whoops from the crowd. It was obvious
that we weren't regulars, but new money was still money
and nobody seemed to mind too much. The long stretch
of bar was packed with sweaty bodies jostling for position, and crumpled ten pound notes were being waved in
the air like SOS distress flags. The barman appeared to
be programmed only to respond to the word 'lager',
unless you were a girl, in which case you could have a
lager with a nip of lemonade or blackcurrant juice.

While we sucked gassy, coloured froth off the tops of
our plastic glasses, Professor Lolly and Cambridge threw
themselves around the dance floor. The collapsed girl
and her spandex-covered friend were still huddled on the
fringes of the action, waiting for salvation, when Kevin
called for everyone to do the 'Funky Chicken'.

No one seemed to think that perhaps the dancing
should stop until the ambulance arrived. Sweet Phil did
his best, suggesting a musical truce, twice, to the less-
than-empathetic barman. 'You've got to be joking,'
seemed to be his professional opinion on the matter.
'Alright babe,' the barman waved at the unconscious girl,
her arm involuntarily lifted in the affirmative by her
increasingly impatient friend. There was 'pulling' to be
done and she was wasting time.

Gay Opera Singer had rushed the dance floor as soon
we got in the door, and by the time he'd downed his
fourth blackcurrant lager top, he was baying for the

Village People. For a man who thought Classic FM was populist rubbish, he certainly seemed to be getting the hang of it. *'I wanna be like common people,'* he bellowed, to the delight of his fellow revellers.

Meanwhile Spooky, dressed as always in stilettos and a mutated nightie, was attracting the attention of several heavily tattooed admirers. Two of them sat down either side of her. She could take her pick, they said. They were going to fight over her anyway, but they thought she might like to choose one first. It was suggested to Cambridge that perhaps he should intervene to save her from this bizarre courtship ritual. 'Are you nuts?' he screamed, and bought the two men a drink instead. 'Cheers,' they said. 'You don't mind us chatting up your bird, do you?' Cambridge said he thought they made a lovely threesome and that the 'bird' was nothing to do with him.

The girl in the purple spandex trousers said she'd 'pulled' and so could someone else help her get her friend outside to wait for the ambulance? Sweet Phil said it would be his pleasure, but wasn't it a bit cold out there for someone in her state? Perhaps a taxi would be a better idea? The girl in the spandex trousers said he was probably right, thanked him for the proffered £10 note and went outside to hail a cab, leaving her friend to collapse back on the floor.

Matt Boomy returned from what passed for the gents to find Spooky's would-be suitors occupying his seat. 'Excuse me,' he boomed, oblivious to their combined bulk. 'You seem to be in my spot.' Then he knocked a drink over. Like the moment when the saloon doors swing open, we knew there was going to be trouble.

'That was my drink,' hissed one of Spooky's suitors. 'There wasn't much left anyway,' replied Matt Boomy, nonchalantly. 'He deserves to get a smack,' screamed a helpful spectator from the next table.

We stared at Matt Boomy, mouths gaping. 'Get outside and we'll show you how much of my drink was left,' shouted the larger of the two suitors. Strangely, none of us had noticed earlier how they both had the word NUT tattooed on their foreheads. 'I think you're over-reacting, chaps,' said Matt Boomy. It was a language they didn't speak. With no announcement, Nut One lost control and started dragging Matt Boomy across the floor by his left ankle.

'How much drink was left?' Sweet Phil, the voice of reason, shouted through the hysteria. 'About 50p's worth,' snarled Nut Two. Quick as a flash, just as Matt Boomy's torso was disappearing out onto the pavement, Sweet Phil produced a seven-sided coin from his back pocket and handed it over. 'Will that do?' he pleaded. 'Nicely, mate,' agreed the Nut Men and they strolled off to the bar, dumping Matt Boomy on the sticky carpet. There was joy, relief, then sober reflection on the embarrassing realisation that Matt Boomy's life had just been bought for 50p.

The Deer Punters

The Penny Stamp public house was used to serving pints of bitter to hardened metropolitan postmen who liked the television left on but the sound turned down. Nobody else used it. It had never been co-opted into the north London frenzy for all things trendy, until tonight. Tonight the Penny Stamp was renting out its upstairs function room to a bunch of Siberian reindeer poets and their assorted followers. When the Poetess and I arrived at the bar they were still busy serving the early shift from the sorting office.

A collection of hirsute hippies was queuing in the corner, smoking roll-ups and fine-tuning their attitude to Rimbaud. 'We're here for the poetry,' I whispered to the barman. 'Corner,' he snarled and pointed to the bedraggled group of non-posties. After declining the Concord red wine on tap, we settle on two gin-and-tonics, one ice cube, no lemon, and follow the rest of the literary skulkers slowly making their way upstairs.

The Siberian reindeer poets had a warm-up act, a two-piece consisting of a male cellist and a female sax-player. They wouldn't actually be playing their instruments, they explained; instead, they would be banging them – and they did, for 40 minutes. Occasionally the sax-player screamed into her mouthpiece, but mostly they just banged, until the cellist broke his bow and they stopped. I wanted to leave but The Poetess was keen we hold for on the Siberians. 'They're unique,' she kept saying.

Cambridge had agreed to get down to the pub for the second half. By the time he arrived, I'd had three medicinal brandies and was assuring the Poetess for the fourth time that whatever happens next I wouldn't laugh.

The lights dimmed, the chairs stopped shuffling and from a corner of the room two middle-aged blokes from Siberia slowly crept towards the front of the makeshift stage area. They were naked except for two pieces of straggly rabbit fur tied around their midriffs, and bell-encrusted bracelets accessorising their ankles. On their heads they were wearing flying hats with full-sized antler horns attached with gaffer tape. A high percentage of the audience simultaneously developed coughing fits. I didn't dare look at Cambridge, who was staring at the ceiling while reciting the team line-up for the 1966 World Cup.

The Siberian reindeer poets started hopping around the stage on tip-toe. The bells jingled, other bits jingled, one of them banged a pig skin drum. The Poetess was mesmerised. They started wailing and violently throwing themselves around in a circular movement that left nothing to the imagination. Then suddenly, without warning, they emitted a high-pitched noise, a kind of cross between an unneutered tomcat and a Friesian cow minutes before milking. Several enthusiasts in the audience joined in. The man on the next chair got so excited that he showered the makeshift stage with cheese and onion crisps.

The reindeer poets leapt around regardless. The gaffer tape on their hats came loose and their antlers took on a half-cocked look. It did nothing to dampen their enthusiasm. From out of the darkness, an oversized carrot was produced. The smaller of the reindeer, the only reindeer I've ever seen wearing horn-rimmed glasses, enthusiastically set about shredding the carrot whilst hopping on one leg. His partner wrapped himself in a sheet and made like a mountain. A lone postman at the back, lost on his way to the gents, joined in: 'Leave it out!' he shouted.

Thankfully the poets had no comprehension of the English language. After ramming the shredded carrot into a specially prepared mouth hole in the sheet, the two took a bow and left, discarding the giant vegetable as they go. Silence fell on the upstairs room at the Penny Stamp. The Poetess clapped, loudly.

'They've been communing with the deer in Richmond Park every day,' she beamed. 'Don't you think they're fantastic?' She said she wanted to introduce us to the poets and before we had a chance to make our excuses and leave, we were shaking hands with the previously naked pair. They had an interpreter and were anxious to get feedback. 'What's with the carrot?' I asked. 'The rat eats the carrot,' the interpreter explained. 'What rat?' I said. 'The rat was a figment of the reindeer's imagination,' came the interpreter's solemn reply.

Cambridge, desperate to bridge the growing cultural gap, interceded. 'Did you discover that in Richmond Park?' he asked. The poets were ecstatic. A breakthrough. 'Yes, yes,' shouted the interpreter. 'There are many psychologically damaged deer in Richmond Park.' 'Right,' said Cambridge. 'So they get on well with the poets then.'

Not-It Boy

Perhaps there had been some dramatic body resculpting. Perhaps it was the skin-tight black sateen trousers. Whatever the cause, the effect was the same. Fungus had undergone a dramatic transformation.

'Does it show?' he asked, smoothing his hands over his newly tinted strawberry-blonde hair and arranging his profile in the best light. 'Would you say it was a shade too far?'

For those of us gathered around Fungus's birthday canapés and bottles of Chilean red plonk, it was a difficult one to answer. Ever since his eminently sensible wife had upped sticks on the honeymoon, we had feared the worst. And clearly it had happened. Fungus had donated his nine-piece suits to the third world and become an It Boy.

The reason for his new look was soon revealed. 'I have decided to return to the cabaret stage,' he announced to his stunned guests. 'And I shall be rediscovering my youth.' For anyone who had been there the first time around, it was a terrifying concept.

It seemed that to help him fund this radical reinvention, Fungus had been given free lodgings with a gracious lady benefactor and was paying for his keep in a rather unorthodox manner.

Daily, it was rumoured, he was called upon to inject her posterior with an age-defying serum, a secret recipe extracted from sheep and concocted in a high-security Swiss cosmetics laboratory.

In return, she had shown him a window into the world of the eternally youthful. His days were now spent submerged in mud baths, perfecting the art of corsetry and devouring *Tips For Ageing Swingers*, all while honing his soon-to-be-revealed new stage act.

As he worked the drawing room, unable even to sit down due to the constraints of his crotch-garrotting trousers, Fungus explained in great detail how this was going to be his major comeback. The comeback to end all comebacks. Sinatra had done it, Tom Jones had done it, and now it was his turn.

'Spread the word,' he urged. 'Competition for tickets will be intense.' Not only would tickets be hard to come by, but, by all accounts, they would also be expensive.

'The cost of living has increased,' he quipped at those

startled by the proposed three-figure entrance fee. 'And stardom costs,' he added. However, he was prepared to make a concession to those who demanded quantity with their quality.

In short, there would be a number of what he liked to refer to as 'warm-up acts', his Uncle Larry for one. Although now in his late seventies, Uncle Larry was keen. If there was to be 'relics return' he wanted equal billing. After all, he did own the amplifier.

Of course, there would be myriad costume changes. 'I shall, naturally, be having several new outfits made for the occasion,' Fungus assured us. 'My public would expect nothing less,' he continued, before pointing out that the sateen trousers were simply a prototype for a body-hugging cat suit designed to make any woman's eyes water.

But the *pièce de résistance* of tonight's festivities was yet to come. The mike positioned in the centre of the mantelpiece wasn't simply a toy. Fungus had a captive audience, and he was determined not to waste it. The long-suffering downstairs neighbour cracked first. 'God, no!' she cried, as he leant over to lift the microphone out of its gold lame covered cradle.

Her eyes, once the sparkling jewels of a twenty-some-thing model, were baggy with lack of sleep and nervous exhaustion. There were only so many nights she could take another rendition of *My Way*. The 'for sale' sign was going up tomorrow, and she wasn't coming back.

'Give it up,' she screamed at Fungus as she fled the flat. 'If only my fans would let me,' he sighed, as he tapped the microphone.

After-Dinner Streaker

Poshy and Glammy were back. The unused horse blanket had been hocked on eBay, the chintz-flecked cottage given over to heritage-seeking holidaymakers. Kissy-Poo had been packed into her travelling basket and the litany of claims for personal damages and distress had finally been settled with the villagers. The countryside experiment was over. Or, as Glammy preferred to describe it: '*So* over.'

Determined to resurrect her involvement with the arts and generally reignite her passion for promoting all things aesthetic, Glammy quickly set about joining a dedicated circle of like-minded types. Weekly, they would meet to discuss the finer points and painful struggles of artistic endeavour. The funding crisis. Unimaginative directors. Unique venues. Amazing young actors. Drunk old has-beens. The themes were much as she had left them five years earlier. Except for one.

Since her re-emergence into city life, there had been an increase in a genre colloquially known as 'bootie dancers', though some unreconstructed critics still liked to call them 'strippers'. No longer confined to the seedy basements of Soho or bachelor parties hurriedly organised by anxious best men, these new proponents of the art of disrobing were keen to be seen as serious performers. Ever the trailblazer, Glammy was keen to help.

It seemed that the main problem the disrobing-artists faced was getting their work viewed by sophisticated audiences. But Glammy felt she had just the answer. With plenty to celebrate, she decided to throw a large dinner party for a select line-up of guests culled from her contacts book. True, many of these people hadn't seen her or Poshy since their voluntary incarceration in the shires, but all the more reason to invite them. Besides, it was Poshy's birthday, so why not push the boat out?

By the time she had whittled down the list, there was a tight 20-seat arrangement in the kitchen-cum-dining room of their recently acquired late-Victorian terrace. She was looking on it as part supper club, part salon for the arts, she explained to Poshy. With a couple of old friends thrown in. In short, he wasn't to stint on the booze.

As soon as the first guests started arriving, Poshy decided against a family hold-back policy towards the drinks trolley. At best, he confided to an old pal, the evening might involve some long recitals of Yeats over the cheeseboard and, at worst, a choreographed interpretation of Beckett by a couple of leotard-clad men with a penchant for shaving their heads. Either way, in his experience, self-medication was the answer. 'Get it down you,' he urged him.

So imagine his surprise when, soon after the venison scraps were cleared, the lights were dimmed, the stereo teed up, and a muscular young woman dressed in a hoodie and track suit bottoms burst through the French doors. It was a long way from *Waiting For Godot*.

To a backing track of terrifying rap music, the woman proceeded to take her clothes off. Her name was 'Chavarella', she shouted, and she was here to shake her bootie. For most of the female guests, this was a first. And perhaps for many of the men too, although they were quicker to see the artistic merits of the event, especially by the time Chaverella had revealed her nipple-tassles, and a pair of skimpy briefs emblazoned with the words 'bad arse'. The removal of these caused a collective intake of breath that put most of the candles out.

For one of the older guests, seated towards the rear of the room, it had been a confusing blur. 'Did something saucy just happen, old boy?' the man asked, having located his glasses. Poshy sighed and explained that something saucy had indeed happened, but that sadly, as is often the way, it had been over remarkably quickly. 'Have I missed the sweet as well?' the man continued. 'You certainly missed the chocolate buttons.' Poshy replied.

Flash Photography
'The social event of the year,' the invitation announced. *'Bring £50.'* In these cash-strapped times £50 can buy you a great deal. Or not. For Fungus, a man with a heightened sense of his own worth, £50 was the price of a seat at his birthday dinner. It was good value for money he told us. After all, it was for him.

Over the years, friends, neighbours, his Uncle Larry and even his mother had become accustomed to paying for the privilege of his company. This year, however, with the larger-than-average number of refuseniks endangering his minimum spend deposit, Fungus had been forced to spread his invitation net wider.

Among the unsuspecting new recruits were the shampooist at his hair salon, the Eastern European trainee charged with organising his 'personal waxing' and Cambridge, who had recently returned from a creative tour of South Africa and was desperate to attend any gathering that didn't involve an armed guard. The meal had been economically constructed beforehand – three courses, no choices, and wine that Fungus introduced as 'experimental', but which its recipients recognised as 'cheap'.

The placement had been an ad hoc affair, with the result that the conversation was strained and in some quarters non-existent. With little or nothing in common, many struggled to get beyond their starters. But as the cash had been collected on the door and no one was prepared to leave before they'd had their money's worth, the disparate party soldiered on. Besides, there had been the promise of Fungus singing. It was to be a first for his new girlfriend Dee Dee, and as one recidivist warned her, most likely a last.

Sandwiched between an East Coast American woman who hadn't touched a carbohydrate since the Nineties and a lone male diner who had been told this was the overflow table from the main restaurant, Cambridge did his best. But things were not easy. The lone male diner's conversation consisted of only one repetitive, question: 'Where am I?' It was a question that Cambridge felt ill-qualified to answer, not least as he had been struggling with it himself ever since arriving.

To jolly things along, and in a bid to divert her attention from the breadbasket, Cambridge attempted to engage East Coast neighbour in a discussion about the merits of South Africa. The wine was good, he said, unlike the stuff in her glass. The food was excellent, if she ever intended to take up eating again. And then there was the scenery. Undeniably, it was a striking country. He had some snapshots on his mobile phone, would she be interested in seeing them? He took her lack of response as an affirmative, and produced his Nokia. 'It's beautiful,' he insisted. 'Honestly, I don't think you'll have ever seen anything like it,' he added, before flipping onto the first image.

Two seconds later, a blurry picture of his member appeared on the small screen in front of them. It was not what either of them had been expecting. 'What is it?' the startled woman cried, shifting her chair away from his. Not wanting to state the obvious, but finding himself doing so anyway, Cambridge said that it was a terrible mistake. 'I can see that,' she replied, her eyes fixed on the tiny organ. 'But what's it doing on your phone? Why isn't it on your body?'

Hurriedly switching the device off, Cambridge mumbled something about being jet lagged, the phone ringing that morning when he was in shower, grabbing it without his bathrobe, the shutter going off accidentally. He knew it didn't look good. As she struggled to regain control of her eyebrows, the lone diner leant over and pleaded, one more time: 'Where I am?' he said. East Coast neighbour sighed: 'Believe it, honey – you're in a much better place than me.'

Blackberry Jam

Since flipping his mobile phone onto an uncensored image of his private parts, Cambridge had managed something of an upturn in his social life by switching to a BlackBerry. This afforded him the chance to develop a new contacts list (many of his old ones having deserted him) and easier control over the camera.

One of these new contacts had agreed to have supper with him. The restaurant, chosen for its set-price menu and easy proximity to his flat, was a favourite with

Cambridge. His date, once a child model and now a well-preserved 35-year-old brunette with aspirations to being a television presenter, seemed keen.

The evening went smoothly, and by the time the bill arrived they had agreed to retire to his flat for a nightcap. Things were going well, he felt. It was possible that the two of them were at the start of something wholly romantic, or at least something that would pass for wholly romantic in the pages of a lads' magazine.

But then, as they climbed the stairs towards his flat, he felt his new BlackBerry vibrate in his pocket. A furtive look revealed it was a text from another new contact – a single, vivacious blonde he'd met the night before. She was desperate to chat. Realising that now wasn't quite the right time, but feeling confident that he could juggle the situation, he decided to feign an emergency. 'Sorry,' he whispered, handing his date the keys. 'I really have to take this.' 'Sure,' his date replied, accepting the keys and heading towards his door. These things happened when one was dating a thrusting and in-demand young man about town. 'I'll just let myself in, shall I?'

Back on the street, Cambridge hurriedly punched the call button. The number was busy. He tried again. And again, and again, for several minutes. In the space of 30 seconds, the single blonde had found someone else to chat to. Eventually, just as he was in the process of giving up, and leaving her a voicemail, his actual date reappeared, her face set in a sheepish grin.

'Sorry,' she mouthed at him as he was finishing his message. In her hand was half of the door key. The other half had apparently broken off in his lock. Not wanting to believe her, Cambridge dashed to his door. True enough, wedged firmly in the Yale's bossy grip was the missing business end.

'What happened?' he wailed as he tried manipulating the mangled pieces of metal. The brunette would-be presenter shrugged. It wasn't really her specialist subject, she explained. Or her door. After 15 minutes of microsurgery it was obvious that the latch wasn't budging, and Cambridge's mounting list of expletives was attracting the attention of the other residents.

Panic set in. It was one o'clock in the morning and cold. 'I have a meeting at 8am,' he screeched. 'I have to get in.' His date gurned another apology, before looking at her watch and reaching for her purse. 'I think I should go,' she said. 'But take this for the locksmith,' she added politely, offering him a crisp £20 note. Desperate not to appear mean, and fully aware that £20 wasn't going to cover it anyway, Cambridge refused her offer and hailed her a cab.

'Let's do it again sometime,' she yelled as the taxi pulled away. But Cambridge was already dialling the emergency call-out number. As it wasn't a matter of life and death, and he didn't have cash, help didn't arrive until four a.m.

'Rough night?' the locksmith asked rhetorically, as he dismantled the barrel. Cambridge said that was an understatement and proceeded to reveal the chain of events. 'You know what they say,' the locksmith laughed, writing out the bill (£240 plus VAT). 'A bird in the hand, surely worth two in the BlackBerry bush.'

Cha-Cha-Cha
Fungus rarely got more than one twirl round the ball-

room, and not even that if he wasn't paying. But times change. Rising divorce rates and falling standards had released a new breed of physically active women onto the market: *Strictly Come Dancing* fans whose desires stretched to little more than a well-starched pair of spats and a decent pulse. Years of practising the paso doble in front of his wardrobe mirror had finally paid off for Fungus.

Weddings, supper dances, office parties, upbeat memorials, downbeat reunions, Fungus's basic ability to put one foot in front of the other was suddenly in high demand. True, by the time carriages were called his services were usually dispensed with, but he was sanguine. The band played on and so did he. He had even started taking advance bookings. As he explained to one friend, 'Why turn down the opportunity to wear a mauve sateen frill-necked dinner shirt?'

On a recent outing to a 60th birthday party, midway through a particularly energetic version of the cha-cha-cha with an ebony-tressed HRT devotee, he felt a tap on his shoulder. Tall, slim, athletic, with a full set of teeth, Dee Dee had just arrived in London and was on the prowl for what she described as 'a work-out'. A child of the Fifties and a young woman of the Sixties, Dee Dee had lost none of her frontier feminist spirit. 'May I?' she asked as she peeled the other woman's white knuckles from her target's lapels. 'He's just what I was looking for.' For Fungus, it was a first.

Within seconds the band had moved into a high-tempo version of the foxtrot and they were off. Fast and furious, with Dec Dee's patent stilettos hammering the recently varnished dance floor, their expansive engage-

ment virtually cleared the hall. Four numbers in, and
Fungus was struggling to keep up. 'Would it be possible
to get a glass of water?' he pleaded into his new partner's half-turned ear. 'No!' she instructed, firmly. He was
thrilled by her domineering approach, but fearful of a
hernia, so three jives and a so-so rumba later he insisted
they take a pew before his legs gave way. She insisted on
leaving, but not before she had taken his photo-
embossed calling card. Two days later, she rang.

Was he available to escort her to a dance? He would
be expected to perform for at least two hours. Non-stop.
Keen to make up for his previous showing, Fungus readily agreed. A crimson cummerbund stretched round his
middle, and two cans of extra strength energy drink in
his gullet, he arrived at the allotted address.

Dee Dee had come dressed for action, her side-split
silver lamé cocktail ensemble revealing a sizeable chunk
of thigh and just a hint of miracle pants. Tune after tune
they twirled until eventually there was only one other
couple left standing. The band struck up a tango.
Fungus glanced across at his opposition. Young, taut,
and sporting a white tuxedo, the man could have been a
pro. The man stared back at them and then blew Dee
Dee a kiss.

'Do you know him?' Fungus panted, as their pace
quickened and he plunged his date's head backwards
towards the floor. 'Yes,' she replied, rearing back up at
him. 'He's my number one partner. Unfortunately he was
already booked.'

Fungus felt the perspiration creep across his brow. He
hadn't realised it was a competition. 'Strictly speaking,
darling, it isn't,' she consoled him, as she threw her leg

over his left shoulder. 'But I like to keep a scorecard.' Fungus was mortified. 'So how am I doing?' he asked, anxiously. 'Well,' she replied. 'Let me put it this way. I don't think Fred Astaire would have had anything to worry about.'

The Escape Artist

It was 10pm, the supper was burnt and the star guest had failed to materialise. The phone rang. 'I'm sorry I'm late,' came the plaintive cry. 'But I need help, and I don't mean metaphorically.'

The Culture Kid, critic-cum-artist, beloved of the avant-garde art world, a man who had spent his life breaking moulds and expanding boundaries, had somehow locked himself inside his east London studio. As no-show excuses went, at least it was an original.

After a recent spate of door-to-door gunpoint robberies in their increasingly fashionable neighbourhood, he and the rest of the artists had convened a meeting and decided the best line of defence was a hefty padlock secured across the front door.

A notice was posted, threatening immediate expulsion for anyone failing to observe the new lock-up rules. It was the artists against the outside world and the artists were determined to win. Unfortunately, this particular evening no one had noticed that the Culture Kid was still inside, taking a well earned nap after a hard day's daubing.

By the time he woke, it was too late, and he was locked in. For more than three hours he had tried to effect an escape. He had called the fire brigade, called the BBC, called his mother and finally he had called to say he wasn't going to make it for the entrée.

Hysteria had clearly begun to set in when he explained that he felt he had come up with the final solution. 'I'm only on the second floor,' he elaborated. 'So I could tear up some old paintings, tie them together to form a rope and slowly lower my way down to the ground. If it works I could turn it into a conceptual art piece. I'll call it Lucky Escape. What do you think?'

The Culture Kid was famous for his lucky escapes. As a spotty youth, he'd survived being kidnapped by two anarchic lesbians determined to give him an enlightened life in a Canadian hippie commune. He very quickly got Stockholm Syndrome and would still be there knitting yoghurt if the place hadn't been raided by a crack team of free-love-hating Mounties. He had even survived what could have been a fatal moment when the steering wheel of his clapped-out Golf had come off in his hand. Fortunately, he had been stalled at the lights at the time.

But jumping out of the window while clinging to a collection of ripped up pictures – that seemed to be pushing his luck too far. 'I'll bring a ladder, and some rope,' I managed to shout before the credit rang out on his phone.

Willy's Walker, who had been patiently nursing his knife and fork while doing his usual impression of a long-suffering boyfriend, was less than pleased with the new timetable for supper. 'Can't he wait until we've eaten?' he moaned. 'I'm not sure I can face human carnage on an empty stomach.'

Despite his protestations, five minutes later, we were in the car, which was crammed with assorted washing lines pressed into service as ropes, one collapsible ladder, two bemused dogs and a first-aid kit. Sadly we were too late.

Unable to bear his entrapment any longer, the Culture Kid had taken his life in his hands and plunged down the side of the building clinging desperately to the remnants of three recent canvasses. Admittedly they hadn't been his strongest work, but the thud with which they had brought him down to earth had still come as something of a shock.

His trousers were torn. His lip was bleeding. He was suffering from gashed knees that any five-year-old would be proud of. He was barely able to stand, but he was smoking a celebratory cigarette, posing like a madman's Bond.

'I made it,' he cried, as we got out of the car. 'Art triumphs over adversity,' he crowed. Amazed, I congratulated him on his bravery and offered him a sip of medicinal brandy from the first-aid kit. There were smiles all round.

Finally I suggested we go home and eat the remnants of the supper. 'Okay,' agreed the Culture Kid. 'But I've just got to collect my bag.' I looked at him aghast. 'You can't climb back up,' I pleaded. 'It's okay,' he replied. 'I've got the keys in my pocket. It's just that they only unlock the padlock from the outside.'

I looked at the padlocked door and his studio window directly above it, his gashed knees and then the ripped canvasses. A simpler scenario came to mind, one in which the Culture Kid had thrown the keys down and I had released him from his artistic prison in time for the entrée. Then I moved on. Somehow, it seemed churlish to point out this clearer picture.

Not His Bag

Very occasionally, even in East of Islington, the postman
delivers a gold-embossed, vellum-lined envelope that
hints at an evening of top canapés washed down with
vat-loads of expensive champagne. For Boy Wonder, this
moment came courtesy of a former school network,
reinvigorated through Friends Reunited and dedicated
to getting its more financially challenged members invited to as many free parties as possible.

His hostess had told one of their number that she was
keen to incorporate more 'alternative' types into her
contacts book, and Boy Wonder certainly fitted the bill.
Since his student days, he had been an enthusiastic
member of the Socialist Workers Party. But recently, he
had been in search of a new group, one that placed less
emphasis on 'work' and more emphasis on 'party'. This
was the perfect opportunity to pursue his new agenda.

Arriving in surf shorts and flip-flops, Boy Wonder initially had some trouble getting past the burly security
guard. Eventually he gained admittance on the grounds
that his attire was 'tycoon wear'.

Men with large amounts of cash often 'dress down' as
dispossessed youths to avoid attention – it was a conceit
that had served Boy Wonder well over the years.

Thankfully, his interlocutor had come across the phe-
nomenon before.

Outside on the terrace, the party was in full swing,
the canapés as luscious as anticipated, the drinks chilled
to perfection, and the other guests dressed for corporate
success. Confidently, Boy Wonder made his way through
the throng, slapping backs and clasping elbows as he

went, ignoring the blank looks cast by the majority of those he accosted. Grabbing a glass of demi-sec in each hand, he settled by the shrubbery, where he set about promoting his dubious talents and littering the carefully manicured blossoms with the spent filters of his Camel full-strength.

Things were going quite well, he felt, and as he was making his fourth lunge for the tray of mini spring rolls, he even collided with a familiar face. It was a former landlady of his, and miraculously, she was pleased to see him. They chatted over old times – his unpaid bills, the legal letters from the neighbours, his refusal to accept that the revolution might not happen and her refusal to fund his campaign – before she eventually made her excuses and moved on.

Half an hour had passed before his former landlady glanced up and noticed that her ex-lodger had taken up residence on the raised dais. He was beckoning earnestly at her. 'Don't worry,' he said, as she drew close. 'I've got your bag,' he added, before proudly handing her what she immediately identified as a mint-condition £700 Fendi. She looked at the bag, looked at him, and then looked down at the considerably cheaper leather holdall already lopped over her arm. 'That,' she replied, 'is *so* not my bag.'

No sooner had the words come out of her mouth than the manager arrived, accompanied by a sobbing woman who grabbed proprietarily at the pricey object. Having already frisked all his waiting staff and instructed that no guests should be allowed to leave until further notice, the manager was in no mood for excuses. Nonetheless, Boy Wonder tried his best. 'Technically,' he said to the red-faced bureaucrat, 'all property is theft.' The manager, mindful that an assault charge would be a very black mark in the world of high-class hospitality, thanked him for his words of wisdom, before ushering the stunned bag lady off to the after-party party, a discreet gathering held in the VIP bar, where the ratio of staff to guests was two to one. After a polite interval, Boy Wonder followed them.

At the door, an orderly queue had formed as one by one the anointed few air-kissed their way to the inner sanctum. Boy Wonder drew close. As it was such a high-level affair, the manager himself had taken charge of the door policy. The manager, not for the first time that evening, looked Boy Wonder up and down. 'I'm sorry, sir,' he sighed, finally. 'No flip-flops.' But Boy Wonder was prepared. 'You know, tycoon wear,' he whispered, knowingly. Briefly glancing across at the traumatised bag lady cradling her third therapeutic martini at the bar, the manager looked back at Boy Wonder and shook his head. 'I don't think so, sir,' he smiled.

Singing in Tongues

In a bid to raise his game, and attract the kind of attention usually reserved for small children and the psychologically disturbed, Fungus had booked a 12-piece orchestra and a room large enough to house the second coming for an evening of crooning to his nearest and dearest. They would, of course, be expected to pay. '*Book early to avoid disappointment,*' the invitation said. '*Bring your friends*', the follow-up email commanded.

Having failed to secure a sponsorship deal with any

major corporate brands (the universal question being: 'Who are you?') he finally gave in and called on Uncle Larry. Suave, sophisticated, a hit with the ladies and a man who had once bought a drink for Sinatra. Despite now being in his eighth decade, Uncle Larry still had all the prerequisites for stardom, in particular the ability to put bums on seats.

His decision to return to the stage had been an anxious one. Would the fans remember him? Would he be loved and adored as he used to be? Would Fungus give him half the takings? A deal struck, they went into overdrive. No connection was left untapped and no acquaintanceship unexploited. Eventually, on the night, the place was packed, although not necessarily with committed fans.

Motivated by sheer pity, Fearless had invited The Muffia, her all-female quiz team from south London. 'It'll be fun,' she assured them. Taking their seats at a candle-lit banquet table, last-minute crib-sheets in hand, the horn section took them by surprise. 'There *are* going to be questions, aren't there?' one of them shouted, as Fungus swept into the opening number of *Chicago*. 'There will definitely be questions,' the man on the next table offered. 'Perhaps even a full inquiry.'

Fungus worked the stage. As Uncle Larry later conceded, he had put in some practice. With every round of applause, Fungus's confidence grew, although admittedly his charms were wasted on some. By the interval, The Mufia was still unmoved. Hard questions would be asked on the bus home. Obscure subjects might have to be explored. Like, what did Fearless mean when she used the word 'fun'? Still, others were having a good time, particularly the statuesque, 25-year-old blonde accompanying Cambridge, whose enthusiasm for the songs was almost as impressive as her embonpoint.

As the curtain rose on the second act, Uncle Larry strolled onto the stage. He knew he had ground to make up, and it didn't take him long. 'This reminds me of the night I spent with Frank,' he intoned like the seasoned trouper he was. 'Just him, me, a bottle of bourbon, and a couple of tunes.' He needed to say nothing else. Even The Muffia looked up from their pass notes.

Occasionally, he would invite the young pretender to join him in a duet, but in the manner of Rod Hull and Emu, only one of them was ever going to get the credit. Eventually the band struck up for the finale. *'I've got you under my skin ...'* the bow-tied duo belted out in sync. But Uncle Larry had already moved on, as the closing chords approached, his eyes had locked on stage left. Years of experience had taught him one thing: the women worth having were always first to make a dash for the bar, and he had his eyes on the statuesque blonde.

True enough, she headed the stampede for the door, Cambridge trotting swiftly behind. Timing perfect, as always, Uncle Larry sauntered down from the stage, and caught her at the pass. Even in the low light she looked flushed at being singled out for recognition.

She complimented Uncle Larry on his performance. 'I'm glad you enjoyed, it my dear,' he whispered in her ear. For a moment, they lingered, before she leant down and pecked him on the cheek. He returned the favour by slipping her the tongue. Cambridge watched, stunned. Even for him, this was a new experience. 'How was it?'

he asked her, after the octogenarian had eventually taken his leave. The statuesque blonde thought for a moment. 'Cold,' she replied. 'But surprisingly lively.'

3

Property Market

The Brush-Off

The first sign that our small world was about to be changed forever came when I returned home to discover an estate agent's board nailed to the front gate. *'Flat For Sale,'* it said. *'All enquiries to Parvenu Estates.'*

So the rumours were true, Weirdie Woman had finally thrown in the towel and was selling up. Sandwiched between myself and Gay Opera Singer, her lack of cohabiting spirit legendary, she had finally ceased all verbal communication with us the previous New Year's Eve.

It had been Gay Opera Singer's annual party, a night to remember. As the bells chimed midnight and the dulcet tones of Abba's *Waterloo* hit the turntable, a vision in a pink candlewick dressing gown suddenly appeared, brandishing a broom handle and a stop-clock. It was Weirdie Woman.

Over the din of Big Ben, she had stated her aims. 'No more Abba,' she shouted. 'You have exactly 60 seconds.' Then, to the bemusement of 35 dancing queens, she had set her stop-clock and, in the manner of a die-hard Seventies punk rocker, pogoed her broom on his dining room carpet.

As terrorist demands went, it didn't. The guests, assuming her protest to be the evening's cabaret, whooped and cheered. Eventually she was forced to retrench. 'You haven't heard the last of this,' she hollered, waving her broom wildly as she beat her retreat. 'I'll be listening.'

And true to her word, like an audio Big Brother, she had been on noise patrol ever since. At the merest hint of a tune from either flat, she would loudly semaphore her disquiet. Bach, Beethoven, Beach Boys, even a little light chamber music on a Sunday afternoon would fail to make it onto Weirdie Woman's exacting playlist.

Banging the ceiling or the floor, no note would escape the blunt end of her broom. Invites to parties, hints at friendly drinks, even front row tickets to hear Gay Opera Singer perform in the flesh were all met with a blanket 'no'. Bang The Broom was really the only game she wanted to play with us. It took some time, but eventually we were forced to conceive a counter-attack. Knowing that she was really only capable of banging one broom at a time, we realised that synchronising stereo systems, ideally playing the same record, at the same time, would eventually wear her out.

Some artistes made her bang louder than others and anything from the Seventies was always guaranteed to cause actual plaster loss. As party games went, playing Bang The Broom with Weirdie Woman became quite popular. But now it seemed the plug had been pulled.

'Do you think it was the Elton's greatest hits or

Beethoven's Fifth that finally sent her packing?' I asked
the man from Parvenu Estates as he waited for a would-
be purchaser on the doorstep. 'Or was it the Pet Shop
Boys evening?' He said he was under instruction not to
give out any information. 'Client confidentiality,' he
explained. 'The vendor doesn't want any details of her
next move to be revealed,' he added conspiratorially.

'Has she already moved out?' I asked him, as casually as I could. 'No,' he replied breezily. 'Did he know
when she was planning to go?' I probed. He sighed. He
knew a lot more than he was saying. Eventually he
smiled. 'Well, I suppose it won't do any harm to let you
know. She's off tomorrow.'

Apparently she was giving up the city in favour of the
quiet life: a croft on the Orkney Islands, to be precise.
There was no time to lose. For old times sake we had to
have one more round of Bang The Broom.

Gay Opera Singer was cooking his supper when I
went upstairs to fill him in. 'She smiled at me today,' he
said. 'It was frightening.'

The real question was what should be our swansong.
'It has to be one of her old favourites,' I said. We had
learnt long ago that she had no favourites. But we did.
Without question, it was *The First Time Ever I Saw Your
Face* by Roberta Flack. It was smoochy, it was the classic end-of-the-party record, it was the tune that had
notched up the greatest number of broom-banging hits
in our collective history of the game. At 8pm that
evening, our stereos synchronised, we simultaneously
pressed play. Within seconds the whole house reverber-
ated with the mournful moanings of Roberta's failed
love life.

But the silence from upstairs was deafening. We replayed the record four times before it became obvious. The broom was missing. With heavy hearts, we admitted defeat. Not so Weirdie Woman.

As the first light of dawn hit our windows, the bagpipes started up. Three hours later, they were still playing. Unable to take it anymore, I marched up to her door. It was then that I spotted her parting shot. Propped against the door frame was her beloved broom, and attached was her heartfelt goodbye note. '*Door locked. Bagpipes recording on continuous play inside. Good luck!*'

Working Girls

Laden down by the fruits of four hours spent at Ikea, Naivety moved into her newly rented flat. It wasn't in the smartest of streets; East of Islington's gentrification trickle had turned into a mere drip by the time it reached her doorstep. But it was cheap and the landlord seemed very friendly. 'You need anything,' he had said in his thick Turkish accent, 'call me. I offer full service.'

True, there were some obvious drawbacks, but in her initial enthusiasm she had decided to overlook them. The lack of a cooker, for instance, had seemed a little odd. But, as she had often been told as a child, 'You can't have everything.' In this case, it seemed, 'everything' was hot meals.

But Naivety didn't care – she had found her little place in the world and was happy. That evening her boyfriend, armed with a bottle of Chilean red to help her baptise her new wine glasses, ordered a cab and was surprised to discover that the driver was very familiar with the address. Apparently it was a regular local booking, and he often dropped fares there.

'Oh, yes,' the driver said. 'Really popular, that one.' Naivety's boyfriend said that that was funny. He'd personally never been there before. 'I'm going to visit my girlfriend,' he explained. 'For the first time.' The driver nodded. 'That's what they all say.'

As they drew up outside, the door was already open and Naivety was standing on the doorstep looking a little startled. It seemed that ever since she had pasted her name on to her doorbell alongside that of Destiny, her new neighbour, she had been receiving confused callers, man of whom seemed to want to know if she was working.

Before she had had the chance to explain to any of them that dental hygienists weren't usually allowed to bring their work home, the door to the ground-floor flat had been pulled ajar and the misguided visitors hastily beckoned into the gloaming. Naivety had yet to meet Destiny, but it was becoming very obvious that her new neighbour knew a lot of people. All of them men, and all of them seemingly conducting surveys on working practices in the area.

As the days passed, Naivety's brand new battery-powered buzzer became more and more active, particularly in the early hours of the morning. Muffled voices would repeat their mantra down the intercom: 'Are you working?' Naivety's answer was always a firm 'no', followed by compassionate but professional advice that callers should contact the surgery, first thing.

The appeal of her new flat was wearing off fast. No hot meals she could handle, but sleep deprivation was not something she had signed up for. She had a perfectly good bed, she just wasn't being allowed to sleep in it. It was her mother who pointed out that perhaps things were not all they seemed with the nocturnal visitors.

'There are some men, dear,' she said to her wide-eyed daughter, 'who want to have their cake and eat it.' Naivety nodded, hoping that clarity would at some point form part of their conversation. 'And there are some girls, dear, who are prepared to do that kind of baking.' Naivety nodded again. 'But you don't have any cakes for sale, dear. You don't even have an oven.' Naivety said she really didn't feel that the callers were after cake. 'Oh, they're after cake all right,' her mother insisted. 'And icing,' she added as an afterthought.

She mentioned her mother's theory to her boyfriend. He said he wasn't sure about the cakes, but he was fairly sure that the woman downstairs wasn't a baker. 'I'm not even sure that she has a kitchen,' he added. 'She dragged me in there the other day by mistake,' he blushed. 'And it didn't look too domestic.'

After she had been living there for about a month, Naivety bumped into the woman who lived in the house next door. They got chatting and exchanged potted histories. The woman had two cats and no boyfriend, but was hoping to get one soon. So if Naivety knew of any available men, she would be grateful for the nod. She also worked in IT, designing websites. Naivety was very impressed. Her own work was a bit mundane. Teeth were teeth and after a while, particularly after veneers, they all looked the same. But web design, that sounded fascinating.

The woman said that it was interesting, thank you,

and that in fact she was working on something at the moment that Naivety might find extremely interesting too. 'Ooh, yes,' Naivety cooed. 'What's it called?' 'www.myneighboursrunningaknockingshop.com,' the woman replied.

Back to Nature
To the best of my knowledge, there were very few naturist colonies in London. But it seemed East of Islington had spawned one of the first, and in our own modest back garden.

As in all things English, the weather had to take some of the blame. With temperatures designed to take the tarmac off the M1, caution was abandoned, shorts donned and acres of raw flesh exposed to the red-hot elements. Something had to give, and the first thing was Weirdie Woman. Even before the temperature dial reached scorching, she had already thrown in the towel. Having failed to sell her flat, the man from Parvenu Estates had rented it out while she waited for the market to 'pick up'. 'Nice Young Lovebirds, I'd call them,' he said, describing the new tenants. 'Won't know what's hit them.' As soon as he heard the news, Gay Opera Singer seized his moment. 'Let's have a house garden party, darleeng,' he announced, as we awaited their arrival. 'A big one.'

He felt we should start as we meant to go on. Things with Weirdie Woman had been too weird, and we needed to take a firmer hand. By the time the lights first went on in the Young Lovebirds' sitting room, the invitations had already been sent out. 'Party this weekend: our garden,' it said. 'Please feel free to come,' he scribbled as an afterthought on theirs.

Word spread fast. By the time the doors opened, the invitation list stood at almost a hundred people and that didn't include several stragglers who strolled in from the bus stop.

The supporting credits were equally lengthy. The six Ukrainian builders, originally recruited to repaint the window sills, offered to slaughter and char-grill a large sheep in return for an evening of large amounts of free beer.

Piano Pete, accompanied by 15 Brazilian rappers and a Japanese oboe player, grabbed the opportunity for a captive audience, and ear-marked himself as the evening's musical attraction.

Not to be outdone, several radical vegetarian friends, fresh from an anti-fur rally, set up an alternative corner providing barbecued tofu for those unable to stomach the contents of the groaning Ukrainian meat table.

For the elderly guests, Gay Opera Singer's sprightly mother and his Aunty Doreen, it wasn't quite what they were expecting. Imprisoned as they were by the lethal combination of rheumatism and low-slung deckchairs, even getting a drink proved a problem. 'Sherry, dear?' they pleaded with anyone passing with a bottle.

Meantime, the Young Lovebirds were busy making friends. It seemed they believed in peace *and* love. Free love in fact. But they were against furniture. Weirdie Woman's once nick-nack-filled flat was now a temple to austerity. Their only piece of furniture, a donated coffee table, was languishing outside the back door.

'Possessions,' they explained to Dazzling Darren. 'It's not where we're at.' Apparently, they were 'at' going to

India. In fact they were heading straight out again the next morning, to an ashram. In short, the Young Lovebirds were of the hippy variety.

This took the rest of the guests somewhat by surprise, although they were quick to compete. 'Yeah, well, we're all hippies at heart, man,' Piano Pete interjected. 'Possessions, who needs them, right,' he added, while surreptitiously hiding his Nokia.

Even the vegetarians were caught on the hop. 'We don't own anything that involves cruelty,' they explained, flailing around for the high moral ground. But the truth was that a hippy was a hippy, and hippies were all but extinct. As social cachet went, it was virtually unbeatable in this neck of the woods.

As the evening drew on, the Young Lovebirds were mobbed by guilt-ridden property-owning liberals desperate for absolution. Eventually, they could take it no more. 'I'm afraid we have to go to bed now,' they announced to the mesmerised throng. 'We start our journey to the ashram tomorrow,' they added apologetically.

We nodded in awe, and parted the way for them to leave. But they stood their ground. Silence ensued. 'We're sorry, but we really have to go to bed,' the Young Lovebirds reiterated. Confused expressions spread. What were they saying? Was it a metaphor? Did anyone actually speak hippy?

Finally, the international language of physical action took over. The Young Lovebirds pecked, stripped down to their birthday suits, lay down on the lawn and bid everyone, 'Night, night.' It seemed they had been sleeping al fresco since their arrival a week ago. 'Go in peace,' they eventually murmured to their flabbergasted fellow guests. The party came to an abrupt end. The spirit of Weirdie Woman lived on.

Fang Fatale

Gay Opera Singer and Dazzling Darren had decided to give a free home to a struggling artiste. 'We want to do up our bit for the arts, darleeng,' Gay Opera Singer announced, as they penned the classified advert for *The Stage* newspaper. 'Help give an injection of New Blood into our tired old theatrical household,' he elaborated.

True, they still had their lodger, Matt Boomy (the man who lost everything in the Eighties except his Stonyhurst accent), but like an ageing pet, they had long ago stopped looking to him for entertainment. No, what they really wanted, they explained, was someone new to play with. The responses came quick and fast. Jugglers, mime artists, would-be rock stars, celebrity impersonators, the list was endless. It seemed there wasn't anyone who wasn't keen on a free bunk.

To make life easier, and ensure that their largesse was going to a good cause, the new art patrons decided to impose certain rules. The criteria were stiff. The beneficiary would need to be talented, nice to look at, and, most importantly, available at a moment's notice to help out with any domestic chores. 'And the capacity to cater for large groups would be looked on most favourably,' read the small print. It was a tall order.

Hundreds of applicants were seen, none passing the strict tests. The arteries of New Blood were rapidly drying up. And then, one evening, just after nightfall, came a knock at the door.

Standing there, dressed from head to foot in a fetching black cape, sporting leather boots and a slash of bright red lipstick, was a black-haired beauty straight from central casting. Piano Pete, who had somehow inveigled himself onto the judging panel, could barely believe his eyes.

'Come in,' he gushed, staring up at the goddess towering a good foot above him. 'Make yourself at home.' Her credentials seemed impeccable. She made perfect steak tartare, had a penchant for pale, clean surfaces, and, most importantly, didn't seem to mind that the room on offer came without any visible source of sunlight.

'I dislike the sun,' she smiled, flashing a set of piercingly white teeth. 'I like to keep my flesh cool,' she added, by way of explanation. She was a newcomer to London, but was already in great professional demand. Her passport, she explained further, said 'actress', but she liked to think of herself as more of a 'performance artist'.

Had she had many reviews? Dazzling Darren enquired. 'I believe,' she replied, 'that at the very least I always leave my co-star breathless.' Her stage name was Fang Fatale. And her preferred genre was 'Transylvanian film noir'. 'So much more subtle for the blood scenes, don't you agree?' she mused to her mesmerised interviewers.

Piano Pete had entered a trance-like state. His mouth was dry, his eyes vacant, his limbs a mass of useless jelly. In short, he was love-struck.

'Perhaps we could meet up later,' he blurted out as the visitor rose to leave. 'I'd like that,' she purred into the nape of his neck, her teeth gently brushing his hairline. New blood rushed to Piano Pete's head.

It was agreed that Fang Fatale would move in the following day. 'I'll supply my own bed,' she told Gay Opera Singer. 'And I like to sleep alone,' she added, as an afterthought.

That night, it was gone the witching hour when the doorbell rang. Fang Fatale had been neatly ensconced in her new room for only a few hours. The rest of the house was in total darkness, Gay Opera Singer and Dazzling Darren having long since finished their evening cocoa.

Outside on the porch stood an aftershave-soaked Piano Pete, his finger firmly pressed against the buzzer. 'Hi,' he mumbled to a bewildered Dazzling Darren when the door was finally opened. 'I wondered if I could borrow some sugar?' he lied. Before he had marshalled the expletives to make his reply, Dazzling Darren was pushed aside.

'He's come to see me,' announced Fang Fatale. 'Don't wait up,' she purred before leading Piano Pete by the hand and into her new quarters. Dazzling Darren was stunned.

'What's happening?' he whispered anxiously to Gay Opera Singer in the privacy of their room. 'Is he going to be her boyfriend?' Dazzling Darren wittered on. 'Oh, no,' replied Gay Opera Singer laconically. 'I think she's just invited him round for a quick bite.'

For Whom the Doorbell Tolls

Spurred on by the televised fantasies of those paid to ruin other people's perfectly charming houses, Mr & Mrs Fit had developed a penchant for taupe and giant staple guns. But much as they tried, their tiny one-bedroom flat offered no further opportunities for growth or improvement. 'We'll have to move,' Mrs Fit announced one morning. As usual, Mr Fit simply nodded.

By coincidence, a house had just been put up for sale across the road, offering something all property pundits dreamed of: potential. Admittedly, it was going to take more than ten meters of MDF, six gallons of eggshell and a John Lewis account to remake it in Mrs Fit's dream vision of domestic heaven. But it would be worth it. Oh yes, an entrée into all those metropolitan after-dinner conversations would be theirs. Mrs Fit wasted no time in developing an immediate bond with the Polish landlord who was selling the house, assuring him that they would pay top dollar and spare no effort in flogging their own place quickly. The deal was sealed.

Back home, Mrs Fit followed the estate agent's advice to the letter. Their flat was small, so their belongings needed to be smaller. Sofas, tables, chairs, ornaments and tapestry rugs, anything that took up any space or hinted at actual residency had to go. White paint, two dinner plates and a single-stemmed gladiolus in a see-through vase were in. 'Let them imagine themselves here,' the agent said. 'And don't forget to have the coffee percolator permanently on the go.'

Eventually, the clutter piled into the back of the hatchback, they called to ask if I could store a few things for them. It wouldn't be for long, they stressed. After all, the agent was sure that their flat's new look would have the desired effect and the whole thing would be over and done with by the end of the Saturday viewing rush. Sure, I said.

Three hours later, Mr & Mrs Fit had deposited virtually the entire contents of their flat in my living-room.

Bidding adieu, they promised to report back as soon as there was any news. 'Honestly, it won't be for long,' she assured me as they drove off.

The following morning, the phone rang. Would it be possible to extend the furniture storage period? There had been a little hitch with the new house. Giddy with the prospect of their new dwelling, and now lacking even the basic implements for frying an egg, Mr & Mrs Fit had celebrated their great property score by going out to dinner.

On returning home, they couldn't help but notice that the area surrounding their new dream house had been cordoned off. Neighbours were lined up along the pavement together with several dog handlers, two police vans and an emergency ambulance. True, it had often been rumoured that Bob Dylan was planning to move to their sleepy corner of north London, but somehow this wasn't really how they imagined his arrival would be hailed.

'It's my house!' Mrs Fit screamed, as they fought their way through to the *'Do Not Enter'* tape. 'Calm down,' said Mr Fit. But there was no calming her, and so instead he followed, two steps behind, as she sought out the officer manning the barricade.

'Is it something to do with number 14?' she asked, anxiously. 'Are you a relative?' came the reasoned response. Mrs Fit could sense this wasn't good. 'No,' she said truthfully. 'But I'm buying the house,' she continued. 'And I was supposed to be going round to measure up for curtains tomorrow morning'.

The officer looked at Mr Fit who raised his eyes in a practiced, nothing-to-do-with-me, kind of way. 'I think I'd better get a detective, madam,' the officer said. 'Wait here.'

The detective approached with head bowed. 'I'm sorry to inform you, madam, that the owner of the property has just been discovered in his bed, dead. Looks like a stab wound in the back. Very nasty.' As he finished speaking, a young constable arrived and took up vigil outside the front door of Mrs Fit's dream home, where a plastic ribbon printed with the words *'Crime Scene'* had been hastily stretched over its fading paintwork.

Mrs Fit was inconsolable. She had set her heart on refurbishing this house, and the small matter of a bloody demise was not going to deter her from her makeover vision. Silence fell for several minutes. Finally, Mrs Fit turned to the detective. 'I wonder,' she said. 'Do you think it will still be for sale?' The detective smiled. 'I think I could almost guarantee it, madam.'

Of Mice and Men

It wasn't the worst case he had ever seen, Ian The Mouse Man conceded. Far from it, actually. Last week, for instance, he had been called to a house where four of their fluffy little faces had popped up from the toaster during breakfast.

The week before, the tailor on the high street had lost a valued seamstress when a fast-moving furry blob had fallen on her shoulder as she was putting the finishing touches to a bespoke trouser leg. And then there was the flat round the corner – several dozen had nested in the dog's basket before anyone had noticed. 'The dog didn't seem to mind at all,' he said, of the bewildered spaniel. 'Bit of company for him, I expect.'

But he had to admit this was the first time he had been called in by the fire brigade. Not that he minded. 'It was good that they had my number,' he said, while cheerfully laying poison behind the inbuilt kitchen cabinets. 'It's nasty work and I'm happy to do it.' Earlier that day, Piano Pete had come to the attention of the emergency services after his novel attempt to rid himself of an unwelcome house guest had gone seriously wrong.

He first noticed its small, brown form scurrying across the sitting room floor and back into his disused fireplace, just as he was putting the finishing touches to a CD compilation designed to seduce even the most reluctant of targets. Piano Pete's heart sank. That evening's dating plans looked set to fail before he had even pulled the cork on the special-offer Macon. He might not know much about women, but he knew that even an ironic dose of Barry White was no match for a stray rodent.

Brought up on a diet of Tom and Jerry, Piano Pete also knew the score. Mousey always wins. Yet he had little alternative but to give it a go. His options were limited. Traps were too obvious and might be spotted. Bait would take too long, and an air rifle would be too risky – even if he had one, which he didn't. So, after not enough careful consideration, he decided to smoke the interloper out. It was an unorthodox move, but one he felt sure would deliver him results. Besides, he was desperate. Stuffing the fire grate with a large pile of damp kindling and a few misshapen logs, he set it ablaze. He also set the chimney on fire.

It was Gay Opera Singer who first alerted the fire brigade, driven by self-preservation in the form of the desire to save his adjoining flat from extinction. By the time the sirens were at the door, a collection of concerned residents had already drowned the problem in several buckets of water, delivered in an impressive relay from the garden tap. They had also drowned Piano Pete's living room carpet, covering it in two inches of sooty wash and leaving him with a smoke-filled flat that would challenge even the most dedicated of jazz fans.

Fortunately Ian The Mouse Man seemed to take it all in his stride. Admittedly, he didn't have any advice on how best to seduce a woman on a soggy carpet – not really his department. But he did know there was no such thing as a single mouse. 'Right goers, this lot,' he said as he continued to spread his toxic entrapments all over the pitifully damaged house. '*They* have no have trouble getting girlfriends. Not like the rest of us,' he laughed conspiratorially. 'And the girlfriends aren't choosy either.'

Somehow Piano Pete didn't think he was going to have the same luck. And nor did the firemen. After draining their mugs of tea and handing him a leaflet on safety in the home, they wished him well. 'Have you thought about getting a cat?' they suggested. Pete said he felt sure that Ian The Mouse Man would be able to deal with the problem. 'Maybe,' the firemen smirked. 'But what you really need is a pussy.'

Destiny Awaits

There were few things in life more upsetting for a girl than a boyfriend with a roving eye, although in Naivety's case her straying beau might be forgiven as she did appear to live above a brothel.

She couldn't be sure, but from the start there had been some tell-tale signs. Her neighbour, Destiny, appeared to be extremely popular and there had scarcely been a night since her arrival six months ago when Naivety's bell hadn't been inadvertently buzzed with the hushed enquiry: 'Are you working? ' She had long grown tired of explaining to these unwanted callers that dental hygienists rarely did gum work in their sitting rooms.

For her boyfriend, a trainee underwriter from the Home Counties, popping round to see her for a quiet night in with a takeaway was becoming increasingly difficult. On more than one occasion he had found himself on the doorstep at the same time as one of Destiny's visitors, and twice he had been dragged over the threshold of what the calling cards scattered in the hallway described as '*Destiny's Diamond Massage Parlour*'. Being spoken for, and, more importantly, on a tight budget, he would quickly make his excuses and leave, but not before he had had his horizons broadened just a little.

It was on one such occasion that he embroiled himself in what became known as 'Coca-Cola-gate'. Clutching two pizzas and a two-litre bottle of the world-famous pop, he had just been buzzed into the hallway when the door to the parlour swung open and there in front of him, dressed only in a leopard print silk scarf, was Destiny. Or, to employ her full working title, Princess Destiny.

The shock had a profound effect on him and, more importantly, his bottle of Coca-Cola. Mesmerised and terrified in equal measure, he reeled backwards, cartwheeling his arms as he tried to regain his composure. The sticky liquid, stirred up by all the sudden movements, blew its lid and deposited its contents all over the communal walls. Two litres of the stuff.

Petrified at the thought of the consequences, he scrabbled around on his hands and knees making a vain attempt to clear up the evidence. But there was no denying it. He knew it and Destiny knew it. He had left an unsightly stain and a fairly big one at that. Not wanting to alarm his girlfriend, nor share the full details of the lurid vision that had preceded the calamity, he confessed he'd had a small slip, but thankfully no one had been hurt. Naivety was very understanding. He shouldn't blame himself, she cooed. Besides, he probably had a lot on his mind. 'More than you can imagine,' he agreed.

The following week, while putting out her recycling, Naivety bumped into a middle-aged woman leaving the parlour and carrying a large bundle of laundry. Naivety smiled and the woman stopped. She didn't live there, but she did own the flat and she had done so for 40 years. She said that Destiny was one of her 'girls', although clearly not literally. 'Bit better tanned than me, dear,' she laughed.

The minor introductions over, the woman asked Naivety if she knew anything about the Coca-Cola stain. Naivety paused. She didn't want to lie, but somehow felt that perhaps on this occasion it might be helpful to be circumspect with the truth. The woman sighed. She hadn't held out great hope, but she had thought it worth mentioning anyway.

It was a mystery, the woman explained. Apparently a man had arrived, unannounced, and helped himself to a free eyeful of Destiny's assets, before beating a hasty retreat. Unfortunately, in the excitement, he clearly hadn't been able to contain himself and his bottle of fizzy drink had exploded everywhere. It had left a nasty mess all over the paintwork and was very off-putting for the other visitors.

Naivety wobbled slightly. Regaining her composure, she politely suggested that perhaps it might have been an innocent mistake. The man might have just fallen over, or stumbled against the door as he was passing. Besides, what is there to look at in a massage parlour?

The woman looked at Naivety incredulously. 'When you've been in the game as long as I have, dear,' she said, 'you'll still be surprised at the effect a bit of boob can have on a bloke, especially if he hasn't seen one in a while.' Naivety's jaw dropped. 'Actually,' she confessed. 'The man you're talking about is my boyfriend.'

The woman looked her up and down. 'Well, I don't suppose I can begrudge him a freebie,' she said. 'But you owe me £200 for the redecoration.'

Mind over Matt

Eddie The Psychic Decorator would not be hurried. His was an exact art. 'If the force isn't with me, the force isn't with me, madam, and there is nothing I can do.' Three days into repainting my sitting room and the force still wasn't with him. It seemed that such a creative desertion rarely happened, but when it did, sitting in the lotus position in the offending room was the only cure. So, until the force returned, Eddie The Psychic Decorator was encamped in my undecorated sitting room.

Poppy and Willy were confused. The comfy sofa was covered in dust-sheets, the television, removed due to its toxic rays, was languishing in the hall, and there were several obnoxious-smelling candles burning on the window ledge.

For Willy's Walker it was a disaster. 'I'm missing the test match,' he said. 'You have to sack him.' But telling him to leave was a risky option. Having your home painted by Eddie The Psychic Decorator was the latest cult to hit the style-conscious home-owners of East of Islington. To date not one soul had dared cross him.

According to Eddie, it was something of a privilege that he had agreed to daub our walls in the first place. Many had tried to engage his services, but few had succeeded. 'Some homes have a mutant energy,' he had explained when he first arrived. 'I can tell right away, because my bristles stand on end. But your place seems okay so far.' Flattery. Difficult to resist.

Unfortunately, my home's energy had not been as benign as first appearances had suggested and things had taken a down turn. 'Is there anything we can do?' I pleaded, after he been in the lotus position for six hours. 'Is it something to do with the colour choice?'

The colour choice had been a bone, or bristle, of contention from the moment the room had been stripped bare. Client intervention was not encouraged in Eddie's artistic orbit. In fact, it was positively discouraged.

His preferred mode of working was to walk around the room, stroking the walls and feeling their needs. 'Walls don't just have ears, you know,' he had said on more than one occasion. 'They have feelings too.' In short, my walls were going to decide for themselves what they wanted to wear. Unfortunately, not all four of them were in agreement.

'Their decision will come to me,' he kept saying, as we

waited with bated breath. 'These things can't be rushed.' But impatience had got the better of me, and after a day-and-a-half of wall-stroking, I had taken matters into my own hands, and arrived home with a *'Shades of Cream'* colour chart.

From the moment I took it out of my bag, I knew I had made a mistake. 'Madam,' he had sneered. 'You have employed Eddie The Psychic Decorator, not Dulux The Dumb Dog.'

Even though I had apologised profusely, then shame-facedly thrown the ill-judged leaflet in the rubbish, the vibe had been affected – irrevocably. By midnight on the second day, Eddie had maintained the lotus position for almost 48 hours and his psychic skills were at crisis point. 'I may never be able to feel walls again,' he cried. 'Or my legs.'

Meanwhile, having already missed three day's of play, Willy's Walker was desperate. Quietly, he wheeled the television set back into its position and joined Eddie The Psychic Decorator on the sitting-room floor.

In the half-dark they sat, side by side, Eddie praying for the return of his painterly force, Willy's Walker praying for a test match miracle, the dogs simply pining for the return of the sofa. As play drew to a close, it seemed no one was going to get their heart's desire. But then, suddenly, as Hussein's eleven walked off the pitch, and Willy's Walker reached for the off button, Eddie The Psychic Decorator jumped up.

'Stop!' he screamed. 'I feel something! I feel colour! I feel energy! I feel the force!' He pointed at the players on the screen. 'What?' we screamed back, desperate for it all to be over. 'Those men. Their outfits. My inspiration has returned,' he pronounced. Unable to believe our luck, we leapt to our feet, speechless, waiting for the final score to be announced.

'The walls shall be white,' he announced regally, before picking up his psychic bristles and heading out the door. It was several minutes before Willy's Walker broke his silence. 'It could have been worse, I suppose,' he mused brightly. 'They could have been dressed for a one-day international.'

The Islington Sock

For almost 20 years Fey Jay had, for a song, occupied a crumbling Georgian wreck in the very heart of trendy Islington. So grand was his address that few could refuse his offers of hospitality, although admittedly far fewer ever returned.

The house, like Fey Jay himself, had a surreal quality about it, trapped as it was in a time warp, heated only by carefully rationed coal and lit by several hundred life-threatening candles. It had originally been a short-term housing stop-gap, the keys handed to him by a then ide-ologically deranged council desperate to be seen as polit-ically correct.

Fey Jay had once written an obscure academic paper on the interplay between the shrinking working class and the wallpaper choices of its dwindling members. In the Eighties, as far as the Stalinist decision-makers on the council were concerned, he was worthy.

For two decades Fey Jay had lived the life of a regency gent, holding soirées for culture-vultures and admitting coach parties of misguided tourists keen to experience the flavours of Olde Worlde London.

Armed only with a palate knife and a misshapen serving spoon, he had methodically dug away the layers of his home's chequered history, attempting to unearth great national treasures. Discarded buttons, swatches of Fifties curtaining, two candlesticks of an indiscernible date, three old pennies and several postcards written in faded blue ink made up the bulk of his haul. But the item for which he became famous, his most treasured possession, was a dusty, moth-eaten woollen sock. It was not, as he was fond of telling his bemused guests, just any old sock.

Like a bottle beached on a high tide, it held a message. Hidden inside the toe, carved on a piece of wood, a mystery man had left his mark.

'I've run away,' it said, 'John Smith, 1830.' For Fey Jay, its discovery had been a life-changing event. Locally, it became known as 'The Islington Sock'. Soirée attendances boomed, glossy magazine articles were written, visits from English Heritage and murmurs of blue plaques abounded. This mundane piece of clothing took on a larger-than-life quality, housed permanently in a specially built timber box, to be dramatically revealed to a hushed audience at specially staged events. In short, on the swing of the cultural barometer, wallpaper was now out, and ancient woollen footwear was in.

But then, disaster struck. The free market had finally made it into the town hall and the council changed its flag of allegiance. The councillors wanted their house back, and they wanted it fast. Fey Jay's protestations fell on deaf ears. The building's cash value was so huge, they argued, that its sale would wipe out their years of overindulgence. Finally, Fey Jay had to concede defeat and join the homeless queue.

But that wasn't good enough for The Sock. The Sock, Fey Jay believed, deserved a special place in the world. The Islington Sock, he felt sure, would attract a celebrity benefactor. He was even prepared to throw in the specially designed timber display case.

And so it was that he held one last soirée, inviting all the grandees he had met in his years at the top. Stocked up on low-grade Chilean red, he welcomed his footwear followers for one last look. Taking the Oscars ceremony as his template, he promised that the newly privileged owner would be revealed that evening. Secrecy was so important that he had decided not even to forewarn the chosen one. Who, he argued, could refuse the ownership of such an historically important item anyway?

As the evening progressed, rumours grew rife. Who would be the person awarded this huge privilege? Would they be able to maintain the artefact's integrity? Might Fey Jay be permitted to visit? Finally, with a rap on the table with his favourite digging spoon, Fey Jay called for hush.

The chosen one, he announced, was Mr Very Big, a handsome, surreal storyteller who Fey Jay felt provided just the right shade of appreciation of the baroque and the bizarre to be the custodian of The Sock. Mr Very Big seemed a little taken aback by the honour, not least as he couldn't imagine how he and the item could get along.

Fey Jay was mortified. 'But this is a special sock,' he said. 'And it will only fit the right foot.' Mr Very Big nodded, sagely. 'In that case,' he said solemnly, 'I will accept it. Once my left foot falls off.'

4

Religious Quarter

Rite on, Rev

Since setting up shop as the local minister, Rt-On Rev had become quite a hit. Handsome, erudite, prone to spontaneous outbursts of song and laughter, his Irish charm was equalled only by his other essential East of Islington quality. He didn't really believe in God.

Tucked away in a small, discreet cul-de-sac, his Unitarian chapel provided solace for liberal non-conformists in search of a good tune followed by a decent cappuccino. And on high days and holidays, or simply when he was in the mood, the entire congregation was encouraged to pull up a pew at the local hostelry.

In this way, he had made quite a reputation for himself, as the people's preacher – for people who didn't really want to be preached to. His repertoire was inclusive, non-judgemental and customer-friendly: alternative weddings, non-religious baptisms, eco-funerals, garden blessing, pet internment, and now, in a Unitarian first, resurrection.

Like so many strange happenings, it came in the middle of the night. Peacefully asleep in his modest harbour above the chapel, Rt-On Rev was woken by the dramatic sounds of men banging hard on the vestry door. Pausing only to cover his modesty, he dashed downstairs to answer their calling.

Outside stood three waiters from the nearby Turkish grill. They were distraught and desperate. They needed help, they explained. One of their colleagues had fallen through the roof while trying to dislodge a blockage in the grill's chimney. It didn't look good, they explained, and the customers were taking it badly. Could he come and say some final, soothing words?

Keen not to offend, but at the same time not wanting to take on a job that that wasn't strictly his, Rt-On Rev took pains to explain that he didn't really do intercessory prayers, the last rites, nor any other kind of pleading with God. His position was more of a philosophical one. 'Also I'm not very good with blood,' he elaborated, 'so it's probably a job for the Catholic boys down the road.'

But the Turkish waiters were adamant. The Catholics didn't eat in their restaurant, and he did. 'You are one of our brothers,' they said persuasively. So finally he relented.

The scene that awaited him was not pleasant. The fall had been dramatic and the poor man was motionless and silent. He and the floor were both covered with the shattered remains of the glass roof panels. An ambulance had been called, but the Turkish waiters were right, it wasn't looking good.

Declining the offer of a medicinal brandy, Rt-On Rev

assumed the kneeling position and tried to keep his eyes off the red-spattered carpet while he ad-libbed some comforting thoughts appropriate to the occasion. A Sufi mantra, some Tennyson, a line or two from a Cat Stevens song, all of these were tossed in. But mainly he chanted for the medics to arrive.

It seemed like an eternity, but eventually his prayers were answered. Down from the sky came an air ambulance, bright red and sponsored by Virgin. 'I'm Mary,' said the ambulance woman, without a hint of irony. 'It's okay, we'll take it from here,' she added, prising Rt-On Rev's rigid hands off the stricken patient. 'What are his chances?' he called after them as they carried the stretcher out. Mary smiled benevolently. 'Miracles can happen,' she replied. 'You should know that.'

Three nights later, the banging on the door happened again. Rt-On Rev hurried to answer it, barely believing that disaster could strike twice in one week. Outside were the three Turkish waiters, but this time they were sporting wide grins.

'Praises to you,' they said to him. 'You have brought our brother back to life and every week we shall honour you with these gifts,' they said. They then handed him two crates of beer and 40 packets of black tobacco.

It seemed too good to be true, but apparently, after only a couple of days in the hospital, the motionless man had got out of bed and walked outside for a smoke. 'He was dead, and now he is alive,' the waiters said. 'You have the gift of life.' Their faith was touching, but on his new booze 'n' fags diet, Rt-On Rev didn't think he was going to have the gift of life for long.

Knocking on Heaven's Door

The Jehovah's Witnesses were the latest in a long line of religious sects to erect their temple on the already cramped ley-lines criss-crossing their way through East of Islington. Jostling for position alongside the Catholics, the Buddhists, the evangelical Christians, the Unitarians, the Hassidics and the Rebirthers, the Jehovah's Witnesses had arrived to warn the residents that the future was bleak. But for most of them this was old news. After all, they'd already bought houses in the area. How much worse could it get?

Daily, the doom-laden believers would set out from their recently constructed hall, behind the 24-hour Turkish supermarket, and head off in search of new converts. Dressed in formal low-key suits, they looked more like insurance salesmen than religious gurus and were greeted as such. Door after door went unopened, and they would generally return to base with not a single soul on the score sheet.

Until one day they decided to change tactics and start their rounds in the evenings. They figured that people would have seen the gloom of the six o'clock news by then, and might be looking for answers. It was a bold initiative, and one that did reap some rewards. Two of their members were offered dates and another was mauled by an overly enthusiastic dog.

It wasn't exactly the reaction they were looking for, but at least they had managed to get their feet in some doors. And then one night a couple of enthusiasts working overtime knocked on the door of Les Mums. For most non-locals, two married women with no husband was a mildly unorthodox arrangement. For the

Jehovah's Witnesses, it was completely off the song sheet.

Mum-Mum opened the door. She smiled warmly. Dad-Mum was out at work and she could do with the company. They were saving up for a sperm donor and Mum-Dad was working extra hours, she explained to the men standing in front of her. 'Although its fairly cheap, we want to have the pick of the crop,' she said. 'A doctor maybe, or an actor, an astronaut though, that's a bit passé don't you think?' The formally dressed young men recoiled from the burbling woman.

Mum-Mum certainly wasn't what they usually looked for in a potential convert, but numbers were at an all-time low and needs must. 'Have you ever wondered why there are so many disasters in the world?' one of them asked, desperate to get on with his sales patter. 'Or why there are so many bad people in the world?' Mum-Mum smiled knowingly. 'Sorry, I'm a Unitarian,' she said, giving them her stock reply for religious hawkers. The visitors were taken aback. 'What do they believe in then?' they asked.

Mum-Mum had to admit it was a bit difficult to pinpoint. She only went every now and then, and only because they had a gay minister and didn't seem to talk about the crucifixion too much. They also ran a babies-of-gays playgroup so she wanted to keep in with them, for when the time finally came. 'I'm sure you understand,' she said. They didn't. Undeterred, she explained that she thought the Unitarians liked everyone really including Jesus, although they thought of him just as a nice guy – a bit like Bob Dylan, but more upbeat.

'You know,' she said, finally, waving her hands sky-

ward, 'they're part of your gang.' The Jehovah's
Witnesses looked shocked. 'What gang?' they asked in
unison. 'The religious lot,' she replied. 'Cults, that kind of
thing. I thought you all knew each other?' The two visitors were momentarily silenced. This woman really
needed salvation, although they weren't really sure how
popular it would make them back at HQ. Still, they
decided to give it one more shot.

'Armageddon is coming!' they blurted out. 'And there
are just 144,000 places available in Heaven!' Mum-
Mum said she found this a bit difficult to believe. After
all, that was barely enough to fill a sizeable council estate
let alone the corridors of eternity. Who was in charge of
handing out the tickets?

That, they insisted, was beyond their control. But one
thing they did know for sure – being a Unitarian wasn't
going to cut it. 'Jesus would be there though,' they said,
and she should take comfort from that. 'What about
Cliff Richard?' she demanded. The Witnesses shook their
heads firmly. 'So there is a God,' said Mum-Mum, and
gently closed the door.

The Last Supper Book Club

Rt-On Rev had agreed to be a guest speaker at the local
East of Islington book club. Strictly speaking, it wasn't
actually a book club, more a supper club really, as it was
held in the local Vietnamese restaurant. But books did
feature, and in his honour the chair had chosen the Bible.
'A perennial favourite with our members,' she had lied
when extending the invitation.

An odd choice, I thought, but it seemed that everyone
had glanced through some version, even though very few

had managed to read it cover-to-cover. Rt-On Rev had read it, of course. Theology at Oxford and a stint in a seminary had seen to that. But he didn't actually possess his own copy any longer. After all, he was a Unitarian, and they didn't bother with the Bible.

Of the members present, two were Jewish by birth and had since switched allegiances to self-help books and Buddhism. One was an occasional Catholic, but her three illegitimate children didn't make her very popular with the local priesthood. Three were unsure of their calling and two, including myself, had attended church schools, but never with any great enthusiasm. Which left Sixties Starlet, Alan Angst and Susie Round The Bend. Each had their own particular affiliations, none of them particularly holy.

'Let us begin by welcoming our guest,' announced the chair. 'And thank him for taking the time to come and break bread with us tonight,' she added piously. 'If any of you have an issue you would like to raise, please don't be shy, ask away.'

Susie Round The Bend was the first to launch into the fray. 'Are there any straight men at your church?' she asked. 'Preferably rich and single.' It wasn't exactly the opener he was expecting, but Rt-On Rev fielded it well.

'We have all types in our congregation,' he said. 'And we certainly wouldn't turn a man away for being rich and single.' At which point Alan Angst threw his own hand in the air. 'What about gays?' he asked. 'Do you have any gay men?'

The chair started to look anxious, but Rt-On Rev was keen to be inclusive. 'We have gays, too,' he said. 'Single ones?' Alan Angst wanted to know. Apparently, in the congregation, there were straights, gays and people who simply hadn't made their minds up yet. And a lot of them were available. In short, the Unitarians could be all things, to all persuasions.

'Perhaps we could return to the Bible,' the chair chided. But it was dating, not deconstruction, that was being demanded.

'Would you be able to introduce me to any of your men?' persisted Susie Round The Bend. 'Yes, me too,' said Alan Angst. The chair was desperate. 'Please, members, let us not forget why we are here,' she said. 'We have only one night with our esteemed guest, let's not ruin it.' The esteemed guest, however, was trained to be graceful. He said that he was happy to help people meet one another. After all, it was part of his job. 'I just don't want any God-squadders,' Alan Angst instructed.

Eventually, after all possible relationship-avenues had been sauntered, the Poetess managed to wrestle the conversation back to the book in hand. 'Has anyone actually managed to read it?' she said, holding her own King James version aloft. Sixties Starlet, who until now had restricted her verbal intervention to ordering more merlot, confirmed that she had. 'Took me an afternoon,' she drawled, her accent more affectedly Mockney than ever.

Rt-On Rev was staggered. 'Was that just the New Testament?' he said. 'Or the whole thing?' Sixties Starlet said she had read the whole thing before cocktails, and couldn't see what all the fuss was about. 'I mean, Jesus Christ, it wasn't like he was a great writer,' she spat out contemptuously.

The table fell silent. The chair tried to retrieve the situation. 'It's a metaphor, isn't it?' she nodded to Rt-On Rev. 'Like this evening, for instance. There are 12 of us. We are in a restaurant. You're our guest. It's like the Last Supper.' There was a long pause before Rt-On Rev gave his considered reply. 'It certainly will be for me.'

Dana International Relations

Dana International was beaming down at me from Gay Opera Singer's drawing-room window. 'Isn't she wonderful, Darleeng?' he screamed. 'Six foot three in her stockings. What more could a man ask for?'

There were some men, however, for whom a cardboard cut-out of a huge transsexual in a low cut Jean Paul Gaultier evening gown was not the stuff of romantic dreams. They included the six rabbis and several of their yeshiva students pelting the Dana-adorned window with soggy cabbages. Gay Opera Singer, dressed in a very becoming turquoise silk kimono, was standing his ground.

'*It* is a disgrace to Israel,' the lead rabbi was shouting, fastidiously avoiding the use of the words 'he' or 'she'. Gay Opera Singer's blatant display of support for Dana's Eurovision entry had divided the street, with most of the residents lined up outside on our front steps. Mrs Eisenhower had brought along her Canon long lens and Gay Opera Singer was threatening to draft in a chorus of drag queens to provide artistic support. He was also planning to stage an impromptu Dana appreciation concert on the flat roof at the rear of our house.

Sultan the garagista and his Muslim mechanics from across the road were divided. They had voted for Dana International because she was the best-looking, her poster hastily pasted up in their outside loo. But since learning of her previous incarnation as Yaron Cohen, the bar mitzvah boy who went on to discover Rimmel and high heels, they weren't so sure.

For Mr Fatwa, the street's very own fundamentalist Muslim would-be MP, the quasi-religious, semi-sexist, pro-minority bust-up was a gift. Fresh from his own shot at fame in the local council elections, he was delighted to have stumbled across such a large gathering of potential new voters. 'I will deliver us from this evil,' he promised, in a reprise of his electioneering speech. People started listening, if only in the hope that he might make the noise stop.

Ever since Dana International had pipped Great Britain to the coveted post of Eurovision Singer of the Year, her record had been spinning continuously on Gay Opera Singer's aged turntable. The lyrics were like a red rag to an Orthodox bull.

For two days, the rabbis had deserted the hallowed confines of the synagogue to keep permanent vigil outside our house. Plod was about to make his third visit, but Mr Fatwa believed he could heal the breach. 'I have seen what my political leaders can do,' he burbled. 'We can also make the peace.' The rabbis usually voted Conservative, but in the interest of community relations they handed him a cabbage. 'Throw, throw,' they chanted. 'Then maybe we will have peace.' Plod arrived just as Mr Fatwa was letting rip with his fourth cabbage. 'For peace,' he shouted, before taking full aim at the Victorian glass window. 'Bound over,' Plod replied, before taking down his details.

Just as dusk started to fall, Gay Opera Singer's retinue

of drag queens arrived for his Dana Party. 'You all look great,' a six-foot ex-builder in a crimson sequinned number shouted at the protestors. The lead rabbi, although wearing a faux 16th-century Polish costume, complete with white stockings, insisted they were not in drag. 'Wow, love your style, dearie,' the sequin-wearing ex-builder screamed, before skipping up the stairs in the style of Judy Garland.

I was beginning to feel some sympathy for the rabbis. The Dana din was relentless. Plod returned for a fifth visit, and suggested that in the interests of community cohesion maybe the opposing parties should try to reach a compromise.

It was Mrs Eisenhower who came up with a sensitive solution, of sorts. 'We should have a raffle – whoever wins gets to keep the cardboard cut-out.' Gay Opera Singer was secretly relieved. There was only so much popular music a man of his sensibilities could take. And besides, a raffle might amuse his excitable guests.

Mrs Eisenhower hastily tore up some pieces of paper, wrote down the names of the interested parties and put them all in a bucket. It all felt very British. To a drum roll played by three drag queens, Plod drew the winner. Tense anticipation. 'Shlomo Leibowtiz!' he announced with a surprising sense of occasion. The rabbi contingent had won and the lucky young yeshiva student stepped forward to accept his six-foot-four prize.

'The dignity and honour of Israel is restored,' declared the senior rabbi. 'Now let's burn it.' But Shlomo wouldn't let go of his huge cardboard cut-out transsexual. 'We can't burn her,' he cried. 'Why not?' came the scream from all quarters. 'Because I want to take her home to meet my mother.'

Book of Revelation

Miracles are rare and bargains even rarer, but this doesn't stop most people from believing they can buck the odds. Every weekend, car boot sales and village fetes are mobbed by prisoners of hope in search of that Holy Grail: an Antiques Roadshow Hallelujah Moment.

For Rt-On Rev this blind faith was touching, and something that he thought he might be able to exploit in his desperate bid to increase church funds. So, on Sunday, over cappuccino and a service dedicated to the relative merits of Jamiroquai as a spiritual leader, he announced to his fellow Unitarians that the church would be going into the second-hand book business.

Every other Saturday, in return for freely donating their own unwanted paperbacks, he would be offering book lovers the chance to buy someone else's. Nothing would be too expensive and the quality on offer would be set according to their own consciences. 'Eco, ego-free, economics,' he said. It was the way forward.

Within weeks, his modest vestry was piled high with the yellowing spines of a thousand discarded tomes. Literally overwhelmed by the generosity of his parishioners, and more accurately, by their obvious need to rid themselves of excess material baggage, he hastily instigated a 'buy one, get one free' initiative, Unitarian-style.

Therefore, a recent copy of Joan Collins's biography (anonymously donated), priced at £3, would also net the buyer a *1987 Guide To Barcelona*. For the more intellectually rigorous, and those with room to spare, the entire works of Proust, priced at a mere £6, came with a free copy of *Geri Halliwell's Yoga*. Like the sermons, the marketing approach was littered with teasers to attract all tastes.

On the first day of business, the bargain-hunters flooded in. Gardening guides, self-help manuals and anything with the word 'organic' in the title were a sell-out. The eclectic 'buy one, get one free' gimmick was hailed as a huge success, a chance for people to broaden their literary horizons without shrinking their wallets. Until the following morning, at least.

Shortly after breakfast, Rt-On Rev's phone rang. Accompanied by his mother and devoted grandmother, a seven-year-old boy had apparently spent a happy morning at his bookstore buying up old *Beano* annuals. Although a little dog-eared, at only 50p each they had represented excellent value for money, especially for a little shopper on £2 per week.

With his Harry Potter backpack filled with booty, plus freebie bonus books, the shrewd little shopper had returned home to an afternoon of intense reading. Several hours passed before he finally emerged from his bedroom, glassy-eyed and pale, and wandered over to his mother busily making his tea. 'Mummy,' he asked casually, 'what's a "manless lovestick"?'

It seemed the stacking system in the children's section had gone slightly awry. Although many schoolboys might dream of being given a 1965 illustrated copy of *Fanny Hill* free with their *Beano*, most mothers would take a dim view, and the caller was no exception. The offending item had now been confiscated, but, the boy's mother wanted to know, what was Rt-On Rev going to do about it?

Mortified, the embarrassed minister was keen to help make amends. 'Perhaps I should come round straight away and give him some pastoral counselling,' he said. 'Or perhaps I might suggest some alternative reading. Age-adjusted of course.' However, this wasn't exactly what the mother had in mind. 'We don't want your counselling,' she snapped. 'We want his 50p back.'

As he hadn't really thought through a returns policy, and technically the book had been free anyway, Rt-On Rev wasn't that keen to hand over hard cash. 'What about a credit note?' he tried. But she had shopped with him for the very last time. 'I know my rights,' she said. 'I want his 50p.'

Within the hour, the irate mother had returned her son's first glimpse of the dark side and pocketed a cash refund. Rt-On Rev was again the proud owner of a Georgian novel so racy that it was still banned in Australia. But his ownership was short-lived.

A parishioner, who asked to remain nameless, arrived offering a £50 reward for the return of a book somehow donated by mistake. Rt-On Rev suspected he might have just the book. 'It's a miracle,' the man said, on seeing its precious cover. 'And a bargain,' Rt-On Rev replied, as he held out his hand.

Lovable Mop-Heads

For a couple of years, Yacob, the reasonably handsome son of Mr and Mrs Rabbi four houses along, had been posting through our front doors Moppeze catalogues, strange pyramid-selling, domestic-cleaning product brochures.

We in turn, finding no need for cloths specifically

designed to shine the soles of our socks, had been discreetly putting them back out on the doorstep for re-collection as instructed, the order forms always left blank.

But the day came when, in a bid to do our bit for the post-Dana International community relations, I decided perhaps it would be politic to buy something. Just once. Just to show willing. A quick scan through the Moppeze catalogue was called for.

It seemed to come in two parts. There was the Fairly Useless section: sock cleaners, sock shavers, neon-coloured floor cleaning liquid and the like. And there was the glossier, more expensive, Utterly Useless section. It was here that I found what I felt would be the solution to our neighbourly disharmony. The Free Standing, Chrome-Plated, Fake-Savoy-Hotel Toilet Roll Holder. £19.99.

Not the most expensive item – too obvious – but expensive enough. Perfect. I filled in the order form, placed the catalogue on the doorstep as usual, then waited. Yacob turned up two days later, bearing a large cardboard box.

He spoke, admittedly to the floor, but he spoke. It was a breakthrough. I paid in cash – he seemed particularly pleased – and I boldly asked if his mother had recovered from the Dana International weekender. He mumbled that he thought so, and then as he left thrust in my hands two new bigger and even more useless product catalogues.

Later, upstairs at Gay Opera Singer's kitchen table, I boasted of my diplomatic prowess. 'I really think I've achieved peace,' I said. 'And all it took was one toilet roll holder,' I added.

Suddenly the Moppeze catalogues were coming thick and fast. Pretty soon, between us, Gay Opera Singer and I had bought, and thrown out, two frog-shaped soap dishes, one tortoise-impersonator lawn sprinkler, and a magnetic window cleaner that fell apart on first use. Still, it was worth it. Yacob was now going out of his way to chat to the floor in front of us.

It was during one of these little chats that we noticed the salesman-recruitment sticker on the bumper of his Volvo. He didn't just do pyramid sales it seemed, he did pyramid recruitment too. *'Earn £20,000-£30,000'*, it said. *'No experience necessary'*, it claimed. 'That's amazing,' I said, pointing at the figures. 'You must be loaded, darleeng,' Gay Opera Singer said to our new friend.

'I know,' Yacob smiled. 'It's Big Business. Are you interested? I could introduce you to the right people.' 'Sure,' we said, in an unsure kind of way. '*You'd* be good,' Yacob said, throwing an appraising look at Gay Opera Singer. 'You have the salesman in you,' he insisted. 'If only, darleeng,' Gay Opera Singer purred in reply.

Twin Souls

It seemed like a good idea at the time – a retreat for those in search of spiritual enhancement and perhaps a little weight loss. For Rt-On Rev, it was to be a much-needed rest, away from his bleating flock. For his old school friend, Father Eoghan, a semi-lapsed Catholic priest with a passion for racehorses and saloon bars, it was a safe place to hide from his creditors.

The retreat was run by an order of Irish monks more than equal to the task of whipping misguided souls into shape. Although strict – the male-only paying guests had to adhere to a routine of prayers, abstinence and zero sexual congress – the monks were also realists. After all, they were in the service industry and repeat business was king.

There was a television in the lounge, carpets in some of the rooms, hot water in three of the best bathrooms and an evening allowance of hand-pressed lemonade. There was also the chance for curious friends and family to take tea in the parlour, or join the residents for high supper in the refectory.

Most of the guests elected to have visitors, but only Father Eoghan chose to have a visitor whose long-held ambition was to 'turn' a monk. Her name was Mona and she worked behind the bar at his local. 'Let me at them,' she said when he extended his mischievous invitation.

Sporting a skimpy black, shiny cocktail dress, a slash of red lipstick setting off her waterfall of sooty hair, Mona arrived for supper dressed to impress. The look wasn't wasted on the older members of the community, two of whom asked to be excused pudding in order to seek urgent spiritual guidance.

There were many reasons why Father Eoghan had long ago given up wearing the dog collar, but a large hint was dropped at breakfast the following morning when the Abbot held up a pair of ripped panties and a packet of 'Superman' condoms. Both items had been found down the side of the parlour sofa. A first, the Abbot sighed, and certainly for the housekeeper.

Although it wasn't his job to apportion blame, the Abbot continued, looking around the room at the startled guests, then alighting on Father Eoghan, he said he expected a healthy contribution to the cleaning bill and a hundred hours of dedicated prayer for the poor. And he wanted it to start immediately.

Accepting his punishment with good grace, Father Eoghan set about praying for the salvation of all those men and women facing a Saturday night rollover without a winning lottery ticket. He prayed for the bingo fans and scratch-card addicts. He prayed for his impoverished friends at the bookies and their irate wives. But quickly he lost interest: He knew the odds better than they did, and praying just wasn't going to cut it. What they needed was a lucky break, and so did he. 'Tell them you saw me on my knees in the oratory,' he shouted to Rt-On Rev as he jumped over the wall. 'I'm planning to be there all night.'

Five hours later the Abbot banged on Rt-On Rev's door. Where was Father Eoghan? Sticking to the agreed script, Rt-On Rev explained that his friend was in the oratory, praying for the poor.

'Well, the Lord moves in mysterious ways,' the Abbot replied. 'It seems Father Eoghan has achieved the miracle of bilocation.' Apparently a man fitting Father Eoghan's exact description had also managed to get into a fight over a woman in the Rose and Crown and was now in the cells waiting to be bailed.

Rt-On Rev blushed. 'Should we go and collect him?' he asked. The Abbot smiled. 'Oh no, son', he said. 'With his special powers, he'll surely be here soon enough.'

Do-do L Ron-Ron

The squat man standing in the dim doorway on Tottenham Court Road made Gay Opera Singer an offer he couldn't refuse. 'Perhaps we can offer you a glass of cooling water?' he said, stepping out from the shadows.

It was 90 degrees on Tottenham Court Road and barely noon. Gay Opera Singer had come in search of a satellite dish, but had so far drawn a blank. A refreshing drink seemed just the thing, he thought, as he accepted the squat man's invitation gracefully. 'It's hotter than Venus out there,' he joked, as they stepped into the cool reception area. 'Never my favourite planet,' the squat man replied.

Once inside, they headed for a bright-white lounge, past a life-size drawing of an interstellar space-plane that looked just like a Douglas DC-8 and several bookshelves housing loudly dressed science-fiction books. Comfortably seated, Gay Opera Singer drank the first of several glasses of chilled Evian.

The squat man drew up a seat opposite him, a clip-board and tape recorder by his side. As his guest drank, he asked if Gay Opera Singer would agree to answer a few questions. He and his colleagues were very interested in the outside world and they hadn't received many visitors that day. They were always on the look out for like-minded souls, and he thought perhaps he might have just met one.

'Ask away, darleeng,' Gay Opera Singer said. 'My mind is all yours.'

The squat man thanked him and swiftly reeled off a list of questions. Where did he live? Had he been here before? What was the purpose of his visit? Had he ever seen any shining lights? Had he known his parents? Gay Opera Singer answered all his enquiries patiently and politely, his enquirer diligently recording and noting down all answers.

'And what do you do for a living?' the squat man finally asked. 'I'm an opera singer,' Gay Opera Singer replied, his chest expanding to fill the sentence. The man looked startled, his pen trembling over his piece of paper. 'That's fascinating,' he said. Gay Opera Singer beamed and thanked him for the compliment. Not everyone liked opera, it was true, he continued. But he liked to think that one day the masses would suddenly switch on, so to speak. 'I like to believe I've already made lots of converts,' he added, buoyed by the attention.

The squat man became very excited. He too was interested in making converts. In fact, he had made it his life's work. 'I assume then, that you are familiar with space opera,' the squat man said, conspiratorially. Gay Opera Singer explained that it wasn't a genre he was wholly familiar with. 'But I am always open to emerging markets,' he added, keen not to alienate his host.

His host leant forward and patted the side of his nose. 'It's okay,' he said. 'You are among friends now, you can speak freely.' Gay Opera Singer thanked him but confessed that truly, he really wasn't au fait with this particular branch of the operatic community. 'Perhaps they are at the ENO?' he asked.

The squat man laid his pen down and whispered softly into his visitor's ear. 'Perhaps it would help if I told you that I myself am an Operating Thetan Level 3.' Gay Opera Singer nodded enthusiastically. 'That's fabulous,' he replied. 'But personally, darleeng, I really haven't done that much experimental work.' The squat man grew quite agitated. 'Look,' he said. 'Just because I've been put on door-duty doesn't mean that I don't know my stuff. I've done my time. You try surviving as an intergalactic walrus who was once thrown from a flying saucer.'

Fearing his host's rising anxiety, but not quite ready to hit the furnace-like pavements outside again, Gay Opera Singer attempted to humour him. 'The important thing is to keep working,' he soothed. 'You never know when your big break will come. One minute the door, next minute, the moon.'

The squat man rose from his chair and pulled himself up to his full height. 'Have you been to the moon?' he demanded. Gay Opera Singer had to confess that, no, it wasn't somewhere that life had taken him thus far. 'Well I have,' he replied. 'And let me tell you, those people are rock eaters. They know nothing.'

It wasn't quite the answer that Gay Opera Singer had been expecting. But by now, he wasn't really sure what he had been expecting. Whatever it was, it certainly wasn't this.

The conversation had ground to a halt, with both men reduced to staring into separate areas of space. Eventually, Gay Opera Singer broke the silence. 'You don't sell satellite dishes, do you?'

Make Mine a Monk

The beautiful young woman holding a clipboard leant in towards Piano Pete's eardrum. 'I SAID,' she shouted over the roaring traffic. 'Would you like to adopt a monk? Or perhaps an old man.'

She was from the newly formed Revive Seventies Politics Party. They were dedicated to discussing why the revolution hadn't happened – in Reichian terms – while at the same trying to raise sponsorship for Tibetan monks and old men.

She admitted that it wasn't an easy path to have chosen. Nobody cared about the revolution any more and the sponsorship-raising was hard work. True, some people would take a monk, 'as a status symbol,' she explained, but very few were interested in the old men. It was a shame, as the old men were lovely, spiritual types and just as worthy of the £6-a-month sponsorship fee.

They had very simple needs, didn't drink or smoke and as far as charitable donations went, they represented good value for money. 'Just think of the positive vibes you'll be sending around the world,' she said. 'And you'd get monthly updates on their lives.' What did he think?

Piano Pete was thinking lots of things, but mostly he was thinking, 'Thank God.' As far as he was concerned her sales approach meant only one thing: this beautiful nymph of a creature didn't think he was an old man. He was in with a chance.

'I'd like to know more about it,' he said. 'Perhaps we could go out for a drink and discuss it.' Hardened street hawker that she was, the beautiful young woman barely flinched at his suggestion. 'Why don't you come along to the Revive Seventies Politics Party party, tomorrow night,' she urged. 'I can't promise anything, but I'm sure you'll find it enlightening.' As far as Piano Pete was concerned, it was a date, and he promised to bring his chequebook.

The following evening he arrived, as instructed, at the rear entrance to the Red Bull pub. A hand-painted sign directed him along a route that promised authentic political and spiritual enlightenment, circa 1970. He was greeted at the door by a man sporting a ZZ Top beard and open-toed sandals. Over in the corner, there were various mug-shots of old men and monks, and above them hung a banner saying '£6-a-month and I'm yours'.

Along the back wall, a table was laden down with foodstuffs not seen since, well, the Seventies, which were being served out by more men in beards and several women who looked like Nana Mouskouri. There was a heavy scent of patchouli oil in the air, mixed with the unreconstructed smell of Old Holborn roll-ups. Nobody else was wearing Hugo Boss.

He scanned the room several times, but Piano Pete could not see the beautiful young woman. Eventually he gave up and went to the bar to console himself with a free pint of Carling Black Label. The man with the ZZ Top beard came over to join him. 'Hey, comrade,' he said, before putting his arm round Piano Pete's neck. 'See anything you like?'

Piano Pete was horrified. It really was just like the Seventies. Free love was about to happen, and here he was, trapped in a room full of men with beards and woman with batwing glasses. The man with the ZZ Top beard sensed Piano Pete's tension and squeezed his shoulder. 'The monks, comrade, and the old men, see any that you fancy?'

Piano Pete let out a relieved sigh and explained that they weren't exactly the reason he was there. 'I was approached by this beautiful young woman with a clip-board,' he said. 'She asked me to come along this evening. I suppose she just got delayed,' he added.

The man with the ZZ Top beard told him not to worry, there were plenty more gorgeous women at the party. 'Just look around you,' he said. Piano Pete smiled politely and ordered another warm lager. 'Take that woman over there,' he continued. 'Now, that's what I call a beautiful woman.'

Piano Pete could barely contain his alarm. 'You've got to be joking,' he said. 'She looks like Putin in a kaftan, how could you fancy that?' The man with the ZZ Top beard straightened his back. 'Because she's my wife,' he replied.

Scottish Assembly

Downtown Aberdeen isn't the first place you might consider sending a gay Unitarian minister, but the world's spiritual compass moves in mysterious ways and even the non-conformists are occasionally forced to heed its call. Besides, it appeared it was Rt-On Rev's turn. Wrenched from his liberal perch in East of Islington, he was dispatched with a mission: get the numbers up, up north.

Naturally his flock in the south were devastated. 'Aberdeen?' they wailed. If they wanted converts in the north, what was wrong with Hendon? But head office was unmoved. 'They'll welcome you with open arms,' his superiors insisted. 'Just don't try anything too fancy.' The Scottish ministry had been left unmanned for several years now and it showed. There was barely time for him to unpack his suitcase in the concrete motel block before the demands for pastoral attention started arriving.

His living quarters, a badly lit room with nylon-covered twin beds, a faulty shower and a cracked mirror, were barely conducive to the kind of caring and sharing he liked to offer, so Rt-On Rev arranged to meet his new flock in the bar. Which was something they generally seemed quite keen on. His first visitor, and almost his last, was a diminutive red-headed man who had managed to reach the ripe old age of 35 without ever having had a girlfriend. 'What can I do to get a girl?' he pleaded with the concerned clergyman. It was a question to which Rt-On Rev admitted he had very few answers. But he agreed that something would probably come to them over another drink.

On his way to refuel their glasses, Rt-On Rev met a gregarious young woman called Mona. Apparently her father was an integral part of the failing ministry, his organ-playing often relied upon for high days and holidays. She was pleased to meet Rt-On Rev, although ashamed to admit that she hadn't been to church in decades. Perhaps she should return. After all, it would make her dad happy and she was in need of a little spiritual guidance right now. Working as a pole dancer – that took its toll.

Rt-On Rev gave Mona his telephone number and urged her to call: in the bid for souls, everyone counted. He returned to his parishioner's problems with renewed vigour. There were obviously nice girls in this town, he explained to loveless young man. He had just met one. The important thing was to be sensitive. He had no doubt at all that this was exactly what women like Mona were looking for.

Rt-On Rev warmed to this theme for several minutes before feeling the weight of a very large hand on his shoulder. Turning round, he was confronted with a snaggle-toothed man who bore more than a striking resemblance to a bulldog with a penchant for steroids. 'See ma woman?' the man snarled, pointing in the direction of the lovely Mona. 'See ma fist?' he added, waving his clenched forearm at the terrified theologian. 'You've goat it cummin'.'

The man was convinced that Rt-On Rev had been attempting to 'pull his bird'. Something of a social faux pas in his etiquette book. 'But ... I'm her minister,' he squealed. 'Prove it,' his deranged assailant snarled. But reiterating his long-held belief that there was really no need for dog collars and other religious signifiers in the modern world, Rt-On Rev only managed to antagonise his assailant further.

The man's eyes bulged and his grip tightened. 'Outside,' he barked gutturally, nodding towards the plastic-coated swing doors. Rt-On Rev felt his knees dropping from beneath him, and just as he began to sag towards the prayer position, he saw Mona striding towards them.

A long barrage of expletives were exchanged between the two lovers, before Mona thrust a mobile into her irate boyfriend's ham-fist. On the other end of the line was her father, the church organist. Minutes passed as the snaggle-toothed madman grunted into the phone, his glare never leaving his victim's orbit. Finally, he hung up and refocused his complete attention on Rt-On Rev.

'So, yer a Sassenach?' he quizzed. Rt-On Rev admitted that, yes, technically he had moved from the south, but originally he was from Ireland. 'Aye,' he nodded. 'The auld guy said thut the new meenister wis a short, fat, mincing Paddy. And he wisnae wrang there.' Rt-On Rev was speechless. He looked over at his parishioner for some friendly support. 'Sensitive,' the parishioner mouthed back.

Highland Fling

Rt-On Rev had received an email asking if he would officiate at a wedding in a remote highland village. Since being sent up north to spread the Unitarian word, he had begun to wonder where his pastoral boundaries lay. But one thing was for sure, he was clearly the only minister north of Watford with a functioning website. This was his third crop of marital tourists this quarter and they didn't pay extra.

The bride, a lapsed American Catholic, and her intended, a second-generation Russian immigrant, had met as language students working off their loans at the new Starbucks in East of Islington. Neither of them had ever been to Scotland, but the idea of returning to The Bride-To-Be's ancestral roots had appealed. 'They're always doing it in films, aren't they,' she said by way of explanation.

Following the directions he had been given, and on the date booked, Rt-On Rev arrived at a small, unassuming, workers' croft. The door was opened by a bewildered-looking man in his early sixties. Waving the special licence, Rt-On Rev explained that he was the minister and had arrived ahead of the wedding party in order to get set up. 'Whatever,' the man sighed.

It wasn't the warmest of welcomes and the reason for the croft-dweller's lack of enthusiasm soon became clear. Two days earlier, he had received a knock at the door. A woman he had never seen before was standing on the doorstep: it had been the bride-to-be and her sheepish looking intended. Cutting to the chase, she had explained that her great-great-grandfather had once lived in the croft and under an ancient law of the Highlands this gave her the right to get married there. 'It is what he would have wanted,' she said.

Naturally, the home-owner had been more than a little taken aback. 'Naturally,' Rt-On Rev concurred. But, not wanting to appear mean-spirited, and because he was a newcomer with a limited grasp of local custom, he had agreed to their bizarre request. 'I'm not happy, though,' he said. 'My neighbour said I should have told them to sod off.' Rt-On Rev said he could see it was a difficult situation. 'But maybe lasting love would be it's own reward,' he added in his best pastoral voice. 'I'd prefer hard cash,' the home owner replied.

After several minutes of awkward silence, there was another knock at the door and the rest of the wedding party filed into the tiny living room. The young lovers were accompanied by the groom's Russian-speaking mother, and a man called Raoul who happened to have been staying at the same hotel. 'This is a first for me,' said Raoul. 'You're not on your own there,' said the home-owner.

Conducting a ceremony over the back of a frayed velour sofa was also a first for Rt-On Rev. But who was counting? After adjusting his ceremonial robe, he placed the candle for love and peace on the coffee table and pulled a bottle of merlot from his bag. As a representative of the spirit of life, he found it worked as well as any other liquor and he usually got to drink it afterwards.

At the sight of the bottle, the groom recoiled in horror, and his mother sucked air through the gap in her mouth where her teeth should have been. 'We don't drink,' the groom hissed. 'I do,' replied the home-owner, thrusting a glass forward.

With the formalities about to commence, the groom's mother anxiously motioned to the inside of her voluminous overcoat. 'Mama wants us to display the family icon,' the groom explained. Rt-On Rev nodded sincerely while the home-owner groaned as he was forced to clear his best china from the mantelpiece.

Out of the coat came a faded photograph, trapped in a hand-made frame that had been fashioned in the shape of a crucifix. It was a semi-nude image of what appeared to be the groom's parents. 'Another first,' said Raoul. At the risk of losing his concentration, or being thrown out by the home-owner, Rt-On Rev raced through the rest of the service.

Finally he got to the end of the lawful requirements and lit the candle of love and peace. It was over, they were wed. Man and wife kissed and Mama spat on the carpet.

'Jesus,' said Raoul, as he leant forward and lit a cigarette off the burning flame. 'Yes,' said the home-owner. 'Make sure you never buy a second home in this village.'

5

Lover's Lane

Seasonal Cheatings

Susie Round the Bend had been taking stock. She was almost 40, single and living in a neighbourhood full of confirmed bachelors and Hassidic rabbis. In order to get a date for the festive season she would either have to go kosher or learn the dance moves to the Village People. Or she would have to broaden her horizons.

The internet seemed to offer the largest range of possibilities. People in search of love, happiness, marriage, low commitment, high maintenance, one night stands, party animals and obscure cultish activities were all catered for. But there was something about Felipe's advert that caught her eye: *'Wanted. Woman for office Christmas party.'*

There would be free food, wine, dancing, and good company for a girl with an evening dress and a good sense of humour. In broken English, Felipe typed out the horns of his dilemma. He worked for a very traditional company. Not having a date suggested he couldn't get a girl or didn't want one – neither possibility was seen as career-enhancing.

In return for being his fake girlfriend for the evening, the respondent could be assured that he would escort her home in a taxi and that he could be trusted to behave himself. 'I don't need anything from you after the party,' his posting ended. For Susie Round the Bend, this last sentence set something of a challenge. After all, what man wasn't open to persuasion? True, he had set any potential dates an age limit of 28, but surely everyone lies about their age. And what were a few years once you were having a good time?

Ignoring the advice of all her friends, Susie Round the Bend answered the ad. She said that she loved to party, true. Was currently single, no questions there. Had a good sense of humour, she was answering the ad wasn't she? And that she was looking for nothing more than a good time from the evening, no strings attached. This last statement was a complete deviation from the truth but one that she felt more than capable of managing on the night.

Due to his apparently punishing work schedule, Felipe was unable to actually meet her before the event, but over a period of several weeks they conducted something of a mild flirtation via email. Or rather, Susie Round the Bend conducted a flirtation and Felipe became increasingly anxious about their compatibility.

It wasn't just the cultural references that he found difficult to recognise (he hadn't been born when Abba were in the charts). There was also her refusal to reveal any details of her age or physical make-up. 'I beg you,' he typed on a couple of occasions. 'You are important date

for me, I would very much like picture of you.' But Susie
Round the Bend was playing hard to get. Besides, what
use was a virtual 2D image when he would soon be able
to embrace the reality of her full-bodied charms?

On the anointed evening they arranged to meet in the
foyer of his company HQ. Although the invitation had
said cocktail dresses, Susie Round the Bend had opted
instead for a full-blown taffeta; she intended to make a
big impression.

Felipe caught sight of her as soon as he came through
the revolving doors. 'Felipe!' she shouted as she saw him
heading back towards the exit. 'Over here darling.' All
heads turned to the rising young executive as he scuttled
over to meet his date. 'You are not like I imagined,' he
mumbled, as she thrust her cheek expectantly towards
him.

She could tell that he was alarmed at their age differ-
ence but simply put that down to inexperience. He was
only 25 and probably hadn't been out with many
women. 'You'll get over it,' she assured him as she
grabbed his arm and steered them in the direction of the
canapés. But Felipe was having trouble 'getting over it'.
In fact, he didn't think he would ever 'get over it', certainly if the looks from his bemused colleagues were anything to go by.

As they rounded the corner into the hub of the
party, they came face to face with the chairman and his
wife. There was an awkward silence as the two couples
stared at each other, Felipe not daring to introduce the
woman on his arm. Eventually the chairman's wife
broke the ice for him 'It's very nice to meet you,' she
said, extending her hand to Susie Round the Bend. 'It

can't be easy having a gay son.'

Never-Never Land

Fungus had ridden the rollercoaster of romance with more vigour than most. Along the track he had his lost heart and soul, but never his faith, in a quest to meet that special person – the true and rightful one. A woman who would finally, unequivocally, fulfil his fantasy requirements, and do it all on a tight budget.

There had been serious contenders before, even a momentary stroll up the aisle. But the sad fact remained that Fungus's lust for love had remained largely unsated. Until, that is, three weeks ago, when he strolled into a bar, pulled up a stool, ordered a happy hour cocktail and spotted her in the smoked glass mirror. As he told me later, it was the face he had been waiting for, staring back at him as he admired his own reflection.

It was too good to be true. She was wearing designer clothing, but nothing too flashy. Her hair was perfectly coiffed, but not more bouffant than his own luxurious mane. Her teeth were white and appeared to be all her own. She also appeared to have a sense of humour. She was going to need it.

Pausing only to adjust his theatrical tie, Fungus manoeuvred himself into her orbit. He discovered she was an American – foreigners were always top of his wish list. A part-time actress (he was a great supporter of the arts) and a qualified pastry chef, a woman who knew how to stretch her dough, perfect.

Her name was Fondant Fancy, and little did she know it, but she had just met the man she was going to spend the rest of her life with. Unfortunately she wasn't going to spend the rest of the evening with him as his credit card had just been declined and he had been forced to make his excuses and leave. But not before he had secured her number and a dinner date.

In the cold light of the following day, Fungus assessed his situation. It wasn't as good as it might have been. Courtship was expensive and, as the barman had already reminded him, he was far from solvent. Undeterred by this minor detail, Fungus shuffled through his wallet before finally alighting on one obscure piece of plastic that hadn't been abused to the limit.

Doing some swift calculations, he estimated that if he was careful, chose the establishments wisely and starved himself in between, he had about four weeks worth of credit in which to woo Fondant Fancy. Plenty long enough, he concluded. After that, it would simply be a matter of long nights in, snuggled up in front of the TV, until his electricity supply was finally cut off. Who knew? She was American, there were bound to rich parents.

The first couple of dates at his local brasserie went extremely well. He was careful to stuff himself with store cupboard carbohydrates beforehand, thereby allowing his unsuspecting date the full rein of the 'French-influenced' menu, sensibly priced for midweek low-season diners. Mercifully, she was happy to let him do the wine ordering, and seemed content, even charmed, by the carafes of house plonk provided.

Then disaster struck. A hiccup that he hadn't accounted for. One of her actor pals suggested she get her new beau to take her to a 'fabulous' new restaurant. It had received rave reviews, apparently. The chef was the latest hot thing, and anyone who was anyone (and their agent) was there every night. There were virtually queues round the block, but her pal could get them a table.

What about it? Fondant Fancy wondered at their next meeting. Fungus could visualize the scissors of the *maître d'* on his magnetic strip as she spoke. If he was lucky, he might just be able to stretch to one course each, no wine, and definitely no tip. But it seemed unlikely. 'Can't wait,' he lied.

As they were being seated, he was swift to explain to the waiter that he would only be drinking tap water, no wine, and definitely none of the champagne cocktails recommended as an aperitif. 'I'm in training for the London Marathon,' he said, tapping his bread-bloated belly. 'Have to keep an eye on the figure.'
He skipped starters using the same excuse, ordered the cheapest cut on the menu, and watched Fondant Fancy unwittingly eat up all the money he had set aside to finish the courtship. 'Would madame like to see the desert menu?' the waiter asked, as he cleared away the remains from his date's chateaubriand.

Fungus acted swiftly. 'Madame is sweet enough,' he purred as her hand reached for the gold-embossed dessert carte. It had a suitably dewy-eyed effect on her. But the waiter was on to him. 'Of course, madame,' he said. 'But I can see that you are partial to something cheesy.'

Enchanted
Ever since Piano Pete had moved to East of Islington he had been on the prowl for a girlfriend, and tonight was to be no exception. His determination was admirable,

although primarily motivated by the almost certain knowledge that if he didn't settle down and breed quite quickly his highly fertile sisters would have emptied all the coffers in the family trust. To protect his interests and find a mate, he was prepared to travel far and wide into new and bold social arenas and join any social group willing to have him.

'At this stage I would date a penguin if I felt it would do the trick,' he said as he left for the bus stop. That evening's unknowing victims were the Kensington and Chelsea Freedom of Expression Society, a predominately female group looking for new members.

The party was already in full swing by the time Piano Pete arrived. His hostess smiled benevolently and ushered him into the busy throng. 'Everyone', she announced to the room. 'This is Pete, he's single.'

He wasted no time getting acquainted. 'Hi,' he said nonchalantly, to the red-headed woman sitting cross-legged on the elegant drawing room floor. 'Can I join you?' The red-headed woman nodded, serenely, and Piano Pete crumpled into a heap next to her.

The name she liked to call herself was Chakra and she was a Buddhist who spent most of her time chanting. When she wasn't chanting she thought good thoughts, but mostly she chanted.

In short, it appeared she was something of an earth mother type, but with impeccable taste. Perfect, thought Piano Pete. He could see the key to the family vault falling into his lap.

'I'm not a particularly religious person,' he said, by way of conversation. 'But I like to think of myself as a Buddhist. In fact, some of my best friends are Buddhists.'

The red-headed woman smiled. What, he mused, did she chant for? World peace? Love? The brotherhood of man? A sticky end for Barry Manilow?

The woman adjusted her Armani cashmere wrap and let out a delicate sigh. 'Most recently, I have chanted for a sports car,' she replied. 'And a flat in Mayfair. Although now I am concentrating on a new kitchen.'

Apparently she was a member of a new breed of Nouveau Buddhists; no brown rice and sandals for them. It wasn't quite the answer Piano Pete was expecting. 'But I thought you were all alternative lifestyle and no cable television,' he said. 'More mud huts than Mayfair'.

The woman smiled, again. 'I see you only deal in stereotypes,' she replied, taking a sip from her champagne flute. 'How dull,' she added, before wafting off towards to the catered nibbles.

Things weren't exactly going to plan. Undeterred, he refused to let this little opening hiccup put him off and instead spent the rest of the party following her from room to room, being sure to avert his gaze in a non-masculine manner whenever she caught him staring.

Unbelievably, his dogged determination paid off, and as the party drew to a close, the object of his desire tapped him on the shoulder. 'I wondered if you'd like a lift?' she asked. Piano Pete could barely contain himself.

Clearly, she had simply been playing hard to get. 'Sure,' he replied, as coolly as he could muster. 'Good,' she said. 'It will give me a chance to really show you what it means to be a Nouveau Buddhist.' Piano Pete could hardly wait.

The journey home was spent discussing places she

had been that he would like to go. Her dreams, always fulfilled, his dreams, still just that. Eventually they drew up outside his flat. Sitting in the darkened car, he made his next move. 'Would you like to come in for coffee? Or herbal tea, perhaps?' he added, fashionably. But her ignition key stayed firmly in place.

'You've driven all this way,' Piano Pete persisted, the desperation mounting in his voice, 'why not come in for a break? After all, you promised to tell me more about Nouveau Buddhism.'

And it was true, she had promised. 'Nouveau Buddhism,' she said finally, 'is quite simple. It is about chanting and doing good deeds. So, I chanted for my sports car and got it, and tonight I have done a good deed. I have given a lift to man who will never own a sports car.' And with a rev of the engine the lesson was over.

Greek Goddess

Fungus was many things to many people, but to himself he was a man of the world. He ate pizza. He drank good French wine, when he wasn't paying, he wore specially commissioned safari suits with monogrammed epaulettes and he always made a point of talking very loudly in English when approached by confused foreigners.

But his allegiance to the global village really came into its own while pursuing his favourite pastime; ensnaring unsuspecting females. 'They need guidance,' he was fond of saying when introduced to the naïve, newly arrived Eastern European au pairs employed by his more successful friends. 'Someone to take them in hand,' he would suggest to their horrified employers.

No people was safe from a potential invasion. Spanish, German, Scandinavian, Slavic – he had, he liked to boast, 'been there, done that'. But not the inventors of democracy. For some reason the Greeks had always refused his attempts at romantic diplomacy – until now, that is. A chance encounter at a local taverna had recently added a new flag to his collection.

He had been invited along to a friend's 40th birthday party, an occasion that the man's wife believed gave her an excuse to smash large quantities of crockery, all helpfully provided by the restaurateur and paid for by her husband. By the time dessert arrived, the floor was awash with the shattered remains of hundreds of once perfectly serviceable plates and the tears of the man footing the bill.

The guests, meanwhile, were throwing themselves into the party spirit, and it was while one of them was attempting to persuade a waiter to 'do an Anthony Quinn' that the door opened and in walked Zorbina, the proprietor's sister. A bold, tanned, fiery divorcee with a mane of wild auburn hair, she was, as far as Fungus was concerned, the epitome of a Greek goddess.

Wasting little time on niceties, he crunched his way over to her table and introduced himself. 'Let me take you away from all this,' he said to her. Her response was to throw a plate at his feet, which he took to be a yes, or at least a maybe. Zorbina, it soon became obvious, was no wallflower, and several glasses of ouzo later he discovered that she been married, then divorced and liked her men to be men. The latter she denoted by raising her arm in the air and pumping her muscles, Popeye-style.

Real conversation was limited, perhaps because she had only arrived from Crete that morning and didn't understand much English, or maybe because she couldn't be bothered to speak to him. He needn't have worried though, she had a way of making her feelings felt and had somehow managed to master a few select phrases, the primary one of which seemed to be, 'huh, waster,' which she spat out every time the subject of her ex-husband arose. Fungus was guessing, but from her hand movements he understood that the man was a writer of sorts who appeared to have a pinky finger stuck in place of where his marital under-carriage should have been. The ex-husband also liked a drink, but then they had had that in common.

Having mimed their way through the best part of a bottle of ouzo, Fungus felt confident that the fledgling relationship was proceeding apace, and suggested that they retire to his place for a final nightcap. Although a state of near-bankruptcy forced him to share a small flat with four other men, he was sure the other inhabitants would all be asleep, leaving the coast clear for him and Zorbina to continue reading each other's body language in the comfort of his eight-by-eight foot studio room.

Miraculously, she seemed amenable to the idea and so off they set with Fungus carrying her incredibly large bag – the contents of which had yet to be revealed. Within moments of entering the flat, she threw him, and the large bag, down onto his badly made single bed.

Like a scene from a pay-per-view movie, they rolled around in an impassioned frenzy, the static from his nylon sheets competing with the heat of their ardour. As workouts went, it was a marathon. Finally, the closing credits arrived and his head hit the pillow for a moment of quiet reflection. Not so Zorbina. 'Encore,' she shouted, pulling a bouzouki out of the vast bag. In a trance-like state – which he felt he could claim some credit for – she began wailing and playing, the machine hung low around her naked midriff.

There was no denying it, she liked things loud. Within moments the entire household was awake and banging on the walls. But Zorbina, oblivious to their pleadings, had started her second act and she intended to finish it. Eventually, after what seemed an eternity, but was actually ten minutes, there was silence. The flatmates, dazed and confused, ceased banging. Zorbina smiled. 'More, yes?' she shouted. 'More, no,' came the calls from beyond the thin partition.

Greek Gifts

Snoring was not something that Fungus usually put at the top of his romantic CV. Rather like his habit of employing underpaid Eastern European beauty therapists to rip the hairs off his back with the aid of a birch stick dipped in burning hot wax, he often found it was not to everyone's taste. And certainly not to Zorbina's.

Since their liaison had cooled from the first flushes of its passionate embrace, he had been at pains to ensure that his nasal outpourings did not incur her further wrath. It was a difficult task. Her fiery Mediterranean temper was prone to explode at any moment and the thought of waking, or not, in the morning with a broken nose kept him on his toes.

It wasn't, she was at pains to point out, that she didn't have feelings for him, far from it. On their twice-weekly trysts she would allow him to express his gratitude for her attentions by carrying her large bouzouki kit bag, and occasionally would consent to his arm around her waist in public, but on the whole she preferred to keep his emotional needs repressed. 'Treat them mean and don't worry about it,' seemed to be her relationship mantra.

But when it came to the issue of his snoring, she was resolutely unmoved. Not for him the cosy feeling of leaving his spare pyjamas under her feather-light pillow. In fact, not even for him the opportunity of staying unclothed for longer than was absolutely necessary. From the moment he had completed his conjugal duties, to the point at which he had realigned his fob watch over his nine-piece suit, his actual presence in his mistress's bedroom could be measured in mere seconds. Timing, he had found, was everything.

He once made the mistake of lying down to recover from what he felt was a particularly arduous attempt to impress his paramour, and awoke some minutes later with the full force of a duck down duvet being pressed over his airways. The heavily embroidered design detail left an imprint on his face for many days afterwards.

Occasionally he would try to find a 'cure' for this tiresome nocturnal affliction. Herbal remedies; heated candles placed in his ears; ice-cold water poured into his inflated nostrils; sleeping on his side; sleeping on his front; not sleeping at all. He even consulted a psychic. He had spent a fortune but the outcome was always the same: no bed and certainly no breakfast. It was putting a strain on the future of their relationship.

Finally, on the eve of a much-anticipated romantic

getaway, Zorbina called him over for a 'chat'. They needed to confront the elephant in the room, she explained. And that elephant was him, quite literally. She realised that it wasn't his fault, it was a problem that affected millions and she didn't want him to take it personally.

What she wanted them to do instead was concentrate on what they should pack for their holiday. Fungus was confused. After all, he liked to pride himself on his capacity for squeezing piles of highly unsuitable outfits into two specially monogrammed suitcases. In fact, on several occasions customs officers had complimented him on his ingenuity.

Still, her reaction had been better than he had expected and there seemed no harm in humouring her. She looked on benevolently as he read through the list of lurid checked shorts, safari suits, Brazilian-style bathing briefs, sun block and four changes of Panama hat that he never travelled without. She even looked amused at the sight of his beloved teddy bear placed in pride of place on top of his sateen pyjamas.

When he had finished she presented him with a small gift. 'For you,' she said. Fungus was taken aback. 'You shouldn't have,' he said. 'Oh yes, she replied, 'I insist.' Inside was a 'results guaranteed' anti-snoring kit containing two long wires marked 'personal electrodes'. They were accompanied by a precise, and rather graphic diagram, that seemed to involve direct application onto his private parts.

He stared at the instruments of torture for several minutes 'For your little problem,' she explained. 'I wouldn't call it little exactly,' he replied.

Greek Ruins

Over the years Fungus had frequently altered his position on what he liked to call 'the opposition'. When he was young, lofty ambitions for high political office drove him in search of girls destined to look good in blue. These fledgling relationships started out fine enough. The happy couple would spend leisurely weekends at country houses, not his, and romantic evenings discussing the merits of a good personal fortune, always hers. But invariably it all ended in tears and on two occasions with the threat of a lawsuit.

Then came the wilderness years. The years spent loitering on the liberal fringes where he lost a fortune, bought some ill-fitting leather outfits and gained some rather unsightly marks on his rear. Momentarily, there was a marriage to an eminently sensible girl who gave it a week before leaving to do good works overseas, her newly signed-up spouse still applying the airbrush to his side of the wedding photos as she slammed the door.

As the decades passed and the hair 'styling' increased, it became universally acknowledged that his was a challenging case. After all, what woman would want to devote their life to a man who spent three hours a day hoisting himself into a collection of specially constructed nine piece suits, then topped the whole ensemble with a fob watch embellished with a portrait of himself?

For a while it appeared that Zorbina was just that person. Demanding, athletic, with little or no regard for what the Californians called his 'emotional needs', her fiery Mediterranean temperament was best expressed when it came to her physical desires. 'You fail to entertain me,' she would threaten as he trod the stairs to her boudoir, 'you fail to live.' Wetsuits, dry suits, lights on, lights off, comedy routines from the best of PG Wodehouse, Fungus was soon out of ideas and struggling to make the grade.

Twice he had accidentally fallen asleep whilst taking what he referred to as a 'performance interval' only to wake with a kebab skewer against his windpipe. It was his final warning. Regardless, he was determined not to give up. He believed he knew what she wanted; what all women wanted. Danger, excitement, a touch of darkness tinged with something sweet. Yes, what they wanted was The Milk Tray Man.

A quick visit to his local army surplus store furnished him with a black balaclava and a second-hand set of crampons. Fortunately he was already well stocked with a variety of lycra outfits that he felt gave him just the right 'come hither' silhouette. True, she might fear she was being attacked by a member of the IRA, but what paramilitary would take on a woman who had been taught to garrotte chickens in her school lunch break?

It was dark when he arrived at her apartment. Instead of discreetly laying the gift-wrapped box of chocolates on her pillow with his calling card, he had decided to make do with a chance encounter in the lift. It was a deviation from the original script, but times change and he had no real idea how to scale a building.

By the time he spotted Zorbina fumbling for her door keys, his unorthodox garb had already attracted some attention and he had been forced to buy off two hooded teenagers with all the hard centres from both the top and bottom row. It wasn't looking ideal but Fungus decided to press on regardless. Just as the doors to the lift were about to close around her, he plunged the mutilated chocolate box forward. The object of his desire stared back at him.

'All because the lady loves Milk Tray?' he said, smarmily, a heat rash rising under his acrylic mask. Zorbina opened the box and had a cursory shuffle around. 'There's no hard ones,' he said, apologetically. Her expert eye fell upon his skin-tight outfit. 'I can see that,' she sighed.

www.love.com

Over the years Cambridge had applied for a great many romantic positions. Straightforward boyfriend, second-string lover, occasional walker, stalker, decoy beau, all with the hope of reaping some fringe benefits and a long-term contract. He had even tried moving countries in an effort to up the hits on his dance card, but invariably the result was the same: he never got called for the last waltz.

But recently he had announced that things would have to change. Like most of us, he was fast approaching 40 and he wasn't planning to do it alone. The internet café on the high street promised the answer. *'Meet your dream partner,'* the promotional poster claimed. *'£1 per hour, two hours free for first-timers.'* What did he have to lose?

Once the local self-service launderette, these days, instead of lonely singles staring aimlessly at revolving foamy orbs, the interior was full of frozen-faced youths crammed into minute booths fitted with metered LCD screens. In a way, the effect was much the same.

Luther, the twenty-something Ukrainian arts-graduate-turned-manager forced to work 14-hour shifts to pay off his overdraft, had come up with the idea of attracting more customers by enticing the 'relationship-challenged' with offers of easy access to love. For a one-off registration fee of £20 an open gateway to the world's dating sites was assured. Seven days a week, 24 hours a day, complete with thumbnail pictures and sassy word portraits.

For most of the men in the room, Cambridge included, it was a steal compared to the costs of propping up an uptown bar and standing several rounds of drinks for a clutch of girls who would invariably leave in time to catch the last train home. 'Oh yes,' Luther assured him as he was handing over his credit card. 'There are no trains in cyberspace.'

In order to keep things simple, and save on computer credits, he decided to focus on those girls who had intentionally ticked the box saying they were looking for men with PHP, otherwise translated as Proper Husband Potential. Luther said that this was generally a safer bet than those who were looking for men with ILB, commonly known as men with Incredibly Large Bits. 'Those women can be trouble,' he explained. 'Some of them have been known to ask for proof of measurements.'

After much searching, Cambridge made contact with a woman who sounded almost too good to be true. She was in her early thirties, a graduate with a keen interest in arts and literature who said she didn't take herself too seriously and whose picture suggested that there was going to be no attractiveness shortfall in her gene pool.

There was only one drawback. She lived in Washington.

But despite the possible geographic difficulties, they embarked on a series of increasingly fruity email exchanges culminating in a midnight suggestion that he board the next available flight to DC. For a man who had essentially played safe all his life, it was a gamble but one to which he felt irresistibly drawn. Eighteen hours later he touched down at the presidential airport and made his way to the restaurant where they had agreed to meet. He had never known an adrenalin rush like it. His potential new girlfriend was waiting for him and they headed off to consume a beautiful meal, backlit by candles and supported by Neil Sedaka's greatest hits. She was every bit as attractive as he had imagined. The substantial bill came and he gladly paid it. It was, in short, the perfect date.

On the way out of the building she turned and gazed into his eyes. 'There's something I'd like to tell you,' she said. Cambridge nodded, expectantly, his face carefully drawn into a loving pose. 'I'm bipolar and celibate,' she said. He felt his jaw drop – he had to admit, it wasn't what he had expected. 'You didn't mention it on your profile,' he finally mumbled. 'No' she admitted, cheerily. 'I wasn't sure what box it would come under.' 'Did you consider MAD?' he replied.

Shop Till You're Dropped

Piano Pete's efforts to persuade a woman to give him what he wanted were still proving fruitless. True, there were woman who had agreed to go on a date with him. There were even women who were occasionally prepared to answer to the title of 'girlfriend'. But passionate love seemed to evade him. Or, to put it more bluntly, he just didn't seem to be able to get them to agree to hanky-panky.

Roses, champagne, Gloria Estefan records and lengthy RSI-inducing foot massages rarely resulted in the Tarzan and Jane-like antics he was looking for. And it wasn't that he hadn't done his homework, he told anyone who would listen.

He had memorised whole chunks of *The Joy of Sex* and was a regular subscriber to *Cosmopolitan* magazine (a well-known source for the modern man in search of bedroom tips). But he frequently had to settle for being what the Americans called a 'pyjama pal': something marginally more alive than a pyjama case but still subject to the same lack of voluntary movements.

His latest inamorata was a Peruvian salsa fan specifically targeted for her love of all things hot and steamy and yet even she managed to resist her genetically inbuilt urges. Nightly, he would take her out and fill her to the brim with expensive cocktails, whisking her back to his basement lair in the hope that her giddy state would persuade her to abandon her newly discovered reserve. But nothing. As with most of his other attempts at carnal conquest, the pattern was always the same.

As they fell into bed and the passion meter began to rise, she would invariably utter the words that he grown to dread. 'I don't feel like it,' she would say. 'I just want you to hold me.' He had learnt from bitter experience that pleading got him nowhere but still, he always gave it a go. And the answer was always the same. 'Why can't you just love me for who I am and not for things I can give you in the bedroom?' she would say. Strictly speaking, her English didn't quite run to full sentences, but he had heard the patter so many times from her predecessors that he had now taken to helping her finish the lines.

Finally, he realized that he could take it no more and went in search of a remedy. A cursory search on the internet led him to a site for fellow sufferers entitled *'Get Your Own Back'*. For a one-off payment of £25, he would regain control of his own universe, or least his own bedroom. *'Follow our step-by-step instructions,'* the site said, *'and you will never have to face the humiliation of sexual rejection again.'*

Piano Pete quickly signed up and devoured the contents of the fool-proof plan. The next week, following the instructions to the letter, he took a day off work to spend some 'quality female time' with the object of his desire. He took her out to a nice lunch and then went shopping at a large, luxurious women's fashion emporium. He walked around with her while she tried on several different very expensive outfits. She couldn't decide which one to take, so he told her that they would just buy them all. She wanted new shoes to complement her new clothes, so he said, 'Let's get a pair for each outfit'.

They went on to the jewellery department where she picked out a gold bracelet and two pairs of diamond encrusted earrings. She was, she whispered, highly aroused by the experience and Piano Pete was the happy recipient of much stroking and hand-holding. After four hours of intensive shopping, her mouth was aching from the pain of constantly smiling at him. 'I think this is all darling, let's go to the till,' she cooed finally, her voice full of panting anticipation, his arms weighed down with gorgeous gifts.

It was the moment he had been waiting for, the first stage of the *'Get Your Own Back'* £25 plan. 'Actually sweetie, I don't feel like it today,' he replied. Her face froze. Warming to the script, he embraced her. 'I just want you to hold them,' he continued, handing her the pile of euphoria-inducing goodies to cradle. Her expletive-laden response quickly drew quite a crowd. 'Why can't you just love me for who I am and not for the things I can give you in the shop?' he smiled, loudly reiterating that last part of the *'Get Your Own Back'* plan. There was a hushed silence from the room full of female onlookers, followed by the sound of their collective howling. It wasn't exactly another sexual rejection, but he didn't think it was a come-on either.

Current Affairs

There is little doubt amongst those of us who knew him that Fungus was, in the immortal words of Frankie Howerd, 'very peculiar.' But his latest affectation had even the most understanding of them confounded.

For a man who spent most of his time staring at his reflection in any available surface, and very little time engaging with the views of others, he had suddenly developed an almost obsessive interest in the news. Or, to be more precise, the delivery of the local news.

He was no longer available for social events, unless he could be assured that there would be a television set tuned for the six o'clock bulletin. At a push, he would accept the offer of video-taping in return for making a personal appearance at a cocktail soirée, but he was itchy to have a replay as soon as the final olive had been consumed.

Begrudgingly, he would share his small-screen experience with other viewers, but only on the understanding that there was total silence. It was imperative that he didn't miss anything important, he claimed. A change of outfit perhaps, or, apparently most worryingly, a new hair do.

In short, Fungus had taken to stalking Nina the Newsreader. And he left no stone unturned in his quest for knowledge of her life and times. Official websites, fanzines, details of Nina's favourite restaurants, pop stars, star sign, choice of lottery numbers, mother's hair colour; such was his dedication that he had little time for anything else.

Work, whilst never a major preoccupation, became a mere passing fancy. Family reunions, dental appointments, trips to the theatre, all passed without notice. Instead, like all stalkers before him, he focussed only on the one thing that he believed would bring him true happiness: a meeting with the object of his desire.

'We are made for each other,' is all he would say when counselled on the error of his ways. 'Just wait and see,' he would add smugly. And then it happened – the impossible.

Like a scene from a romantic novel, he spotted her across a crowded party, in the flesh, the walking, talking embodiment of his perfect female. It was his only chance for happiness, and he wasn't going to miss it. Unfortunately for Fungus, however, he wasn't the only middle-aged man with a fixation. Nina the Newsreader was surrounded.

Those hovering on the outer circle of her orbit were comparing notes. 'She was even more beautiful up close,' one whispered. 'Her eyes were like liquid pools,' another drooled. For Fungus, the competition was unbearable, but he was determined. 'She's mine, she's mine,' he mumbled under his breath.

But then came the earth-shattering news that none of the star-struck fans was prepared for. 'She's married,' interjected a passing female guest. 'To a merchant banker,' she added for good measure.

Audible intakes of breath emanated from the assembled group. Fungus was mortified. How could she be? Months of vital research had revealed nothing about a husband. 'Perhaps she's ashamed of him?' suggested one of his competitors. 'It's probably on the rocks,' consoled another.

And all the while Fungus was slowly edging his way up the informally arranged queue towards the woman he still had every intention of going home with that evening.

To calm his nerves, he decided to mentally run over his notes. She liked wild flowers. So did he, sort of. She didn't like Heavy Metal, ditto. She had a penchant for all things Middle Eastern. He had recently added couscous to his culinary repertoire. And she was very sporty. He liked that in a girl.

But the clincher he felt was her professed love of history. He had a degree in history – it was obvious, they were made for each other.

The other fanciers were getting restless. Fungus was being jostled quite hard by a rotund barrister whose plan was to offer a charge account at Tiffany's. 'What girl could resist?' he boomed at anyone who would listen.

The pressure was on. Then, suddenly, and without proper introduction, Fungus and the object of his every desire were face to face. 'Hello,' she purred, as she extended her elegant hand. 'I'm Nina'.

Fungus was stage-struck. Finally he opened his mouth. 'I'm an historian,' he squealed at her. 'And you need to know that your husband will soon be history.' It took some time for the beating from the security guards to subside, but Fungus still maintains that his relationship with Nina the Newsreader moved to a new level that evening.

Three-Minute Wonder

Piano Pete had reached the point where he had given up hope of meeting the right girl through chance or convention. To everyone, including his mother, it was becoming obvious that he was more likely to dance with Elvis than meet a single woman with a pulse hunting for a barely employable musician.

To date, he had tried dinner parties, theatre clubs and New Age conventions (a good source of gullible souls he figured) but time still marched on and with it any chance of getting his hands on the family fortune; 'no sprogs, no spoils' was the Air Commodore's motto.

Then Speed Dating arrived at the Hen and Chickens. At first glance the basic premise seemed clinical and calculating but for Piano Pete it also had its advantages. It was in the pub, the bar would be full of women, none of whom he would have to buy a drink for, all of whom he would get to chat up. True, he would only get three minutes with each one, a pointless exercise some might say, but actually something of a flirting record for Pete.

What had he got to lose?

On the first night the pickers and choosers were taking no prisoners and Piano Pete was woefully under-prepared. In the tight time-scale allocated there was little room for procrastination and the questions came quick and fast. Favourite film, pop star, pizza topping, character in *Friends*. Cat or dog ? Meat or veg? 'Do you come here often?' just didn't get a look in.

Bruised but not bowed, he did his research. Over the next month he honed his responses specifically for the female market. *Bridget Jones's Diary* (the first one); George Michael; pepperoni; Monica (the uptight one); he loved all things furry and only ate them if they had been given a good life and only then on a special occasion. He also polished his technique. 'I love you,' as an opening gambit seemed to stop a few in their tracks, but it was the much more frank 'I need you' that eventually landed him the ultimate prize – a follow-up date that would span an entire evening.

The woman was considerably younger than him but she said she didn't want him to worry. She could 'feel' his need and she believed that this was a good sign. As Pete could 'feel' his need himself, he agreed that he too believed it was a good sign.

They arranged to meet for dinner at a small candlelit pizzeria and then to go on to a chi-chi drinks party thrown by a man Piano Pete had been at school with and who occasionally invited him to things when he was low on numbers.

The meal went incredibly well. She ate meat, lots of it, and drank enough red wine to make him feel that they were heading for a happy ending or at least a point when she would want to remind him again of how she could 'feel' his need.

When the bill arrived he was taking no chances and quickly brushed aside her attempts to pay half. 'I insist,' he said. She leant over the table and stroked his hand. 'You're so old-fashioned,' she sighed.

The party was about ten minutes' walk from the restaurant and he suggested that perhaps a romantic stroll was in order. Along the way they discussed pop bands he had never heard of and TV shows that had barely crossed his cultural radar but again she told him not to worry. 'As long as we are able to "feel" each other,' she said, repeatedly. He said that he could think of nothing else.

In fact, he was concentrating so hard on them being able to 'feel' each other that he realised rather too late that they were lost. His date seemed unfazed. 'Let's ask someone,' she said, breezily. At that moment a man half his age rounded the corner, headed in their direction. 'I'm going that way,' the stranger replied in answer to the young woman's call for help.

Within seconds the two had fallen into a rapid quick-fire conversation about mutant art forms and obscure musical genres that ended with her inviting the stranger to the drinks party. In effect, she had invited him to join their date. Even for Piano Pete this was a courtship first.

Once at the party, it became obvious to Pete that there had been a sudden shift on the 'feelings' barometer and the needle was no longer pointing in his direction. In fact, it was pointing out the door on the arm of the stranger his date had picked up in the street. 'What's happening?' Piano Pete wailed, as she collected her coat and hurried out the door. 'Very speedy dating,' she replied.

Fifty and Not Out...
To celebrate the fact that he had reached his half-century, Fungus invited 30 of his closest friends to buy themselves dinner in his honour. He understood, he explained in the invitation email, that many people would find it difficult to believe that he really was this aged – after all, he still looked so youthful, and still had so much hair, but the fact was that time had marched on, even for him. Although in one sense it hadn't. Even he realized that the last 12 months had been tough on some of them, which was why he would only be charging them the same prices that they had paid for his birthday dinner the previous year. So in a way, he concluded, the celebration of his birth should also be viewed as a story of economic triumph.

Admittedly he had so far failed to scale the dizzy fiscal heights of tycoon-style success, or indeed made a living of any kind, but these things were mere details. After all, he was on the cusp of resurrecting his career as a crooner and was also happy to announce that he would be selling copies of his personally recorded CD during the supper proceedings. Anyone wanting to order in advance could be assured of a five per cent discount.

By the time the evening arrived, he was one guest down. He had just cut off relations with his latest girlfriend, which he admitted was a shame, but as she had recently refused to pay for any more meals, and he was incapable of paying for any at all, he couldn't really see the point of her coming along anyway. Better that he faced an empty seat, he figured, than an even emptier bank account.

In fact, turning 50 had caused him to reconsider many things about his life, Fungus explained to the female friend hurriedly slotted into the vacant space to his right, the primary one being his attitude to romantic entanglements. It was, he insisted, obvious that there were great differences between men and women. And in his case, more so than most.

He was a very self-contained person, he told her as he topped up her glass with some of the wine she had paid for. As far as he was concerned, he really didn't see the need for any actual emotional connection with the opposite sex. True, there were the unavoidable outbursts of begging, pleading and even occasional weeping that could accompany a particularly gruelling night in with the leather whip and bondage accoutrement.

But as far as the rest of it went – the cuddling, the terms of endearment, the need for human contact – it was all wasted on him, and from now on he had decided to make that very clear from the beginning. There was also to be a moratorium on sleepovers. Indeed, he had developed a new dating template for all future involvements so everyone knew where they stood.

It was all very simple Fungus told her. After sexual congress with him he found any woman was usually 'replete' and therefore fell asleep very quickly. 'I like to give it ten minutes,' he told her, 'and then get up and take the night bus home.'

It's proved very successful so far, he added. The friend agreed that it was certainly the right approach for someone trying to avoid anything even vaguely romantic, especially the bit about the night bus. Fungus thanked her. 'The thing I really love about this plan,' he said, 'is that in years to come my dates will only get cheaper.' 'Cheaper?' the woman wondered. How much cheaper could he get? 'Well,' he smiled. 'There's always the free bus pass.'

6

Kennel Club

Babe Magnets

Willy and Poppy had never liked Piano Pete. Not for him the frenzied greetings reserved for those guaranteed to hand over titbits and coochy-coo chats. Not for him the privilege of having his clothing covered in their hair.

Instead, they barely bothered to glance up as he entered the room, conscious as they were of his indifference to their limited bag of tricks. So it came as quite a surprise to them both when he suddenly appeared at my door, offering the hand of friendship and enquiring as to their availability for a walk around the park.

'I thought it was time we got to know each other better,' he cooed at a suspicious and snarling Poppy. 'I mean, it's not like I'm not a dog-lover.' He was obviously lying, but it was free dog-walking so who was going to argue? On his return from his first cursory trot round the greenery that passed for the local park, he decided to confess all. It seemed his motives were less than altruistic.

Piano Pete had fallen hopelessly in love with a tall, blonde, Polish princess who had little or no interest in swapping her international jet set lifestyle for a shabby existence in a basement flat East of Islington.

But Piano Pete had a plan. Apparently the Polish princess was the proud owner of two extremely precious, madly inter-bred Chinese lap dogs whose sole purpose in life was to be patted and stroked.

As far as Piano Pete was concerned, these walking fur purses were his beacon of light. In their limited conversations to date, the unsuspecting girl had mentioned them on several occasions. Ergo: he needed bait.

'Dogs as babe magnets,' he beamed broadly. 'It can't fail. I just need to borrow them on a regular basis and she is bound to fall for it.'

Poppy and Willy weren't keen, I could tell. 'The dogs don't seem very sold on the idea,' I said. But Piano Pete was adamant. Somehow, despite only exchanging two brief sentences with the Polish Princess, he was convinced she was the answer to his prayers. Having a father like the Air Commodore had long ago helped focus his mind on matters of the heart. 'No sprogs, no spoils,' was the old man's inheritance mantra, and with two fertile sisters ahead of him Piano Pete was prepared to stop at nothing. Even dog theft. Besides, he had already arranged to go dog-strolling in one of the smarter royal parks the following day. 'Her dogs are really posh,' he said as an incentive. 'Your mutts need to get out more.'

It seemed churlish to deny him this chance, cynical as

I was about his limited hope of success. So, with a heavy heart, I agreed. The following morning he arrived bright and early to collect his new allies. 'Haven't they got any pretty little coats to wear?' he pleaded, looking at the unkempt duo sulking on the doormat. 'I distinctly remember her saying that her ones liked nothing better than putting on their Burberry flock doggie coats. I wouldn't want her to think I haven't made an effort.'

It was at that moment that I noticed Willy's lip curl. Obviously nothing, not even a free trip to a swankier park, was going to make them love him. By the time they set off, relations were extremely strained, but the dogs were nothing if not pragmatic. He was holding the leads, they were just being dragged along. Certainly Piano Pete appeared to be heartened by the results. 'I'm sure she's growing to like me,' he confided after their fourth outing to the far swankier park. 'She said yesterday that she would never consider having a relationship with someone who wasn't a dog-lover. I think that's a good sign, don't you?'

I suggested that he come clean, before she discovered the truth herself and reported his unhealthy obsession to the law. 'I can't back out now,' he said. 'Yesterday I picked up her dog's poo-poo and she said I was a darling.' His misguided belief in their burgeoning romance was short-lived. The phone call breaking the news was short and terse. The dogs were no longer required to make the trip across town and frolic around the far swankier park.

He would be returning the library copy of *How A Dog Can Change Your Life* and attempting to get a refund on his subscription to *Dog Lovers* magazine. In short the charm offensive was off. He felt it had been a brilliant plan in every way except for one small detail. 'And what was that?' I asked. 'The dogs belong to her boyfriend.'

Guinea Foul

As a young girl Susie Round the Bend had been in love with a guinea pig. Or, to be more specific, George the guinea pig, her one and only childhood pet. Her mother, never keen on the sight and smell of strange creatures, had allowed her desperate children just the one furry indulgence and told them to make it last. 'Once it's gone, it's gone,' she had said with all the emotional candour of a Sixties parent.

Knowing that it was a once-in-a-lifetime treat, her elder brother had wisely picked a tortoise, hedging his bets against the chances of early loss and abandonment. But the ten-year-old Susie, naively unaware of the need to invest her affections wisely, chose to fixate her feelings on an animal more used to the warmer climes of South America than her parents semi in East Purley.

During his brief lifespan, she worshipped George with an unguarded passion. Dressed in a silk jacquard waistcoat specially crafted at Brownies, he had been her date at several birthday parties, his penchant for nibbling her young earlobes the cause of much alarm amongst her more conservative friends.

When she fell off her bike she sobbed into the warmth of his unwillingly upturned underbelly, his photograph worn with fierce pride in her special collectors' Barbie locket. But tragically, at the tender age of 18 months, he died, his stiff little legs discovered protruding from the bars of his cage one crisp autumn morning. Susie Round the Bend had been bereft.

A funeral befitting a head of state was performed in the herbaceous border, his body interred in a specially adapted, velvet-lined tea caddy coffin. In the 30 years since, no male had managed to make that much of an impression again on her. He might have been a guinea pig, but as far as Susie Round the Bend was concerned, he wasn't just an experiment in love, he was love.

So it came as something as a surprise to her friends to discover that she wasn't quite as accommodating when it came to other members of the rodent family. In fact, her dislike of the more common varieties could be said to border on the clinical.

It was difficult to tell what it was about them that she found so abhorrent, but as with all personal fancies, it seemed to come down to aesthetics. Guinea pigs had it and the rest of them didn't. Ordinarily it wasn't an issue, True, she would avert her gaze when presented with her niece's pet rat, and Disney films that glorified the mouse were automatically avoided. But it wasn't a life-threatening affliction, and generally she managed to keep her feelings of revulsion in check.

Until, that is, her house was invaded. It had started with some familiar scratching behind the skirting board and ended with hysterical screaming and an emergency dash to the local DIY store. The manager was very understanding. 'We get a lot of them round here. And they just won't take no for an answer,' he laughed, basking in the comfort of his well-practised repartee. 'You better take this card.'

He handed her a black embossed piece of plastic with

the words *'Manuel Manual Mouse Removal'* printed on it. 'He's very popular with the ladies,' he added.

Within an hour Manuel was standing in her kitchen surveying the tell-tale signs and sucking his teeth. 'You need help, lady,' he said in his strong Spanish accent. While Susie Round the Bend made the tea, Manuel set about laying the hair-trigger hinges that would be the visitor's final curtain call. It turned out Manuel was from South America, just like George. In fact, Manuel was from Ecuador to be precise. Susie said she was ashamed to admit that she was never really sure where George's ancestors originally came from, but wherever it was she felt sure it must have been beautiful.

Manuel said she wasn't wrong, South America was a great place and he missed it, the weather, the people, the pace of life. But most of all he missed the food. 'Oh the food,' he sighed. 'Magnificent.' What about her friend George, he wondered. Didn't he miss the food? Susie became misty-eyed and got out her old childhood photograph album. There, in pride of place, was a picture of George in his silk-jacquard waistcoat.

Confused, Manuel took the album from her and stared at it for a while, looking several times from the portrait to her tear-stained face. 'Ah yes,' he said finally, grasping the situation. 'In your country, guinea pig is pet. In our country, guinea pig is delicious.'

Obi-Wan Kenobi

Obi-Wan Kenobi had little or no time for social norms. Not for him the pedestrian reality of polite obedience and personal boundaries. His was a parallel universe in which he was no mere border terrier but a warrior, a giant, the king of all he surveyed. Cats, dogs, sheep, goats, in fact any mammals with a small mind and a slow turning circle were fair game to this self appointed superhero. But he wasn't a superhero. He was, in the words of the local plod, 'a very naughty boy'.

His doting owners, Poshy and Glammy, had even once experimented with leaving the big city lights behind in order to give their beloved pet a better life in the countryside, only to discover that rural family outings were at best a chore and at worst a legal case waiting to happen.

Desperate to fit in, they had tried everything. Behaviour modification at the very best classes. Treat withdrawal, treat overload, delicate personal surgery that had rendered him useless to even the most persistent of the female sex. They even bought him a friend, a little pup called Kissy Poo, who took one look at her new mate and refused to leave the boot of the car.

Occasionally, other immigrants would arrive and unwittingly invite them round for drinks. Their rectory doors flung open to make the best of the verdant views, these newcomers were full of the first flush of countryside living and neighbourly bonhomie. 'Bring your dog,' they would say, naively. 'We are very pet-friendly here.'

Invariably, these fledgling relationships didn't last long. Once they had seen what Obi-Wan Kanobi could do to a child's guinea pig, in front of the traumatised child, the hosts soon revised their invitation policy. Poshy had lost count of the number of replacement rodents he had bought, but he doubted that anyone else in the village was offered a bulk discount at the local pet store.

Then one day a lunch invitation came from a new

couple with no pets and a desire to make friends. Months of social exclusion had taken their toll. Poshy and Glammy were desperate to see the inside of someone else's drinks cabinet so they decided to risk it.

With nothing worth chasing, Obi-Wan Kanobi was the very picture of good behaviour. 'He's such a good boy,' their hostess commented as the afternoon drew on. 'Perhaps we should get a border terrier.'

Poshy and Glammy were so proud; during one lunch break he had morphed from an advert for euthanasia to a poster boy for his breed. The feeling was to be short-lived. While the recently acquainted couples opened their third bottle of chardonnay, Obi-Wan Kanobi decided to take a look inside the garage.

The triumphant howls could only mean one thing. 'Ooh,' said Glammy, trying to cover her alarm at the all-too familiar sound. 'What could that could be?' Paolo, the 80-year-old tortoise, had never met a dog before, and from his compromised position, he wasn't keen to repeat the experience.

'Paolo,' sobbed his distraught owners. 'Paolo, Paolo.' Paolo was busy trying to keep breathing while Obi-Wan Kanobi helpfully swung him round by his leg. The specialist vet arrived and said it might be touch and go and it would certainly be expensive. With no alternative, Poshy immediately offered to pay all the bills as the vet retrieved the mortified reptile from the jaws of his assailant.

After several days on 24-hour observation, it appeared that there was no immediate threat to Paolo's life except perhaps Poshy's desire to bring an end to the mounting invoices. Unfortunately for him, the vet was in no rush. Apparently tortoises are as slow to mend as they are to move. It could be 2018 before he was discharged. 'It's the worse case of "tortoise interruptus" I've ever seen,' he added. 'I wouldn't bank on it,' replied Poshy.

On the Buses

For some time now it had been obvious that all was not what it seemed with Eratica, the dog-walker-cum-cleaner. She had come into our lives via a postcard on the notice board at the local supermarket. 'Reliable, caring cleaner needs work, likes pets.'

Initially she went to work for Gay Opera Singer, polishing his surfaces until Dazzling Darren's perfectly aquiline features could be seen at 20 paces. But pretty soon she had branched out, juggling some five guilt-ridden, liberal East of Islington clients who awkwardly employed her services, while at the same time condemning the increasing formation of an underclass.

She hailed from Germany, had an impressive grasp of European languages and a penchant for writing. She also had a liking for a healthy nip of sherry but, having told her to help herself to refreshments, I was hardly in a position to complain.

Once a week, on a Tuesday, she would come to the house, push the vacuum cleaner around and then take Poppy and Willy for an invigorating stroll around the park. Or so I thought. Because, as I have said, all was not as it seemed. A couple of weeks passed, during which Eratica failed to turn up. Her phone remained unanswered, she appeared to have just vanished. While waiting for Tuesdays to return to their normal rhythm, I uncovered the truth about the secret world inhabited by the dogs on a Tuesday afternoon.

The Hopper bus, a familiar sight around the metropolis, would travel less than three miles and then turns and comes back again. Each day it was jam-packed full of commuters, shoppers, young mums, old mums, the long-term unemployed and, I then discovered, Willy and Poppy.

One Tuesday, on my way to waste some time drinking coffee with a friend, dogs in tow, we passed the Hopper bus stop, conveniently located at the bottom of our road. 'Ooh, aren't they looking well!' cooed the two elderly dames standing at the bus shelter, Freedom passes at the ready. 'Poppy looks so much better with her hair cut, doesn't she?' I stood and smiled, while the dogs danced the dance of greeting reserved only for the very few and for all small children bearing jammy biscuits. 'I'm sorry,' I said. 'I don't think we've met.' Clearly the tone of my enquiry was off-pitch, but I was confused. How did the dogs know the two bus pass-holders? What was this secret relationship?

'Ooh, we're old friends, dearie. We have a little chat with them every week, but we missed them on the bus today, didn't we, darlings?' the stouter one continued. As the Hopper approached the dogs started wagging their tails furiously. 'Ah, look!' the ladies chimed. 'They're getting all excited.' It was at this point that I politely explained that the dogs would not be getting the bus today, that we were on our way to visit a friend. 'Ooh, yes,' they murmured in hushed tones. 'Is it because of what happened last week?' What happened last week, I wanted to know? But the doors were opening, and the ladies were getting on. 'Got to rush, hope to see the doggies next Tuesday,' they chorused. The dogs were crest-fallen, as were a gaggle of schoolchildren waving and shouting their names frantically as the Hopper sped off down the bus lane.

The following Tuesday Eratica again failed to turn up. Desperate for information, I presented myself, and the dogs, at the same time, at the bus stop. The two ladies were waiting and, again, the dogs were ecstatic. After a few preliminary enquiries, and several treats for the dogs, it was revealed that Poppy and Willy spent the best part of their Tuesday afternoons travelling the entire Hopper bus route seated right near Stanley, the quiet, unassuming, slightly balding bus driver – and the object of Eratica's affections.

'It's a shame,' one of the ladies explained in hushed tones. 'She seems to get herself a little tipsy, then sits by him for the entire route. Last week,' her voice lowered an octave, 'she sang *Delilah* for him; a couple of customers complained. And she got off before the route had finished.' How long was the entire route, I wanted to know. 'An hour. Some days she goes round two or three times, but the dogs seem to like it. Stanley always stops the bus, you know, so that they can pay a visit.' It seemed that Willy and Poppy were something of a star attraction on the Hopper. 'Stanley really loves them,' they said. 'He just doesn't like her very much.'

The ladies could see I was stunned. 'Didn't she mention it, dearie?' I confessed that I'd had no idea, that none of us had seen Eratica for a couple of weeks now, and that we were getting very worried. 'Oh, you don't need to worry about her, dearie, she's all right.' How did they know? 'She's enrolled as a trainee bus driver. You can see her going through her paces at the depot. Poor old Stanley.'

Hamster Reels

Some people are born animal-lovers and some people have animals thrust upon them. Spooky definitely fell into the latter category. It wasn't that she had a particular affinity with hamsters. After all, she mused, in the greater scheme of things, what did they actually stand for?

But being a newly joined parent at the Vegan Nursery Collective, she was keen to impress and animal-loving seemed to go with the territory. And so it was that she found herself saying the immortal words: 'I'll take the hamster home for the weekend.'

At the Vegan Nursery Collective – the VNC to its more seasoned members – the rabbits, guinea pigs and, of course, Hammy the hamster were all kept in individual cages fitted with water bottles and ripped-up pages of *The Guardian*. They were kept as a testament to the VNC's devotion to all living things. 'We would never hurt a soul,' they were fond of telling visitors as they watched the socially starved Hammy hit 20mph on the exercise wheel.

'If it was up to us, we would release them back into the wild,' they would often add. Sadly the streets of East of Islington were a long trek from the burrows of the Syrian desert so it was never really going to happen. But it was a practiced line in PR and they stuck with it.

Spooky had discovered veganism rather late in life. It was while doing research into the pros and cons of the GI diet that it struck her: what she really needed was an eating system that virtually eliminated all types of food-stuff and the weight would simply fall off.

Her three-year-old daughter had been less keen. Spending her pre-school years in the company of people who thought of the fish finger as the enemy wouldn't have been her choice, but it appeared to have its compensations. Taking the hamster home at the weekend was one of them.

Hammy came with a boot-load of hamster accoutrement and a complete set of instructions. A strictly vegan diet, obviously. No soft drinks other than water. Two hours a day of classical music (to make him run faster on his wheel) and one session each afternoon of healthy 'petting'.

'No problem,' Spooky had called out of the window as her car pulled away one fateful Friday evening. 'We'll have a great time.' The next morning Hammy became Pammy and 12 baby hamsters appeared in the bottom of the cage. A cursory look on a hamster-lovers' website suggested that hamsters were committed breeders, but not how Pammy might have managed it all on her own. It also had no tips on how to stop a squeaking wheel.

By the time Monday morning arrived, Spooky concluded that her short-lived love affair with animals was well and truly over. All she needed to do now was deliver the increased hamster family back to their rightful owners and remember to keep her hand down in future.

The drive back to the VNC was uneventful enough. The hamster's cage carefully strapped to the back seat, her daughter uttering soothing words to the trapped mammals as they went over the speed humps.

On arrival, the excited three-year-old rushed in to

break the good news. As Spooky went to unload the car, she was faced with a sight every mother dreads – a dead pet. Or, to be precise, two dead pets. The speed bumps had clearly been too much for two of the new arrivals

With no time to lose, Spooky had to think on her feet. Swiftly, she scooped the two unfortunate creatures out of their papery grave and stuffed them up her right sleeve, wedged in behind a couple of frayed tissues.

Acting as if nothing had happened, she put the cage back in its place in animal corner, alongside the guinea pigs and the fish tank. The new arrivals were met with squeals of delight by staff and children alike, their little forms peered at and heralded as a positive sign in the vegan universe. Not wanting to detract from the celebrations, and certain that her three-year-old couldn't count beyond five, Spooky decided not to mention the two stiff corpses stuffed into the fibres of her cardigan. Why spoil eveyone's fun?

Besides, it was line-dancing morning, a chance to further impress the other parents. Throwing herself into the proceedings, Spooky led by example, swinging her arms the highest and whirling the hardest. Bizarrely, it was this overt enthusiasm that was to bring her membership of the VNC to a sudden and dramatic end. In slow motion, she could see it coming but was powerless to prevent it. On the third energy-filled twirl, her sleeve shifted, indirectly catapulting the two stiff corpses through the air and into the face of a traumatised four-year-old boy. Needless to say she made her excuses and left.

The Stud
There can be few matchmaking stories like it. It had

started out as a potential romance and ended up like a badly edited scene from an overly saucy lingerie catalogue. All in all, I blame my own social aspirations, and my desperate desire to see Willy matched with a dog from a higher social stratum. Suki was a fellow border terrier who spent her winters languishing in a £2 million pound house in Hampstead and her summers holidaying at a small estate in Dorset.

Her arrival in my life ignited fantasies of drinks party invites and weekends in the country that knew no bounds. Like a pushy stage mother, I ruthlessly exploited our otherwise reticent hound.

Without his approval, or that of Willy's Walker, in Dog Poo Park one day I gleefully handed over our telephone number to a woman I had always secretly referred to as Mrs Money. We were on nodding terms only. She would arrive in a pristine Mercedes, march her pooch round the park barking, 'Morning, morning,' at her fellow dog walkers, then disappear again to the sanctity of her much smarter postcode.

Then one day she stopped me. She was in the market for a 'stud' she said, as she stood and appraised Willy. But he needed to have form. How good was my boy? 'A coconut every time,' I had assured her, without any real shred of evidence. Technically it was true that he had once 'obliged' with a desperate whippet, but that was a while ago, and he really had shown no interest since. Still, I felt sure he would rise to the challenge once he saw the inside of their vast Georgian pile.

Months passed, and I had virtually forgotten all about the encounter, when the phone rang. 'Hi,' said the well-bred voice on the line. 'Can get your Willy round here straight away?' Momentarily taken aback, I twigged, and seized my opportunity. If nothing else, surely it would mean we would be invited in to get a look around the Money Mansion.

Willy's Walker was marginally less impressed. A lifetime spent regretting the loss of the family 'stately' had left him unmoved by house envy. Still, I could tell he wanted his lad to do well.

'Get your pads on, Willy,' he shouted, as he searched for the lead. 'You're going in to bat.' Whether Willy could understand his master's metaphors was unclear, but he seemed relaxed enough when we finally arrived at his intended's door. And he certainly seemed suitably impressed by the delicately landscaped private park at the rear.

It was agreed that Willy would stay there overnight and we would collect him the next morning. But come the appointed hour the next day, it seemed that Willy had not broken his duck. 'He seemed very keen,' Mrs Posh explained. 'But perhaps a little intimidated by the surroundings.' I knew how he felt. Zuki meanwhile was desperate. 'Perhaps I should get a professional?' pondered Mrs Money.

I was crestfallen, the drinks party invites fading before my eyes. 'Or perhaps he would feel more comfortable in his own yard?' Mrs Money added. Grasping any chance to continue our burgeoning relationship, I readily agreed. Zuki was to come and slum it in East of Islington for the whole weekend.

That Friday night, Zuki was dropped at the door by their driver and soon set about making her demands felt. Ousting Poppy from her perch in the fireside basket, she hounded Willy round the flat, eventually causing him to hide under the bed. No shrinking violet, she wanted her conjugal dues and she wanted them now.

'Do you really think you want her to be the mother of Willy's pups?' Willy's Walker sneered at the upper class Jezebel.

But by now, I was determined. Even if it meant 'intervening' in the coupling. Reluctantly seduced out of hiding by a Bonio, Willy was once again urged to perform.

The main problem seemed to be not just his reluctance, but her height. She was just too tall for him. It was then that I hit upon a solution. Two weeks worth of the Saturday *Guardian* provided just the lift Willy needed.

Balancing his back legs on the hefty print pile, while steering his front in the right direction, between us Willy's Walker and I would have made James Herriot proud.

For the next two days the scenes on our kitchen floor were not for the faint-hearted. Spurred on by proffered Bonios and shouts of, 'You can do it boy,' Willy did an approximation of his duty.

By Monday morning it was time for Zuki to leave. Mrs Money came to collect her and was ecstatic with the match report. 'Good boy,' she said, patting the reluctant Willy on the head. 'You must come round for drinks,' she added as she strolled out the door. A positive test result in my book.

Hedge Rows
Reg and Renata the hedgehogs had left the wildlife sanctuary in Cambridge two years before to go and live with

Mr and Mrs Breezy in Battersea. For the first six months they lived in a box, and then one day some kindly folk took pity and built them a Nissen-shaped duplex house complete with ridged ramp. However, shortly after they got their new house they fell out big time, and Reg moved out to live in a plastic bucket.

Except for the unavoidable physical contact when they met each night to consume their tray of upmarket cat food, they avoided any contact with each other. Or indeed any other of their species, being the only two hedgehogs in that particular patch of undergrowth. On the odd occasions when they would accidentally bump into each other on the brick path that ran alongside their Nissen hut, a less than romantic hissing fit would ensue.

Renata, the main instigator of the hostilities, was increasingly unsure of what she had seen in her spiky ex-partner in the first place. Not that they had to look at each other that often. By November they liked to be in bed and, frost permitting, sleep through till March the following year. There were some in the animal kingdom who liked to make more of their lives and get out more, but for Reg and Renata this was it. The world they knew.

Then one day in spring they awoke to dramatic news at Breezy HQ. Mr and Mrs Breezy had drawn up designs for the garden and they didn't involve Reg and Renata. Their garden, 30 feet of brick-walled paradise, knee-deep in slugs and snails, was about to be transformed into a glass cube kitchen extension, leaving a mere ten feet of paved patio, not exactly the hedgehogs' favourite.

Mrs Breezy loved Reg and Renata but they were no competition for extra worktops and a stainless steel Smeg oven with matching extractor hood. Meanwhile,

Mr Breezy had already picked out his place at the eight-
seater dinner table with a view of the aluminium infinity
waterfall through the sliding French doors. There was
nothing else for it, they explained to friends, they would
have to put Reg and Renata up for adoption.

It would be a particular kind of person who would
want to adopt a pair of fighting, snarling, anti-social
hedgehogs, but luckily there was such a person among
our number. Fearless, owner of a huge 80-foot walled
garden in heady Stockwell, complete with a mediaeval
broch, was keen. There was something about their inter-
personal relationship that she found appealing, comforting even. A date was set for preliminary negotiations and
the vetting process.

The garden in Stockwell was in full bloom by the time
they arrived. Mrs Breezy was tearful, but Mr Breezy was
sanguine. It was true that he liked them but they hadn't
made much of an impact on him. 'What was the point of
a pet who was in coma for half the year?' he said, a reply
that hardened Fearless's resolve to go through with the
re-housing scheme. The garden was checked for holes
and neighbouring cats and a suitable spot found under
the evergreen magnolia. Personal care duties for hedgehogs were limited, but Fearless agreed to continue feeding them garlic (to dissuade any opportunistic fleas) and
to serve only premium cat food.

With the practical machinations completed, everyone
retired to the kitchen table to discuss the emotional
implications. Would Reg and Renata notice the differ-
ence? Would they care? Would they need much stroking
(metaphorically speaking of course)?

Mr Breezy suggested that as they were blind and half-deaf he didn't really think it would make much differ-ence, but if it was a help, they might play a tape of the police sirens each night. 'To make them feel at home,' he said. Fearless reminded him they were in Stockwell. 'I don't think we'll need the tape,' she added.

Eventually it was agreed that Reg and Renata would be moved while enjoying their mid-afternoon nap and their mini Nissen hut craned, without interruption, into their new spot. By the time they woke there would be no going back.

There was only one small problem. Fearless ran a tight ship. Her garden was streamlined, seasonally co-ordinated and beautifully coiffed. She could accept the integration of the Nissen hut, re-painted perhaps in her-itage colours, but there was no way she could allow the aged plastic bucket that Reg had made his home. Aesthetically speaking it was a no-no.

'They'll just have to move back in together,' she said. Mr and Mrs Breezy looked a little startled. They recounted the personal problems that the disgruntled couple had been having from the start. The obvious signs that they physically loathed each other. 'They really don't seem to get on,' Mrs Breezy added, finally. Fearless looked a little confused. After all, they were married weren't they? Mr and Mrs Breezy admitted that, yes, technically speaking, Reg and Renata were formally a couple. 'So, no different to the rest of us then,' she replied.

Beggar's Belief

It had become something of a ritual in our domestic arrangements for Willy's Walker to take Poppy and Willy for a brisk early evening stroll. His usual destination was the newsagents, followed by a brief sortie to the local wine merchant, where he would tie the dogs outside to the security shutters, keeping a brief eye on them while he hurriedly made his choices.

But, this being East of Islington, these simple outings were not without their complications and the main one was expense. It had become quite costly navigating the pavements along the high street, lined as they were with a motley collection of part-time beggars.

Armed with empty coffee cups from one of the plethora of lifestyle takeaway emporiums, they would fiercely guard their territory, while sharing the same sales pitch. 'Spare any change, mate,' would be their clarion call to the embarrassed liberals subsequently shamed into coughing up.

Admittedly it was a tactic that never worked with Willy's Walker. 'Get a job,' was his preferred riposte, delivered with all the force that a public school education can deliver. 'Or try the Army,' he would add if he was feeling particularly generous.

Then one evening he returned home full of optimism. He had personally solved the beggar employment problem. 'Dog parking,' he expanded. It seemed that he had struck up a conversation with Bill the Off Licence Beggar, and, for a set fee of one pound, Bill would mind Poppy and Willy while Willy's Walker enjoyed an extended browse though the wine racks of western Europe.

Apparently Bill was keen, not least as takings were down since his rival on the opposite side of the street had added a dog on a string to his tactics repertoire.

'So it suits both of us really,' Willy's Walker explained, before uncorking that evenings purchase. 'And depending on how they do, I could start hiring them out to other beggars.'

Over the following week, the dogs were duly escorted on their nightly tour, each evening's visit to the wine racks lasting longer than the last, Willy Walker's determined to get full value for money out of his new arrangement with Bill. Quite what Willy and Poppy were subjected to while on duty with Bill was unclear, but it soon become obvious that for Poppy it was a less than pleasurable experience.

Initially she displayed this displeasure by dragging her paws as they approached Bill's weather-torn blanket. Willy, sanguine as ever, quickly settled into the routine, snuggling into Bill the Beggar's smelly collection of belongings while Poppy stood firm, refusing to lay down.

As the minutes passed, she would whine, incessantly, until Willy's Walker returned to collect them. She also shunned all Bill's advances. For a dog addicted to stroking from any corner, this was strange behaviour indeed.

Willy's Walker was mystified. Was it Bill's cologne? Did she fear catching a chill sitting on the damp and dingy pavement? Was it the fact that he had considerably fewer teeth than those humans she was used to?

For Bill the Beggar, however, Poppy's distress was a bonus. Takings were up to record levels. The more Poppy protested, the more the animal-loving public took pity on his motley tableau.

But finally, after six nights in her new role, Poppy could stand it no more. And, as they approached the wine merchants on their usual route, she steadfastly refused to move.

Willy's Walker could do little to budge her. As far as Poppy was concerned, her short career as a beggar's moll was over. Bill, on the other hand, was less keen to terminate their arrangement.

'But the punters love the whining,' Bill explained when Willy's Walker pointed out Poppy's obvious lack of enthusiasm. 'And it really makes them cough up when she starts shaking,' he continued.

But there was no budging Poppy. The more Bill pulled her lead in the direction of his patch, the more she dug her paws in. It was obvious, Bill just wasn't the kind of man she wanted to be seen with. Willy's Walker was going to have to call the whole thing off.

It was then that Bill revealed his trump card. He hadn't always been a tramp, he had a law degree and knew how to use it. 'Technically,' he said, 'it's constructive dismissal.' Willy's Walker pleaded for understanding. 'It's going to cost you.' Quite how much, has never been revealed. But it was several months before Willy's Walker could afford to visit the wine merchant again.

Single Mum

Poppy had become the subject of neighbourhood gossip. The once shy and retiring West Highland terrier momentarily lost control of her senses and was now, in the words of Gay Opera Singer, 'done for'. She was about to become a single mum.

Her paramour was none other than Willy, our middle-aged border terrier. 'He can't afford it,' Willy's Walker sighed on hearing the news. Willy himself embraced his new responsibility by ignoring it. A trip to the vet was called for. Willy's walker said that in his opinion (formed during years spent growing up on a Kentish sheep farm) animals generally got on with it. 'It's a natural event,' he muttered over the top of the sports pages. The vet took a similar view. 'Congratulations,' he said, patting Willy on the head. 'Upwards of four of them I'd say. Keep an eye on her and don't let her have them under a chest of drawers, so difficult to get a look at the buggers then. Come back when they're five days old.'

Spooky brought her children round for a visit. 'Are they going to get married?' Starlight, her middle daughter, wondered. Spooky, who had celebrated her own short-lived marriage with a reception at a Kentucky Fried Chicken, was constantly flummoxed by the apparent orthodoxy of her offspring. 'They don't need to get married, darling,' she attempted to explain, only to be beaten by surreal logic: 'But if they don't get married, they won't be able to get a family railcard,' the child pleaded.

Finally, to appease her conservative daughter's fears, Spooky undertook to compose a special dog wedding ceremony – on the strict understanding that we never mentioned it to our more anarchic friends. Meanwhile, prospective parents stepped forward to adopt the soon-to-be-delivered puppies. Like some overprotective madam I was adamant that they were to be given the best start in life. Gardens: a must. Previous experience of dogs: essential. Propensity to over-indulge and leave soothing music on the radio when they're on their own: perfect.

The extra attention was overwhelming for the expec-

tant mum and she responded by refusing to keep her
food down. Eventually we took her back to the vets. We
were greeted at the door by a super-confident Australian
locum. 'And what seems to be the matter with Podgy?' he
drawled as he felt her underside. 'Poppy,' I corrected. 'She
keeps getting sick, and I wondered if it had anything to
do with the pregnancy?'

The man of science stared at me for a bit while continuing to feel around Poppy's lower torso. 'This dog's
not pregnant,' he said. 'She's just got wind.'

Who's The Daddy?

'It'll be all right,' insisted Willy's Walker. 'All you need to
do is get hold of their hindquarters and pull. And have a
length of rope ready.' Having emptied the bookshops of
dog books, I concluded that Poppy was experiencing
what the experts described as the first stages of labour,
or whelping, to give it the proper technical term. She had
been pacing the floor, panting and mildly trembling,
looking for a suitable 'nest'. She had ripped up every
piece of paper in the house and bitten a sizeable chunk
out of my duvet. She had been whimpering for hours and
developed a dry nose, but there was no sign of any pups.

With no other option, I called the vet who three weeks
earlier had diagnosed 'wind'. 'Oh right,' he announced,
without a hint of embarrassment. 'Nothing to worry
about. You'll know when the action really starts.'

Why weren't there any dog hospitals where she could
be taken in with her little pyjama bag packed and a bristle brush for post-natal grooming? 'With smaller mammals, it's often sufficient just to put your foot on their
backsides and give it a good yank,' Willy's Walker sug-

gested after we had endured a further 15 sleepless hours of first-stage whelping. Desperate, I called the nonchalant Australian. 'Okay,' he sighed, sensing my rising hysteria, 'Bring her in.'

Once back at the surgery, things suddenly became quite serious. He didn't want to distress me any more than was necessary, after all, this was my first pup, but things didn't look good 'We'll give her some drugs.' he explained. 'But I think we're looking at an emergency Caesarean.' Several of the prospective adoptive parents rang during the £600 operation. 'Are they cute and fluffy?' they wanted to know. Two hours later, we got our answer.

Poppy, whose relatives had won Crufts for being small, white and fluffy, and who can trace her lineage back 100 years, was delivered of one massive, male, pup. 'It's huge,' the vet announced as I entered the waiting room. 'And black.' The unfeasibly large pup had happily eaten his way through a nine-week gestation period, consuming enough food and biscuits for a litter of four. With the vet's heart-warming words still ringing in my ears, I went out to the car where Willy's Walker was waiting with the travel basket. 'Prepare yourself for a shock,' I said.

Minutes later, he was back, mother and humongous pup in hand. 'Whose is it?' Willy's Walker said looking down at the large, black, pup. 'Because it certainly isn't Willy's.' It was true that the pup bore no resemblance to our small brown border terrier .

We decided to give Willy his Fido Castro celebratory dog-chew cigar from Harrods' pet department anyway, and slowly set about convincing ourselves that this pup, the Lenny Henry of pups, was still, despite the physical evidence to the contrary, in some way related to one of our dogs.

Dangerous Dog Act

The years of begging had paid off and Spooky's children were finally going to get their heart's desire: a real live puppy. Her delaying tactics had been impressive. Newspaper cuttings of children mauled by deranged mutts pinned to the fridge door. Pictures of foam-faced rabid dogs snarling in filthy third world pens held up as examples of what could evolve from a once biddable ball of fluff.

And, most crucially, the removal of the cable TV sub-scription to make way for any Fido. But they were unre-pentant. In their razor wire-fenced comprehensive, if you didn't have a Staffordshire bull terrier pup hanging off your left arm you were no one. Spooky may not have known much about dogs but she did, as the saying goes, know what she liked and the council estate badge of honour was not it. Not that she would ever admit that of course. She was nothing if not a socialist.

But the children were adamant. It had to be a Staffy. At a push they would accept the brindle-coloured ver-sion, but ideally they wanted the white one, with the black eye patch. And the sooner the better.

In a bid to widen their horizons a little, she booked a family ticket to Crufts and dragged two belligerent teenagers and a pet-hungry five-year-old around the show stands. 'They are so many to choose from,' she said, as she steered them towards the cocker spaniels. 'This one looks really cute,' she said, stroking the velveteen ears of a champion. 'And friendly,' she added. 'Wha'ever,' the children replied as they headed off towards the terrier's enclosure.

The Staffy breeder was no help. 'Wonderful around youngsters,' she cooed as they played tug-of-war with one of her testosterone-fuelled young males. 'Bit boisterous, but harmless really,' she giggled as the animal tore the hem clean off the five-year-old's skirt. Mercifully, the woman had a long waiting list for her next two litters and there would be none available before the end of the year. The children were crestfallen. 'Let's keep in touch,' Spooky lied.

On the way home they drove past Harrods, its lights twinkling in a come-hither kind of way. 'They have a pet department,' Spooky mentioned idly. 'In fact, they used to say they could get you anything, even an elephant, in Harrods.' Within what seemed liked seconds they were on the fourth floor and standing in front of several forlorn-looking King Charles spaniel puppies.

A smooth-talking sales assistant approached. The children wanted to know if they had any elephants, or perhaps a tiger, anything really from the nastier end of the mammal spectrum. The King Charles spaniels just didn't cut it. 'We have a pug,' he replied, ruefully. 'And he is particularly unpleasant.'

To date, this over-bred species had not entered her children's doggy lexicon and so there was still everything to play for. For Spooky, pugs had a certain Brighton antiques trader whiff about them, but she kept her thoughts to herself.

The children were intrigued. The pug, Nero, had been there for six months, its puppy sales window long passed. Several times a day it was taken out of its cage by earnest Japanese shoppers looking for something with handbag appeal. Unfortunately a daily diet of visitors' titbits had given him quite a weight penalty and he was now more a suitcase-on-wheels kind of dog than a clutch purse.

The sales assistant offered to bring the bored beast out for closer inspection. Released, Nero strutted across the room like a tiny atomised bull and headed straight for the spaniels, terrorising them into retreating to the back of their pen. 'Cool,' the children said. He snapped at the five-year-old and snarled at the teenager's advances. It was going well.

He wasn't a Staffy but he clearly had major social issues, he could have been made for East of Islington. The sales assistant sidled up to Spooky. 'I could let you have that one for half-price.' Spooky looked a little startled. 'Just to clear him.' Nero had settled himself by the door. He may not have been out much but he could sense a sucker a mile off. 'I'll take it,' Spooky said, decisively. The children punched the air. The sales assistant joined them. Nero relieved himself against the gerbils. 'No returns on sale items,' he added as an afterthought.

Snip

Gay Opera Singer stood astride the kerb, his startled-looking cat Fidelio in his arms. It was obvious all was not well. 'They got him,' Gay Opera Singer wailed. For some time now, the covert operatives from SNIP, the Society for Neutering Islington's Pussies, had been operational in the area and it would appear they had claimed their latest victim.

They were on a mission; the total eradication of free love in the feline world. Their targets, unsuspecting and unwilling, were the motley collection of tom cats regularly to be heard scraping and cruising for sexual favours along the garden walls.

For the most part our terraced enclave had always ignored these nocturnal moanings, mildly envious in fact of the feral feuders' complete lack of sexual inhibition.

For Fidelio, it had been sheer heaven. He had managed to be Top Cat for several summers now. Generations of little Fidelios were living proof that he had frequently triumphed in these highly charged battles. Besides, Ginger Brian from next door, his only real threat, had been 'done' with the full blessing of his owners two seasons ago.

He was now little more than a carpet bag forced to watch voyeuristically from the conservatory window as Fidelio strutted his wares amongst the pheromone-charged females. Gazing on helplessly, the pathetic animal was forced to witness his old adversary fight off young contender after young contender, proudly crawling home at dawn, his ear chewed, white socks sullied, but sporting a rakish grin.

For Ginger Brian, it was too much to bear. Tragically, he had, in the whispered words of his owner, lost the will to live. 'The op' had been a mistake, she conceded, but the SNIP ladies had been so persuasive. 'If you love him, snip it off,' had been their over-riding message.

Given the choice, Ginger Brian would have chosen no love, but he wasn't given the choice and nor, it now appears, was Fidelio. The champion had been floored, and not by one of his own. 'He'd been missing for a couple of days,' sobbed Gay Opera Singer, who took Fidelio's sexual prowess very personally.

'And then, this morning, I found him, dazed and confused, on the mat, barely able to scratch at the door,' he explained to several of the assembled neighbours. This had all the hallmarks of a SNIP nocturnal operation, apparently. It was, according to Mr Eisenhower from number 68, the same MO as the night they did Sixties Starlet's cat, the Beast of Barnsbury.

Armed with a cat box and a felt bag, the SNIP team had crept up on their prey, bagged him, boxed him, and then whisked him off to a sterile veterinary practice for a boyish charm bypass. Then, given 48 hours to recover in a 'safe house', the de-knackered animal was returned to the site of his original cat-napping.

No note, no explanation, nothing. For the Beast of Barnsbury, the one-time Muhammad Ali of the rhododendron beds, it had been the beginning of the end. Like Ginger Brian, he had been incapable of even stepping onto the patio ever since, finally having to be retired to a cattery in Bournemouth where he sat out his days, wistfully recounting his past conquests. The Sixties Starlet had been on a one-woman campaign to warn fellow cat owners about the terrorist threat. Sadly for Fidelio, the warning message didn't reached him and his time in the romantic spotlight was over. Gay Opera Singer could barely contain his grief. 'My boy,' he sobbed. 'What's to become of him?' Try as we might, there was no consoling him.

'He's only ever played lead parts,' he sighed over a medicinal brandy. 'He'll never cope with the cat's chorus.' But miraculously, Gay Opera Singer needn't have worried. That evening, as usual, Fidelio strolled out onto the lawn, leapt up onto the fence, down on to the shed roof and took up his usual position.

Immediately, a challenger surfaced. A bloody battle ensued, but at the end, Fidelio's paw was raised in victory. The boy may have had the snip, but he was no still pussy.

Willy's Last Stand

There are some who would claim that by the time the grey starts to show around a dog's muzzle, he is past it. That by the time he has reached the equivalent of 70 human years, man's best friend should be taking his vitamin drops and keeping his tail down.

But not so Willy. True, the opportunity rarely presented itself these days, the chase in the park seeming rather too much like hard work. But given the choice, and the chance, he was still game, so to speak.

And he still had his admirers. After all, in a neighbourhood obsessed with political correctness, there were very few 'real' dogs left. 'Has he been done?' fellow dog owners would occasionally ask. Willy's Walker was keen to assure them that there was nothing wrong with his old boy. 'All present and correct,' he would reply by way of advertisement.

Not that he had had much experience to use it. There had been that brief weekend with a posh bitch called Zuki, and then he had consummated matters with Poppy and they had settled down to a normal married life. Ergo: she never let him come anywhere near her again. From his point of view it wasn't all bad and there were pay-offs. She rarely finished her meals, so he always got seconds – and she barked at the postman, so he didn't have to bother.

For some time, however, Willy's Walker had been pleading to let his old boy have one more go. Then fate intervened on his behalf.

A friend of a friend was in need of a stud. 'Would Willy be up to it?' she wanted to know. Her name was Nutty, she was the equivalent of a sprightly 30-something human, and according to the matchmaker, she was a great beauty. Barely able to contain his excitement, Willy's Walker jumped at the chance. 'He's raring to go,' he replied gamely. 'Just get her round here.'

There are those who might have argued that a middle-aged man's obsession with his old dog's virility was somehow sad, but not Willy's Walker. 'There's life in the old dog yet,' he would snap in response to any questioning.

So a date was set, and Willy's Walker was put into training. Fearful that the added exertion could prove too much for the old boy, I insisted that he be taken to the vet for a check-up. The vet wasn't that hopeful. 'He's not exactly in his prime, is he?' he commented rather cruelly.

One expensive vitamin shot later and the professionals had done all they could. The rest was going to be up to him. For the purposes of marital harmony, it was agreed that Poppy would be removed from the romantic setting. 'You might put him off,' Willy's Walker explained to the bewildered animal as she was carted off for the night.

Finally the scene was set and Nutty arrived complete with her own sheepskin-lined basket and bumper pack of chews. She was clearly keen, perhaps too keen.

We put Barry White on the stereo, lowered the lamps and pulled the curtains. Nothing. Willy just stood around looking perplexed. 'Come on boy,' Willy's Walker kept muttering under breath. 'You can do it.' Actions, however, were speaking louder than words and there was no action.

Then, suddenly, following a slap-up meal of Chum and biscuit and a tour of the garden, the old pretender seemed momentarily enlivened. 'Yes!' Willy's Walker shouted triumphantly as he spotted the hasty union from the kitchen window. 'That's my boy.' Seconds later it was all over and Willy was back in his favourite armchair. 'Is that it?' Nutty's owner wanted to know. 'That was more than "it",' replied Willy's Walker. 'That was a miracle.'

Bit Hairy…

Willy and Poppy had come to expect a certain standard of living. Walkies: twice daily. Treats: tasty and often. And professional grooming. Four times a year they were taken to see a woman dedicated to fleecing them and us, thereby fulfilling her desire to buy a holiday home in Marbella.

On a strictly hour-by-hour basis, Pat's Pet Parlour was more expensive than a Harley Street surgeon, and certainly less accommodating. Appointments were difficult to come by, telephone calls rarely returned and she operated a barely veiled class system. Simply put, an entry in her diary was a postcode lottery, and our postcode barely cut it.

Following a recent hike in prices and a late cancellation to make way for a well-connected dachshund, Willy's Walker had decided that enough was enough. He

was going to take matters into his own hands. Quite literally. A cursory look through the Argos catalogue
revealed that for the nominal price of £19.99, DIY dog
clippers could be bought and Pat's Pet Parlour slashed
from the household budget. True, there would be the
bathing, and the tricky business of blow-drying, but, he
argued, how difficult could it be?

By the time he had got the clippers home his hands
were already shaking. Argos at sale time is not a pleasant
experience and it seemed there had been a fight over the
last dancing Teletubby which had rather affected his
nerves. 'Nightmare,' was all he could say as he unloaded
his hard-won purchase. There was no doubting it, the
grooming kit came fully equipped. There was the curly-
haired coat comb, the beard trimmer, the 'thinning' tool
for the lower legs and the 'fine work' implement whose
name alone suggested a certain degree of expertise and
the need for a master craftsman.

The instruction booklet recommended that the unsuspecting animal be placed on a flat surface, preferably an
unpolished one, and that the 'groomer' enlist the help of
a fellow dog-lover in order to keep the victim calm. It
also recommended practising on an inanimate object
first, perhaps a sheepskin rug, or 'an unwanted fur coat'.
With neither to hand however, and on the basis that she
was the more biddable of the two dogs, it was decided
that Poppy would be the trial dummy.

Willy's Walker lifted the confused pooch up onto an
upturned fruit box specially found for the task. A cursory comb-through of her unruly coat revealed that she
was in dire need of more than a maintenance trim. 'A
number two for you, I think' he pronounced profession-

ally before switching on the chrome-faced blades.

It was difficult to tell if it had been the lamps or the dog that went first but either way it was a major departure from any of the diagrams in the manual. The flash of purple light and the sudden loss of electricity was some hint that there had been an operational malfunction, but a truer indicator was Poppy herself. Her fur, aside from the newly mowed bald patch along her spine, seemed to be standing on end. And she appeared to be in a coma. In short, Poppy had been electrocuted.

'I've killed her,' Willy's Walker screamed, his own hair also making a rather punk rock fashion statement. 'And I nearly killed myself.' It was true, things were not looking good. 'She's a vegetable,' Willy's Walker screeched at the poor unfortunate animal.

The hysteria took some minutes to die down, until finally I decided to call the vet for advice. It was, apparently, nothing new to him. 'Trying to save money?' he said. I confessed that we were. 'How much?' he wanted to know. It seemed an odd question, but the sums, once added up, did suggest some justification, he had to agree. 'Although I would always advise that you rely on the professionals,' he added, piously.

'You'd better bring her in,' he concluded. Half an hour later, Poppy was laid out on his examining table, her fur still a spiky testament to the hair-raising ordeal. 'Run me through the scenario,' the vet said casually, while giving her vital signs a glimpse. Eventually, when the full story had been told, we asked him what he thought. 'Your dog is just going to be a bit thick,' he said. Taken aback, we asked if the condition would improve. He said he doubted it. We might like to buy some of his

Brighter Light vitamins for the dimmer dog. The receptionist would help us on the way out. She would also be
able to collect the bill. 'How much will it be?' we wondered. 'Enough to teach you a lesson,' he replied.

Foxed

By the time she returned from Bermuda, Fearless knew
there was something seriously amiss. The miniature
gravel driveway leading to the specially constructed
Nissen hut had been disturbed. For four months,
throughout the winter frost and snow, the rescue hedgehogs, Reggie and Renata, had slept for their country. But
alas, as they say in all the best Mafia movies, Reggie was
sleeping with the fishes.

Mr Foxy, fancying a change from all the designer-
sized morsels of Caesar he was fed by the misguided
loonies who inhabited the grander workers' cottages of
south London, had stuck his malicious paw into the tiny
Nissen hut opening and fished Reggie out. For Mr Foxy
it was merely another scalp under his belt.

To her credit, Fearless's garden had fulfilled all the
correct criteria for hedgehog re-housing. But the five-
foot-high wall, topped by several feet of trellis, secure
enough to keep the hedgehogs in, clearly hadn't been
enough to keep Mr Foxy out. Three days after the dis-
turbance was discovered, a very thin Renata stirred,
strolled around in the dusk, and waited patiently for her
first portion of cat food since last December. There was
no sign of Reggie.

Mercifully, his widow didn't seem to notice. She
simply got on with the job of eating both their suppers
until she was no longer able to squeeze through the hut

opening and was reduced to sleeping under the old deck-chair that last saw use when Percy Thrower was still alive. The neighbours who had been feeding Mr Foxy with tasty titbits were mortified at the accusations of carnage. 'It's a cat,' they would say, 'or perhaps a large bird.' Since it was quite some time since a bald eagle had last been seen swooping lustfully over Stockwell, this last excuse seemed unlikely. Any attempts at getting them to curb their attitude towards this ruthless furry killer fell on deaf cars. 'It looks so sweet,' they would coo, like deranged royal baby fans. 'You just don't understand its nature,' they'd shriek, when forced to listen to gory stories of beheaded hens and legless chicks.

The misguided fox fans East of Islington were no brighter. In an attempt to salvage what little hutch life there was left in the bohemian back gardens round the neighbourhood, several bold characters secretly penned a petition for the swift humane disposal of the seven fox dens in the area. At a covert meeting in the local café, the location of which had to kept secret, Willy's Walker went as far as to offer the services of his gun. And, of course, the services of Willy, a hound who had somehow convinced his master that he had what it took to take on any number of dog foxes, and win. For a Border terrier who had once made a career out of being patted daily by wafer-thin society girls from Chelsea, I didn't fancy his chances.

But sadly none of those present, usually fearless to a man, was prepared to risk delivering said document to the council. Such was the pitch of fox fan fever that to suggest that they, like grey squirrels, were simply quite good-looking vermin was tantamount to shamelessly wearing fur. It would surely only have been a matter of time until Mr Foxy's fans, having allowed him to maim or kill every domestic pet in the area under 10lbs, would have been offering up their first-born children in moonlit rituals at the local park. However, that would not, Willy's Walker suggested, have been a complete loss. At least the setting for this perverse tableau would have allowed him to get in a clean shot.

Mad Dogs and Englishmen

The pet psychologist took his time. The examination had been an arduous one and he liked to allow a period of gravitas-inducing silence to pass before dishing out his final diagnosis. Meanwhile Willy's Walker waited patiently, the expensive clock ticking.

'I'm afraid it's not good news,' the expert finally sighed. Willy's Walker whimpered. His charge, oblivious to the proceedings being held in his honour, continued to preen his nether regions. 'I would like to say that there is something that could be done,' he continued. 'But I've seen too many cases like it. He's on the wrong road now and he can no longer read the signs.'

Resisting the temptation to suggest that reading had never been one of his dog's strong points, Willy's Walker asked if perhaps the fashionable specialist might be a little less cryptic. A bit less metaphor perhaps and a little more meat. In short, what exactly was the man saying?

The psychologist pursed his lips. He liked to leave his clients with a little sense of mystery. It was part of being in the caring profession – their embarrassed confusion usually necessitated a return visit, but clearly that wasn't going to be the case here. 'As I said,' the pet shrink sighed, 'He's on a different road now.' But Willy's Walker wouldn't let it go. 'How can he be on a different road?' he argued. 'He's on a lead.'

The psychologist leant forward, the exasperation etched on his face. 'Your dog is demented,' he shouted. 'Good luck.' Once outside, Willy's Walker tried to gather his thoughts. It was one thing to have an aged relative carted off by social services for wearing their pyjamas on the bus, but a dog? How did this happen?

Their walk home was a solemn one. True, every tree was given its usual thorough examination, a box of abandoned fried chicken an enthusiastic going-over, but there was something different, something alarming. Where once he had been one man and his dog he was now one man and his mental health patient. It didn't feel good.

He began to examine his best friend's antics more closely and had to admit, the old boy was acting strangely. There were times when he barely seemed to recognise himself, or anyone else for that matter.

For Poppy, with whom he had shared a basket for almost a decade, this sudden memory wipe had added complications. Each time she came in the dog flap it was as though they were meeting for the very first time, a courting ritual that she clearly found both irritating and unappetising.

But it was in the park that his little local difficulty caused the most complications. Unable to distinguish between one pack member and another, he had taken to following home any short-haired female that hoved into view, a habit that made him less than popular with other dog owners.

Hearing of his mounting crisis, a fellow park-user approached Willy's Walker to offer her advice. She hoped he didn't mind her intervening but she could tell he was new to the game and thought he could do with some practical advice. He wasn't to take it personally. 'It comes to them all in the end, dear,' she assured him.

Her solution was simple, but ingenious. She had discovered that by attaching a homing device on a discreet chain round the wanderer's neck they could be found quickly before too much damage was done. It was sold in all good department stores and ran cheaply on a single AA battery. 'It's supposed to be for finding your car keys,' she explained. 'But it works perfectly well for my purposes,' she added.

He thanked the woman profusely and headed straight off to the shops. Within hours of purchase, his life was transformed. Whenever the confused mutt started to stray, Willy's Walker pressed the remote receiver and simply followed the loud bleeping noise until the runaway was located. It worked every time.

Some time later, walking out of the gates after yet another uneventful visit, Willy's Walker bumped into his Good Samaritan. 'I can't thank you enough,' he said, shaking the woman's hand. 'You've changed our lives.' The woman accepted his thanks graciously, but assured him she was only too happy to help.

'They can be so irritating,' she said. 'Especially when they just wander off after the wrong woman.' Willy's Walker nodded, he knew only too well. 'So, what kind of dog have you got?' he enquired, casually. The woman looked a little surprised. 'I don't have a dog, dear,' she replied. 'Just a demented old boy.'

7

Parenting Classes

Les Mums

The world is made up of many kinds of families: wealthy, healthy, poor, sad, good and bad. But in East of Islington, there was mainly only the one kind: the gay family. This was the centre of the known universe for those people keen on sharing their spouse's wardrobe. And Les Mums were no exception.

The announcement that two members of the female rugby team were planning to conceive a baby came as no surprise to anyone except one of their own mothers, a devout Catholic who had long prayed for grandchildren but had never really expected to get a result.

The logistics of how this miracle would happen initially fazed her, and a look in her bible provided little clue. But a cursory search on the internet revealed that in fact she was not the only widow in rural Ireland whose daughter had taken this rather unorthodox path to motherhood. From what she could tell, and from discreet conversations with her confirmed bachelor priest, it seemed to be all the rage.

Besides, Les Mums assured her, the choice of potential 'fathers' available to them was endless. There were men willing and able, for a small fee, to provide the essential ingredient missing from their own relationship. Tall, small, big, slim, bearded, bald, writers, film-makers, motorcycle couriers: a line-up of anonymous genetic messages queuing up to be catapulted into the next generation.

Eventually, after handing over a substantial fee and poring over the detailed descriptions at the 'Girls Who Only Need Boys For A Few Minutes Agency', they decided on a well-built, blonde-haired Irish actor. The deed done, they went home to spread the word. The expectant granny was one of the first to hear the news. 'It's Liam Neeson, for sure,' she cried, on hearing the finer details of the chosen one. 'Wait till I tell the neighbours.'

Not wanting to dampen her enthusiasm, Les Mums delicately suggested that it seemed unlikely. After all, why would Liam Neeson take time out from his heady Hollywood lifestyle to make a deposit behind a discreet door in London's Harley Street? And would he really need the £15 payable for the job? True, he hadn't been in much lately, but it did seem a bit extreme. After all, he could have always done advertising work if he was that desperate.

But the expectant granny was immovable on the subject. 'God moves in mysterious ways,' she insisted. 'He was probably just passing and received the calling.' By the time Les Mums' baby was well under way, there were very few people in their extensive circle who hadn't also come to believe that they were going to be having Liam Neeson's baby.

The fact that they had never met him was of little consequence. The reality was that East of Islington is full of women who have not formally met the fathers of their children. At the last count, Les Mums' local NCT group boasted the apparent offspring of several poets, two neurosurgeons, one captain of industry, three writers and an astronaut. True, the latter had been hard to find but eventually the agency had come through. He was a retired astronaut, it explained on his CV, though weren't they all?

The idea of having a megastar's baby grew on Les Mums. After all, who was to say that the expectant granny had got it wrong? Miracles, as she was fond of saying, did happen. So why not this one? They pasted pictures of the unsuspecting father on the door of their fridge and hired all his movies from the video shop. 'So we can tell the child all about him when the right time comes,' they told bemused friends.

Finally the day arrived for the baby's big premiere. In common with more traditional arrangements, it was Mum-Mum who did all the work and Dad-Mum who did all the pacing. They also brought a framed photo of Liam with them. 'We don't want him to feel left out,' they explained.

After much brow-mopping, the midwife eventually coerced her charge into the world. Was it okay? A girl? A boy? What was it? 'It's a little mixed race baby,' the midwife replied in answer to their urgent questioning. Les Mums were slightly taken aback. 'That's not what we ordered,' Mum-Mum said.

The midwife looked at the photo of Liam Neeson and agreed they had a point. 'Of course we love, it,' Les Mums quickly chorused, cooing over the new addition to their family 'But it isn't what we were expecting.' The midwife smiled. 'Well there's no refunds, ducks,' she laughed. 'There might be on this one,' they replied.

New Car Cruelty

Willy's Walker had grown up on a diet of *The Persuaders*, sports cars and girls in short skirts who preferred men with long hair. It had done little to prepare him for life in the new century. And even less in helping him adapt to a new life as a new father. It had taken him months to realise what was happening, the rising size of my stomach seemed to offer him little clue, but finally, once little Phoebe arrived, he twigged. His old life was over. Or was it?

Years of vegetarian dinner parties and lesbian marriage ceremonies had so far failed to shake his world view. His was the only shooting jacket for many miles, and certainly the only one with an 'action back' – a device, he was keen to point out, that would allow him to 'dispatch birds' with even greater efficiency.

'If only one had a gamekeeper to break it in properly,' he would muse to bewildered friends. 'Someone to give it a good beating for me,' he would add, oblivious to the shocked expressions around him.

Other men would vent their anxieties about the modern world by playing *Stairway To Heaven* on air guitar. Not so Willy's Walker. Instead, he would stand by the local duck pond, arms raised heavenwards, playing 'air shooting'.

But now, as a new father, his behaviour had taken an even more peculiar turn. His hair, already several inches over his collar, had developed a strange hue, while his beard was close to being visible from Mars.

'I need a convertible,' he suddenly announced one day. 'And I need it fast'. For a man with a small baby, two dogs, a wife and an overly large cricket bag, it seemed an odd choice.

Apparently, his old car, an ageing estate, had suffered enough. And so had he. Apparently there was to be a limit to the amount of users of the new car, and that limit was one. Willy's Walker. And the dogs, obviously.

'I'm afraid that you and the baby will probably have to start taking public transport.' And he wasn't kidding. It was The Convertible Car Cruelty.

Under the rules of The Convertible Car Cruelty, there was no room for passenger rights – mainly because there was no room for passengers, full stop. There would also be no room for buggies, or supermarket shopping, or gardening goods.

And, as the cost of the new convertible far exceeded any sane person's motoring budget, it also meant that there would be little room for financial manoeuvre. For those of us not on the user list, minicabs were not being offered as an optional extra.

Within days of his announcement, the house was wall-to-wall with glossy German brochures. Willy's Walker had entered the world of leather trim and heated seats. I was allowed to look, but not touch.

'Welcome to Mercedes,' said the salesman as we approached the forecourt. 'What can we do for you today?' he purred. Willy's Walker quickly explained that we had come for a test drive. More importantly, that he had come for a test drive.

The salesman smiled. He knew all about The Convertible Car Cruelty, he had virtually invented it. 'Of course, sir,' he replied knowingly. 'Come this way, madam,' he said, ushering me into a small glass child-proof booth at the rear of the showroom.

Inside was a coffee and tea dispenser, and several boxes of tissues. There was also another woman, with two small children hanging off her leg. We smiled politely at each other.

Meanwhile, Willy's Walker and the convertible had disappeared from view, his hair already an electrified mess of G-force and giddy excitement. There was no stopping him now, he thought. 'This is the life,' he shouted to the smiling salesman in the seat next to him. 'Certainly is, sir,' came the practised reply.

Back at the showroom, my booth companion asked me if I would like a cup of tea. I nodded enthusiastically, and asked for a sweet one. 'Is it your first time?' she enquired as she handed me the sickly brown liquid. I nodded again.

'Is it yours?' I asked her in turn. 'Oh no,' she sighed. 'This is our third,' she elaborated. 'Once after each child, and then of course once when he discovered his bald patch. Shame really.' She could see the confusion on my face.

'They don't actually get a sports car, you know. You did know that, didn't you?' I mumbled that I had no idea. That I was new to the world of The Convertible Car Cruelty. Slowly, she leant forward, and patted my leg. 'What do you think the boxes of tissues are for?' she whispered. 'They're certainly not for us, honey.'

Chippy

'What is it, Mummy?' asked the little girl, intrigued, pointing at the large bags hanging from the chip van of pink 100 per cent pure sugar candyfloss.

Her mummy was mortified. 'Come along, darling,' she replied, forcibly dragging her reluctant daughter away from the lurid offerings. 'It's bad,' she said. 'Very bad'.

For the aspirational mummies East of Islington, the sudden bankruptcy of their local vegetarian café in the park had come as something of a shock. The appearance of the chip van in its place had altered their gastronomic world beyond recognition.

For several years they had congregated, their three-wheeler off-road buggies loaded to the gills with lactose-intolerant toddlers, and sipped herbal tea, or occasionally indulged themselves in skinny cappuccinos; the coffee all third world-friendly and the nappies all undyed cotton.

Theirs was a generation of children for whom the narcotic qualities of unrefined sugar were banned substances worthy of a government white paper. But now, Mammon had intervened and the chips were down. Or fried, as the case may be.

The ladies smiling out from behind the lifted shutter of their adapted caravanette were as confused as the children. 'Alright, love,' they greeted each horrified face in turn. 'What can I get you?' The menu, scrawled in red ink across the side and back of their four-wheeler was a football supporter's dream. Hot dogs, chips, hamburgers, ice pops, candyfloss, of course, tea, and coffee: Nescafé, to be precise.

There were also sausage or bacon sandwiches, the charred innards cemented between the floppy sides of Mother's Pride. Ketchup and mustard were stationed on the counter in huge catering size dispensers. There wasn't a vegetable in sight.

But the chip van ladies were eager to be accommodating. 'Have you got anything vegetarian?' pleaded one desperate mummy, keen to feed Horatio, her precious three-year-old. 'The hot dogs come with onions,' came the enthusiastic reply. 'Or what about some chips?' From the safety seat of his three-wheeler buggy two huge eyes lit up. 'Chits, chits,' little Horatio started shouting. 'I want chits, Mummy.'

Horatio had never tasted chips, nor could he pronounce the word properly, yet he knew a good thing when he saw it. But his mother was standing firm. 'I don't think so, darling,' she soothed. 'Nothing for us, thank you,' she continued, turning her attention back to the chip van caravanistas. 'We'll wait till we get home.'

Horiatio's little fingers had to be prised from the edge of the counter. 'Chits, chits,' he sobbed as his mother pushed him away from the sight of temptation. His pleading could be heard all the way to the gate. One by one the other members of the mummies' collective filed up to the chip van, only to follow suit and drag their charges away sobbing and screaming.

'Who could have allowed this to happen?' they murmured. But the chip van ladies had the edge. They were supplying the plastic picnic tables and chairs that the mummies collective had taken to occupying, the eco-friendly wooden benches having gone the way of the rest of the mung bean café's bankrupt stock.

Clearly if their daily meetings to discuss the latest developments in childcare philosophy were to continue, some money had to change hands. Ergo: they would have to look again at the menu. After much consultation, they decided the least they could do was buy a round of some drinks.

And so it was that little Horatio's mummy was deputised to approach the van again. However, since his embarrassing outburst, Horiatio was left tied to his buggy, a good 50 yards from the demon chips, a mushy free-range swede and coriander concoction safely packed in his travel lunch box.

'Could I have seven teas, please?' she asked. 'Three earl greys, one herbal, and three Ceylon,' she detailed. The chip van lady shuffled towards the back of the makeshift kitchen. 'Seven teas coming up,' she shouted back. Within seconds, the counter was awash with polystyrene cups containing a deep orange liquid. 'That'll be £2.80 please, love.'

Horatio's mother stared at the purchases in front of her. 'Excuse me,' she bellowed over the dulcet tones emanating from the transistor radio. 'But could you tell me what kind of tea this is?' she enquired, pointing at the dark orange stuff, the like of which she had never seen before.

'Tea, love. It's tea.' The chip van lady raised her eyes. 'Yes,' continued Horatio's mummy. 'But where did it come from?' A look of disbelief spread over the chip van lady's face before she answered. 'Asda,' she replied. 'In Tottenham.'

On her return to the tables, the mummies' collective was equally confused by the orange liquid. 'What is it?' they asked in unison. 'It's bad,' Horatio's mummy sighed. 'Very bad.'

The Anti-Climax

It was no secret that lesbians had long made up a large chunk of the population in East of Islington. In fact, if you weren't a lesbian, thinking about becoming a lesbian, the child of a lesbian, or the confused parent of a lesbian, it was possible that you had got off the bus at the wrong stop. For those of a Sapphic persuasion, it was the southern equivalent of Hebden Bridge, without the breathtaking scenery and the Two Ferrets pub.

Of course, there were plenty of upsides to this equation. The area was awash with female plumbers and builders. Demos, school committees, car boot sales and even the one o'clock club were all run by impassioned women with a firm eye on the sexual equality meter and a bold line in tie-dye shirts. The downside was that there were barely any girls left for the boys; which went some way to explaining why Cambridge never had a girl-friend, but not all the way.

His social skills were good and he owned a dinner suit, which was great for the legions of middle-aged *Strictly Come Dancing* fans, but as to getting a woman who was remotely interested in men, things were still proving a challenge. Recently he had been stepping out of the area, trying pastures new, but being a home boy at heart, and very averse to paying large taxi fares, he was still hopeful that love would blossom nearer to his doorstep. He had even considered placing a postcard in the newsagents, but this did seem to smack of desperation, even futility, given the demographic.

Still, there had been a clutch of neighbourhood parties recently and he had been an enthusiastic guest, mingling, chatting, collecting phone numbers and pledging support for good causes. To date, he had agreed to take part in a midnight walk for safer streets and run a half-marathon for Breast Awareness Week. If nothing else, he figured that both events would have their fair share of the opposite sex and they couldn't all be batting for the other side.

At a fundraiser party for one of these events, he bumped into someone he hadn't seen for some time – a single woman, now about to turn 40. There had been a moment once a couple of years before when they might have dated, but Cambridge had lost his nerve shortly after she texted him asking if he would donate her some of his sperm. As they had yet to make it to what he termed 'first base', he had declined and she had never improved on the offer.

This time she simply asked him if he would like to come to her birthday party the following week. Things went well. She introduced him to her friends, to her mother and to her one-year-old son. Cambridge was a little taken aback with this last introduction. Where, he wondered, had she got him? 'The sperm bank,' she replied, coolly. Not wanting to appear needy but at the same time needing to know, Cambridge finally asked her the question: 'Was that before or after you texted me?' he said, as nonchalantly as he could muster. 'Oh, after,' she replied. 'Silly really. I hadn't realised how good the choice was at the time.'

Mildly startled, Cambridge thanked her for the lovely party and headed off home. Then 50 yards from his front door his mobile phone rang – it was the birthday girl. She wanted him to know that if he ever changed his mind, she would still be keen to take a genetic donation off him. 'After all,' she said, 'you're a nice guy.' Cambridge was really taken aback. He wasn't sure that the telephone was the correct medium for this sort of conversation. She said he had a point, but at least it was one up from a text. 'Tell me,' he said, finally. 'Are you a lesbian?' The birthday girl laughed. 'No' she replied. 'You're just not my type.'

Southern Comfort

The fantasy plan had been for Willy's Walker and I to escape to a luxury spa in the countryside for the week-end. For little Phoebe, however, the charm of gourmet diet meals and daily beatings at the hands of highly trained sadistic Swedes was clearly limited.

It was a plan therefore that looked destined to remain a fantasy, until, that is, I heard the words every new parent prays for. 'She can come and stay with us,' Somerset announced gaily after elegantly emptying several glasses of vintage champagne. 'I'll just throw her in with the rest, no one will even notice.'

By then, Somerset had produced five children, four pugs, and two personality-deficient budgies. The floors of her sprawling south London villa were like a moving carpet of dogs, children and assorted members of the household operational crew.

Naturally her husband, Mr Grand, played his part, but domestically his role was invariably kept on a need-to-know basis and it seemed there were very few things he ever needed to know. This latest invitation being one of them.

So, after a not-very-convincing attempt to resist this miraculous offer of generosity, I quickly accepted and set about packing little Phoebe off on her south London adventure.

As plans went, it was not without its complications. Little Phoebe's spiritual home was East of Islington, south London was a different world, One into which few north Londoners dared ever tread. Would she fit in? Would she be able to speak the language? And, more importantly, would she ever be the same again?

The following morning, draped exquisitely in Armani and with three pugs hanging off her left leg, Somerset opened her front door and dumped Little Phoebe into the fray.

'Don't worry,' she called out, as my anxious backward glance spotted her little blonde head disappearing into a sea of assorted children and dog hair. 'Amazon will sort her out.'

Amazon was Somerset's right-hand woman, and there were few brave enough to cross her. Least of all Mr Grand, who religiously ate all his greens rather than risk a loss of privileges. There was no denying it, Phoebe was going to be on a swift learning curve.

By the time we arrived at our destination, and after two stiff drinks, it seemed responsible to call for an update. The gardener answered the phone. Phoebe wasn't at home, he explained. She was out, on one of what transpired were going to be many social outings. She had gone to the theatre already and later that evening she would be attending a Pilates class. For someone who was barely one year old, it was pretty good going.

'Do you want to speak to Mr Grand?' the gardener kindly offered. I politely declined, assuming, rightly, that he knew less than me of the household social diary. 'I'll ring back,' I replied before heading back to the bar.

Occasionally, over the weekend, news would filter through. It seemed that Phoebe's days of ready meals were over. 'She really seemed to like the chocolate souf-flé,' Somerset pointed out, during one of the updates. 'And she particularly likes it if you employ someone to play the guitar for her while she is having her bedtime milk.' As I suspected, south of the river really was another world.

By the time we arrived back in London, I was beginning to panic. It was quite possible we could no longer afford to keep our only child in the style to which she had become accustomed. 'Perhaps they'll offer to adopt her?' mused Willy's Walker as we approached the door. 'Just think what we'd save in school fees,' he added brightly.

Somerset opened her door and beamed. Little Phoebe was nowhere to be seen. 'I think she likes it here,' she purred by way of explanation. 'I did tell her you were coming,' she tailed off. But little Phoebe had gone native.

We were ushered through to one of their myriad drawing rooms, only to be confronted by a besieged Mr Grand, surrounded by a cacophony of barking pugs and excitable children.

'Sherry?' he suggested enthusiastically, before pouring himself a large medicinal glass. 'Actually, we've come to collect our baby,' I said, anxiously. A look of confusion spread over his face. 'Have we got a spare, darling?' he enquired quizzically of his wife. Years of training, however, had taught him never to expect an answer.

Meanwhile, I looked around frantically for sight of my errant child. It took some time, but I finally spotted her. 'There,' I shouted at him, 'The one trying to hide behind the miniature Rolls-Royce.' It was tragic but true. We may have had a fantasy weekend, but little Phoebe had signed up for the fantasy life.

Brett The Bionic Maori

Brett the Bionic Maori was not, strictly speaking, a Maori at all. In fact he had never actually been to the Antipodes, nor had he any real claim to its ancestry, but he had a Romanian mother prone to exaggeration and an impressive six-pack so somehow the moniker had stuck.

Tall, a little dark, and more than handsome, he had arrived in East of Islington via Gumtree to brush up on his English and earn enough money to qualify as a gym instructor. 'I learn your body,' he wrote on his CV.

The advert he posted offering himself as a live-in 'manny' had attracted a great deal of attention and he was finally snapped up by Tuba the Life Coach and her three wayward children. Her husband long gone, she felt it would be helpful to have a man around the house, and, at only £60 per week plus board, she said he came a lot cheaper than the last one. He was also a lot more attentive.

Evening meals were cooked with effortless charm, bulbs were changed, sheds cleaned out, lawns mowed, coats dry-cleaned and children corralled into some sort of order. He was, in short, everything his name suggested. And then some.

Pretty soon he was putting her through her paces in the park, honing his keep-fit skills on Tuba in her ill-fitting lycra and handing out flyers to other likely victims. If they were pushing a pram he pushed them a leaflet. 'Get me before your husband gets someone else,' it screamed in lurid pink lettering.

As a PR stunt it had rather limited appeal in an area where lesbian motherhood was in the majority. Still, it showed he had chutzpah and even the girls who said they didn't 'do' boys were impressed with his biceps. Or at least the butch ones were.

Always the trailblazer, Tuba was the first in her circle to employ a male au pair and pretty quickly became the first to take him to dinner parties. Dressed in his only suit and doused in loud imported after-shave, he did his best impression of suave. 'He's so delightful,' she whispered into the ears of goggle-eyed hostesses as he escorted her into their dining rooms. 'And so grown-up don't you think?' At 19 years old, he did seem mature for his years. But then at 47 so did she.

Socially, they made an unlikely couple but it was an arrangement that seemed to suit them both: she got a walker and he got fed. He also got feted by a gaggle of women of a certain age desperately seeking reassurance. 'I like them with the oldness,' he would insist in his broken English when they pushed for his vote. 'I offer full repair service,' he added quixotically, handing out his flyers and imploring them to tell her friends.

He also, it transpired, offered a little more than repair work. The evenings he and Tuba had spent poring over his English grammar had not been wasted; he was finally promoted. Four months after moving in, Tuba announced that she was pregnant, a feat that was described by the GP as nothing short of miraculous.

The news was received with mixed feelings. Her children, especially her 15-year-old son, were mildly confused but easily bought off with an iPod. Her ex-husband was nothing short of ecstatic. He may have left her for an antiques dealer called Julian with a penchant for florid waistcoats but there was nothing like regaining the moral high ground.

Her friends were agog, even the community midwife who thought she had seen it all before was amazed. Gay fathers, bisexual parents, sperm donors, even womb donors, you name it, she'd delivered it. 'But this will be my first bionic baby,' she smiled. Brett thanked her but said that he wasn't bionic really, it was simply a nickname because he was just well-built. The midwife looked at Tuba's date of birth and looked back again. 'Well, if you're not bionic,' she said, 'she's certainly Wonder Woman'.

Head Girl

Every Saturday afternoon little Phoebe attended an African drumming group. Although her blonde hair and blue eyes generally precluded her from claiming any African heritage, she was treated as one of the family.

She had her own miniature drum. Along with the other children, she got fed rice and peas and baked plantain. On occasion, she got to wear brightly coloured clothes and headscarves. And every week she got her hair braided. Intricate, beautiful plaits weaved over her crown with a skill passed down through generations, her blonde locks coiffed in styles that would leave Kelly Holmes's hairdresser on the starting block.

Then, every Monday morning, she arrived at her nursery school, her hair still resplendent in its plaited piles. For quite some time now, she has been the envy of the class. The others, all five of them in total, ogled in wonderment at her elegant bouffant.

Some weeks the plait arrangements were more elaborate than others. On high days and holidays, for instance, they often included beads and baubles, with her scalp drenched in essential oils. All in all, it was the kind of superstar treatment only really reserved for the precious few. In short, she was the Plait Queen.

But lately, all had not been well in plait world. Three weeks ago, she arrived home from her nursery class sans plaits, her hair a startled, crimped Afro with not a hint of braiding in sight. From certain angles, she looked worryingly like Leo Sayer; not a good look in a small girl.

'We have changed Phoebe's hairdo, hope you don't mind,' read a short note from the teacher. It was a new unauthorised styling wave, and I did mind. But it seemed churlish to complain. After all, teachers have a tough time already, I reasoned. They didn't need mothers picking hairs. So instead the following morning Little Phoebe wore bunches and the rest of the week passed off harmoniously.

Then Saturday came round again and she went off to African drumming. As expected, she returned home with a full head of perfectly formed plaits, each individually decorated with their own colour co-ordinated rubber band. She looked resplendent; everyone thought so. Everyone, that is, except her new teacher.

Monday afternoon and the end of nursery school heralded the return of the Leo Sayer look. This time little Phoebe was bearing a longer note. *'We have removed Phoebe's plaits, again,'* stated the obvious.

'She was crying, and we suspect the plaits may be to blame.' it continued. Apparently, it went on to explain, there is a new school of thought that believed that plaits, of any shape or size, might arrest development.

'We are not suggesting that you cannot plait her hair,' the note continued. *'But you might consider other forms of hairdressing. Please call if you wish to discuss the topic further.'* Naturally, I called. 'I'm calling about the plaits,' I said to the secretary.

'Ooh yes,' she replied, conspiratorially. 'I'll just put you through.' Some moments later, the phone was answered by Ms Brown, the new nursery class teacher. 'Hello,' said a firm voice. 'How may I help you?' I said that I was concerned that we might have a 'plaitgate' situation on our hands: that twice now, Phoebe had come home robbed of her hairstyle with the explanation that plaits equalled brain damage. In my youth, I explained, they had simply equalled an early level of self-control. 'Tidy hair, tidy mind,' as my mother was fond of saying.

Besides, she looked so lovely in them and no one in her African drumming group seem adversely affected. Surely a concession could be made? But Ms Brown was adamant. Plaits were not a helpful educational tool. 'It's the tension on the follicles,' she explained, 'I believe it causes children to behave slightly irrationally.'

And then it struck me. 'So is that why the Von Trapp

family were always running up and down the mountain?' I asked. Ms Brown was unmoved. 'I can't possibly comment,' she replied. 'The Von Trapp family don't attend this school.'

Boy George

As the only woman on her street to wear a wedding band and use cork-backed coasters, Boy George's mother had long harboured fantasies of emigration, or at the very least a move to suburbs. For her, East of Islington was a waking nightmare that would finally end. It wasn't a dream shared by her husband, 'You married an unemployed juggler.' He would sigh. 'Give it up.' Still, she was determined; but not as determined as her son.

He was only 15 months old, but Boy George already had all the hallmarks of a successful operator. Mingling by the sandpit at the community playgroup and munching his way through the free slices of orange given out to stave off rickets in the poorer children, he quickly identified the bourgeois families from the smarter postcodes who were killing time until they made a break for prep school. 'Mummy,' he would burble randomly at the coiffed women when they came to collect their Boden-covered offspring. 'Mummy,' he would sob when they left him behind.

Boy George's actual mother was quite sanguine about it. Occasionally, when he was feeling needy, he would call her the 'm' word and she was pathetically grateful. But mostly she knew. He had been born with an intuitive belief that he had been swapped at birth and she could hardly blame him. After all, on a bad day, she felt he had a point. Still, as she often tried to explain to him, they both had their crosses to bear. Then one morning as he worked the toddler room as usual, Boy George's big break came – his mother had a funny turn. The colour draining from her face, she fell to the floor, winded, and was immediately loaded into a mini cab and dispatched to the General.

In the midst of the chaos, Boy George felt his hand being grabbed by a Chanel-scented glove. 'Don't worry,' said a voice from above. 'You can come home with us.' He burst into uncontrollable tears. Finally, his real family had arrived. As his mother was being processed through to accident and emergency, he was being strapped into an Arne Jacobsen-inspired high chair and being fed homemade macaroni cheese by a Latvian nanny in a sprawling Georgian terrace. His fellow diner was a 17-month-old girl called Henrietta, an acquaintance from messy play. Everyone was smiling, but no one was smiling quite as much as Boy George. 'Poor little thing,' they kept saying. 'He's coping so well.'

As the day progressed, there were huddled conversations amongst the adults, even a phone call, but as far as Boy George could tell, this was it. This was home. Eventually bedtime came and a travel cot was taken down from the loft. 'Where's your daddy?' the nanny asked him, quietly, as she dressed him in a pair of Egyptian cotton pyjamas. Boy George stared blankly. 'Shh,' Henrietta's mother said. 'They don't usually have fathers.' Boy George smiled broadly, he was glad that was cleared up.

In the morning he was settled in front of a plate of fresh fruit and wholemeal toast. They continued smiling, he smiled back, it was perfect. 'You're such a happy boy,' they kept saying. And he was. Then the door bell rang. From the stairs below came some muffled voices and then Henrietta's mother walked into the room.

'Look,' she said, gaily. 'Your parents are here.' Boy George stared at the couple who he had been living with since birth. 'Hello, son,' his father said. Boy George's lip began to tremble. He clung to the designer high chair and Henrietta's mother. 'Don't be sad,' she said. 'You're going home.' Boy George started sobbing, hysterically. 'I think he's a little confused,' Henrietta's mother said. 'I think that's an understatement,' Boy George's mother replied.

Liam Neeson Is Missing

Joyce at the family guidance centre thought she had heard everything. Men who liked to dress up in their wife's clothes. Women who insisted on the lights off. Some who insisted on the lights on, the cameras rolling and a full make-up team. Couples who had never had sex. Couples who wanted sex, just not with each other. There was usually a formula and it didn't take long for it to come out over a cup of tea and two fingers of KitKat.

But Les Mums had just proved her wrong. As far as Joyce could tell, and she had been sincerely listening for 25 years, Les Mums appeared to be facing a unique problem. Not that they were a two-mum family, that was almost standard these days. No, their problem was they wanted to have Liam Neeson's baby. Or rather, they wanted another one; they already had one apparently. 'He was so successful last time,' Mum-Mum explained, proudly showing a snapshot of their bouncing toddler posing in a 'children against the bomb' dungaree suit. 'He came out such a looker, so why mess with a winning team?' Why indeed, thought Joyce.

Unfortunately Liam Neeson was no longer available. It had been so easy before. They had gone to the sperm bank, chosen him from a long list of other contenders and hey presto, nine months later Mum-Mum had given birth to the son of a superstar. But this time, nothing. The supply had run dry. They'd tried everything. Other clinics, the internet (in case he'd gone freelance), they'd even tried advertising in *Donor Digest* magazine, but zero response. Family guidance was their last hope. After all, they certainly counted him as part of the family, even if he was an unsuspecting member.

Joyce, like many before her, was surprised to hear that an Oscar-nominated actor had the time or the inclination to donate his celebrity sperm. Was the rest of the world aware that one of Ireland's most famous sons was impregnating lesbians for fifteen pounds a shot? As it were.

'He does it anonymously of course,' Dad-Mum sighed. 'All we really knew about him was that he is a tall Irish actor. But who else could it be?' she said. 'Besides, our son's the spitting image of him.' Joyce nodded. She hadn't liked to mention it, but his lines had looked distinctly more Caribbean than Celtic to her. Still, genetics was a tricky thing and she was no expert. Better to stick to what she knew.

'So how can we help?' she asked, smiling at Les Mums as they sat across the table holding hands and looking earnestly at the *Families Need Fathers* poster. 'We want you to ring his agent,' they said. 'And explain that we need Liam for one more go.' Joyce said that this would certainly be a first for the family guidance centre.

'We usually like estranged family members to come here of their own accord,' she said. 'We don't like to chase after them with a specimen jar.'

Mum-Mum burst into tears. Liam's failure to deliver was causing trouble at home. To put it delicately, Mum-Mum was off colour and Dad-Mum felt she was getting less than her fair share of her conjugal rights. Joyce leant forward; it always came down to sex in the end. 'Tell me about it,' she said in her concerned counsellor voice.

'What's the point of us having sex?' Mum-Mum wailed. 'It's not like it's going to get me anywhere.' Dad-Mum looked crestfallen. She had been a good Dad-Mum, and tried her best, but clearly her fathering skills had limitations and this was one of them. Joyce offered more tea, and a couple of extra KitKat fingers. 'What about getting another film star?' she said, hopefully. 'There must be loads of them out there with time to spare between performances.' Les Mums confessed they had considered it but somehow no one had appealed as much as Liam.

Suddenly Joyce leapt up. 'I think I have the answer,' she squealed. Les Mums leapt up as well, keen to hear it. 'Bob Geldof!' she shouted. 'He's Irish, he's famous and he's on the world stage.' It was true, he ticked all the right boxes, though so far he hadn't ticked the box at the donation clinic. But for Joyce this was a mere technicality. 'Don't worry,' she said. 'He's done Live Aid. I'm sure he'd be happy to do Sperm Aid. And if you're lucky you'll get a Bono thrown in for free.'

8

Gay Village

Grave Errors

Cheap housing, expensive planning mistakes, lively numbers of Hasidic Jews and a 24-hour gun culture were just a few of the crowd-pleasers people could expect when they arrived at East of Islington. But recently this mixed bag of visitor attractions had expanded to include an informal social group solely devoted to exploring the nether regions of the local overgrown gothic cemetery, an area of land long closed to the dead, but apparently all-embracing to the active living.

Its members, young men with a special interest in Judy Garland films and the complete works of Barbra Streisand, were drawn from all corners of the city, their attendance extending well into the twilight hours.

Although someone with zero religious convictions, Alan Angst decided to join their number. He knew the way down the Yellow Brick Road, he could recite the words to *Funny Girl* and his barber preferred to set the clippers to number one. In short, he was well-qualified for crawling around in the undergrowth on all fours.

His knowledge of Victorian memorials and their cool marble surfaces soon became legend. But he wasn't on his own. Mr and Mrs Pearl had travelled the length and breath of the south-east in search of their family tree, loitering in more cemeteries than Alan Angst ever could dream about.

Leaving Purley every Saturday morning, Mrs Pearl would pack a flask of coffee, three rounds of ham sandwiches, one of cheese, and a KitKat. 'When we find them, we like to stay a while,' Mr Pearl explained on his website *Virtually Wake Up Your Dead*. 'Perhaps even read them a bit of the newspaper,' he continued.

Besides helpful information like cause of death, number of dependents left behind and the nearest public conveniences, he also advised fellow genealogists keen on similar endeavours to carry a small pocket-sized spade and a spray can of disinfectant. 'To give them a bit of a spruce-up,' he explained as a postscript.

Mrs Pearl would have liked a bit more variation to their weekends, perhaps a stately home or two, but Mr Pearl wasn't keen. Basically, if there wasn't the chance of finding a dead ancestor he wasn't interested. Besides, he had something of a reputation to keep up. To date, he was leading the field in notching up corpses for the family tree and he wasn't about to be overtaken now.

One weekend, in particularly clement weather, the Pearls decided to venture East of Islington in search of yet another scalp, a distant relative twice removed. He wasn't a rich man and so it came as no surprise to them that he was buried in what they viewed as a rather down-at-heel area.

Due to the date of his demise, and the extensions subsequently made to the cemetery grounds, they were forced to battle their way through several decades of rampant vegetation before finally stumbling on the right area. Unfortunately someone had beaten them to it and it wasn't just the dead Pearl.

As they pushed back the final overhanging branches in their path, there, in front of them, straddling the grave with his trousers round his ankles and his mouth apparently clasped around the private parts of a startled middle-aged man from Ruislip was Alan Angst. Tupperware under one arm and picnic blanket under the other, this was not the scene Mrs Pearl had planned for the afternoon. Or any afternoon.

She screamed, her husband screamed, and the middle-aged man from Ruislip screamed as Alan Angst clamped his jaw down in fear and panic. Instructing his wife to shield her eyes, Mr Pearl acted swiftly. Disinfectant bottle in hand, he doused the compromised duo as they struggled to regain their composure. 'Get off,' he shouted, in an attempt to reclaim his forebear's dignity. 'You deserve a good beating,' he threatened. The man from Ruislip stopped screaming and smiled. 'Well,' he said. 'If you're offering.'

Bags of Fun
Cooking dinner for 12 while sporting a pair of super-black Sunnie Mann sunglasses was a challenging task. So was recognising the faces of the expectant diners. Admittedly there were some who were prepared to endure this self-inflicted handicap in the name of fashion, but generally the effort was beyond most of us. And

Gay Opera Singer was no exception. But recently he had been giving it a go.

The official line was that he had been forced to undergo 'essential' eye surgery. Unofficially though, there had been rumours. 'Darleengs,' he bellowed at his guests as they arrived. 'Be warned, I've been under the knife.'

For days he had been stumbling around in the pitch black, insistent that the glasses stay put. 'Doctors' orders, I'm afraid,' he sighed whenever anyone dared ask for a peek. To date, no one had seen behind the wraparound barrier, not even Dazzling Darren. 'The stitches, sweetie, too awful,' he warned him.

It transpired that the 'essential' eye surgery had been prompted by some kind of hereditary condition. In the Seventies, his mother had also spent some time wearing sunglasses in the house. Admittedly they were living in the tropics at the time, and therefore her strange attire attracted far less attention.

However, she didn't suffer in vain. Miraculously, one side-effect of their family's obscure eye complaint was that the subsequent surgery managed to take years off the patient. In the theatrical twilight world occupied by Gay Opera Singer, this was generally agreed to be no bad thing. His genetic time bomb had been ticking away for some time until eventually he decided something had to be done. 'The older one gets,' he explained, 'the less effective the results'.

Apparently there were some with the condition who had left it too late, and the effect had been negative, or at least not as positive. Naturally, he explained, he had dreaded the idea of surgery, but he knew we would realise that he had no choice.

'Some families suffer from varicose veins,' he explained. 'Mine suffer from a rare droopy eye syndrome. There was really no alternative but the knife.' Some of his guests, although arty types used to suspending disbelief, were clearly experiencing some problems with the storyline. But they stuck with it.

Would he look the same? they wondered. Would he still be recognisable to his friends, or, more importantly, casting agents? And would the scars show? Although of course the operation was not for cosmetic reasons, Gay Opera Singer had clearly thought through the beneficial side-effects.

After all, he had seen his own mother transformed as a result of the family affliction. He knew that it was a possibility that surgery would have the same effect on his own face. And he was prepared. In fact, he had arranged to have some new publicity photos taken the following month.

'By then the swelling should have gone down completely,' he assured his captive audience. 'And don't worry darleengs, it will still be me,' he chortled, before feeling his way to the wine bottle.

As he worked the room, clinging carefully to any available surfaces, gracefully accepting the concerned hands extended out from his guests, he finally alighted on a quiet character sitting by himself in the corner.

On our arrival, Gay Opera Singer had simply ushered everyone in to the room, thereby avoiding the possibility of getting people's names wrong – so easily done while virtually blinded by black-out shades.

As it was, he simply couldn't identify everyone. He approached the quiet man cautiously, desperate not to offend what was probably an old pal. 'Thank you so much for coming, darleeng,' he cooed at the retiring guest. 'It has made all the difference,' he gushed. 'Oh that's alright guv,' the man replied. 'We aim to please,' and with that he offered his glass and his Gas Board identity card.

Doris Dyke
The Nice Young Lovebirds had been settling in nicely, although the recent cold snap had put paid to their penchant for sleeping naked in the garden. They continued to make friends with all the other neighbours, and were extremely gracious when rebuking offers of unwanted second-hand furniture.

'We have no need for material belongings,' was their little mantra, a spiritual position that meant their visitors were forced to perch uncomfortably on the floor. But otherwise their hospitality skills were leagues ahead of their predecessor, Weirdie Woman.

In short, they had been welcomed as the new bohemian dream team. But it seemed that Ms Lovebird had something of a guilty secret, one that very few of her ashram loving pals were aware of. Ms Lovebird had the most terrifying of youthful afflictions. Ms Lovebird had a standard-issue suburban mother.

Unlike most of her circle, Ms Lovebird had neither grown up in a commune, nor been forced to follow her parents lead in wearing ill-fitting orange robes, nor had she had a father who had left home to find himself. In fact, he had never left home. After 44 years, he was still there. For Ms Lovebird, her parents were an ideological embarrassment.

And now one half of that embarrassment was coming to stay. She had tried very hard to dissuade her. 'We don't believe in beds, mother,' Ms Lovebird had pleaded down the phone. 'And we don't have a television,' she added, praying that time away from *Coronation Street* would prove to be her mother's breaking point.

But her mother was adamant. 'I lived through rationing, dear,' she sighed. 'Don't you worry about me. I can rough it.'

Eventually, after much heart-wrenching discussion, it was agreed, Ms Lovebird would allow her mother to come and stay. 'But I won't call you "mother",' she added, firmly. 'In London, you will only be known as "Doris".'

Secretly Doris was rather pleased. It was going be an adventure, she told Susan, her next-door neighbour. They were going to go out for dinner, and perhaps dancing, she elaborated.

'And I'm going to be known as Doris,' she whispered over the fence. 'But that's not your name,' replied her neighbour, confused. 'I know,' giggled Doris. It hadn't occurred to her to contradict her daughter's mistake. And anyway, she was quite looking forward to her new identity.

Two days later, 'Doris' was happily ensconced on a bean bag on her daughter's sitting room floor. The bean bag, together with a blow-up lilo, had been a concession to her visit. Their other concession had been an agreement to take her out with them for the evening.

'Just don't tell anyone who you are,' Ms Lovebird repeated to her mother over and over. 'And try not to stare.' They were going to Amazon Solos, a karaoke club with a twist. A lesbian twist, and Ms Lovebird was beginning to have reservations.

It struck Ms Lovebird that she had never had a contemporary-facts-of-life conversation with her mother, and it seemed too late to start now. Perhaps, she thought, she wouldn't notice that all the girls liked dancing together. Perhaps, she consoled herself, they simply wouldn't get in.

The queue was long and boisterous by the time they arrived. The door policy was tough, but fair. Butch was in, Barbie was out. Bizarrely, Doris's purple rinse and tightly woven perm struck something of a note with the heavy-weight door person.

'What's your name, ducky?' enquired the clipboard-holding gatekeeper.

'Doris,' she replied. 'And I'm not her mother,' she added for good measure, motioning to a mortified Ms Lovebird.

The peels of laughter could be heard all the way to the back of the line. 'Go get 'em, girl,' the doorperson guffawed. And with that, the red rope was lifted. Doris was in, and there was no stopping her now.

Strictly speaking, there was something of a pecking order to the karaoke machine. Regulars took precedence, while newcomers rarely got the chance to pay good money to publicly humiliate themselves.

But Doris was to prove the exception. Her door performance had afforded her celebrity status. Within minutes she was being handed the microphone and being beckoned into the spotlight.

'My neighbours will never believe it,' she whispered to Ms Lovebird. 'And apparently they are going to give me a stage name as well,' she continued. Then, before her daughter had chance to reply, the compere was calling for attention.

'And now, for her first outing this evening, please put your hands together for the truly original, one and only, "Doris Dyke".'

As the karaoke machine pumped out *This Girl's in Love with You* the crowd went crazy and a star was born. For Ms Lovebird, it was inconceivable. Her mother had somehow joined the sexual revolution.

In Stiges
'*Come to Hotel Nanci,*' proclaimed the online brochure. '*And treat yourself like a Queen.*' Hot tub on the roof, tropical theme bar, complimentary continental break-fast, and, crucially, '*Best friends welcome!*' As far as Belle Boomy was concerned, this last sentence was the icing on the planned cake.

Since leaving East of Islington and moving to the wilds of Yorkshire, Matt Boomy, the man who once lost everything in the Eighties except his Stonyhurst accent, was inseparable from Cruiser, his beloved Jack Russell. And Belle Boomy, his new girlfriend, knew her place. The news that man's best friend was welcome at this hotel could mean only one thing, this was the place to hold her boyfriend's surprise 40th birthday party. It was going to be the best one anyone had ever had. Certainly anyone in her small town.

Logistically it wasn't without its problems. Hotel Nanci was in Sitges, a small seaside resort just outside Barcelona. There would be the cost of plane tickets, the small detail that they didn't speak Spanish, a question over how many of their friends would be able to leave their livestock (theirs was a rural life), but Belle was undeterred. *'Best friends welcome!'* was obviously a sign.

'He's only going to be 40 once,' she pleaded with their bewildered circle, most of whom were initially expecting a night at the pub and a curry. 'And it is the off season.' This hint at a bargain proved to be the clincher. Within days four cost-conscious party fans from the Dales and two enthusiastic Londoners had booked themselves flights to a place they'd never heard of and handed over deposits for reduced-rate rooms and a place in the hot tub.

Yes, they were leaving the country to celebrate his birthday party, but there was no need to worry. Cruiser would be well catered for. In fact, the hotel booking clerk had assured her that they got lots of Cruisers.

Anxious that Cruiser might feel a little left out with only Spanish dogs for company, a border collie called Randy was invited along to make up the canine numbers. 'He likes a long run,' Randy's owner said. 'And he doesn't mind sharing a basket.'

Finally the big day arrived. Leading her assorted group through customs, Belle Boomy ordered a cab to take them straight to Hotel Nanci. The receptionist looked a little taken aback at the sight of Cruiser and Randy. Sensing his apprehension, Belle removed a print-out of their sales brochure from her bag.

'Best friends welcome,' she pronounced, slowly, while pointing at the underlined sentence and then to the bewildered pets being firmly gripped by their respective masters. The clerk stared wide eyed, first at Matt Boomy, then at Randy's owner, and shook his head before reluctantly offered them the register and accepting their dog passports.

The description of the hotel had not been wrong. The bar was certainly tropically themed and so were all its occupants. Several of the men were wearing oriental sarongs, two were in swimwear bordering on the feminine cut and the barman appeared to be wearing lipstick. It was certainly a long way from Yorkshire.

The women in the visiting birthday party had changed into their finest chiffon cocktail dresses and high-heeled stilettos yet somehow still looked decidedly underdressed. Cruiser and Randy were a huge hit. Although conversation was limited, there were squeals of delight every time Matt Boomy announced their names. 'Dog-lovers,' he nodded, sagely to his friends.

They had arrived in time for free house sangria, and as the drinks flowed, everyone's sign language skills improved. Strangely, besides the new arrivals, there didn't seem to be any other women staying at the hotel, a fact Randy's owner put down to Latin custom. 'Wife at home with the little 'uns?' he said, repeatedly, to a man wearing a sequinned mini dress sitting alongside him at the bar. 'Night out with the lads?' he continued, before slapping the man on the back, a physical act that seemed to be warmly welcomed.

It was when Dusty Springfield came on the juke box for the fifth time that Belle Boomy began to suspect that something wasn't quite right. 'Darling,' she whispered to her loved one. 'I think we've come on a gay holiday by mistake.' Matt Boomy looked around him. Cruiser was sitting in the centre of an adoring ring, draped in a lamé scarf, being fed titbits by two men sporting slingbacks.

'Oh, I don't know,' he replied, smiling over his best friend. 'I think they just appreciate a good boy when they see one.'

Almost Blue

Gay Opera Singer was many things to many people, but a black blues singer was not one of them. Strangely, this was news to his mother, and it was news that she had decided to keep to herself. There had never been a family wedding that didn't involve her son performing and she wasn't about to change history now. 'He can do anything,' she would brag to distant relatives preparing for the altar.

In the past, he had found himself paying tribute to Abba, Dusty Springfield, Frank Sinatra and, on one particularly odd occasion, the theme tune to *Goldfinger*. But this time he felt she had gone too far. 'I don't have the cheeks,' he pleaded. 'Not to mention the colouring.' But she was determined, the wedding was in Bournemouth and she fancied an afternoon by the coast.

The distant relative in question was a boy called Nigel whom Gay Opera Singer had last seen 30 years ago. He was a cousin twice removed, marrying a woman who would have preferred a performance by Charlotte Church, or at least Aled Jones. Instead she was getting a barrel-chested baritone with a live-in boyfriend. But her husband-to-be was a committed jazz fan so she had reluctantly agreed to his request for Louis Armstrong. Or at least for a man who could 'do' Louis Armstrong.

The bride's mother had been less sure, preferring instead to promote her stage-struck nine-year-old niece. 'She does a lovely version of *All Things Bright and*

Beautiful,' she said each time the in church entertainment programme was raised. But Louis Armstrong it was.

Bournemouth is a long way from East of Islington, in more ways than one. The more sensible guests had allowed plenty of time, leaving the night before in fact, but not so Gay Opera Singer. 'A couple of hours darleengs, that's all we'll need,' he assured his mother and Dazzling Darren as they set off. Five hours later, they arrived in Bournemouth with minutes to spare and without the address of the church. A visit to the local tourist office revealed little except a wrong direction to an idyllic Methodist chapel hosting a Women's Institute jumble sale.

Thankfully the good ladies took pity on the bedraggled trio and rang every church in the parish until their wedding party was finally located. Dressed only in his tracksuit, his dinner suit in a carrier bag, Gay Opera Singer dashed past the assembled throng. 'Where can I change darleeng?' he demanded of the curate. 'In the vestry,' the kindly man whispered. 'You are the vicar aren't you?' When his lack of a dog collar was discovered he was redirected to a shed in the garden.

The church was packed, mostly with members of the bride's family, none of whom could understand why they were being kept waiting for a man who bore no resemblance to their idea of a jazz icon. But perhaps they were in for a surprise. 'Is he going to black up?' they murmured as they watched him disappear from view.

His cue was to follow the Second Psalm, the rector was going to wave a flag out of the vestry window when he wanted Gay Opera Singer to dash across the garden and step up to the pulpit. It gave him just enough time to realise that his shoes were completely different colours. It was not an authentic look, nor did it instil professional confidence but hopefully their aesthetic attentions would be elsewhere.

Unfortunately, the organist was a traditionalist. He had his song sheet and he was sticking to it. 'I don't do Louis Armstrong' he said as Gay Opera Singer approached. 'And nor should you,' he added as an aside.

The news that he was going to have to perform a rendition of *What A Wonderful World* a cappella threw him momentarily, but not as much as the sudden realisation that he had no idea what the bride was called.

But there was no going back. He was just going to have to improvise. 'This is for Nigel,' he announced before launching into song. The romantic lyrics took on a whole new meaning for the bewildered crowd. *'I see trees of green, red roses too. I see them bloom for me and you...'* As the song progressed, Dazzling Darren threw an encouraging smile towards the bride's family. 'Who's the nutter?' one of them mouthed back at him.

The Bearded Bride

The Sapphic Snapper called. She had recently taken to sporting a goatee beard in an effort, she claimed, to play with our clichés of femininity. On the whole I disliked beards on men and would have preferred that my female friends gave them a wide berth. Still, she was from Arkansas and as this was the great metropolitan melting pot her extended circle had been working hard to overlook it. But the latest cycle in her bid for heightened personal development had been tougher to deal with. 'I'm getting married,' she squealed. 'Isn't it great?'

Great wasn't exactly the word, miraculous possibly, unbelievable even, but 'great' perhaps not. 'Who's the lucky girl?' I wondered. 'Honey, you're so cute. It's a gay guy, of course.' Of course. With more than four women to one straight man in London it should have been obvious that the only way to get hitched was to grow a beard and marry a guy keen to wear a dress.

She had a lot to organise she explained, and had heard from Fearless that I had a convertible car. She had also heard from Fearless that I would be happy to act as chauffeur and second string bridesmaid to Fearless's maid of honour. 'I'm thinking Cruella De Vil for you two,' she said of the sartorial arrangements. It's true that I had once yearned to be a bridesmaid, but that was thirty years ago and this wasn't really the fantasy picture I'd had in my head. But I was in a liberal bind. She might have transmogrified into Jeremy Beadle but she was still in the sisterhood. So chauffeur and black widow bridesmaid it was.

'There is one thing,' I said as a final attempt at escape. 'My car is a 2CV.' The Sapphic Snapper didn't seem to mind. 'As long as I'll be noticed,' she said. I felt certain that wouldn't be a problem, I assured her.

The great day approached and I decided to wash the would-be convertible. In the tarmac mess that passed for our road, I set about polishing the 2CV to a shine fit for a lesbian bride and her gay bridegroom.

Opposite, Sultan the garagista and his mechanics were sipping stiff coffee. They offered to help. Business was slack. They didn't get that much work as the area was a strong mixture of Hasidic Jews and Asian shopkeepers who drive Volvos and Nissans respectively. Sultan the garagista objected to both on misguided stylistic grounds so he was slowly going bust. We never discussed the fact that his failure to train as a proper mechanic might also be a contributing factor to his demise.

'How come you wash it?' they chirped while helping me sud the roof. 'Actually, one of my friends is getting married and I'm letting her use my car for the procession,' I replied.

Sultan was difficult to judge. He was a relaxed guy, but somehow I felt that bearded lesbians, like Nissans and Volvos, were not his thing so I skirted round the finer details.

The car came up a treat. With the back seat out and the roof down it looked like a low-grade Popemobile. The wedding was a spectacle: a registry office rammed full with a wedding party that included six women in drag with stick-on beards, a bride with a real beard, a bridegroom with no beard, a semi-naked Sixties fading beauty and assorted artistic types.

I wore a black, full-length velvet evening gown and a large hat. Fearless chose a low-cut black chiffon number with even larger sunglasses. The bride and the groom were both kitted out in tutus, so any fears we had of being a bit overdressed were completely unfounded. However, fears of being beaten senseless by gangs of unreconstructed youths while driving down East of Islington High Street were not. Our worries were not alleviated by the Sapphic Snapper's insistence on standing up in the back of the car and singing: 'We're here, we're queer, we've just got married!'

In a bid to get us out of there quickly, I put my foot down and Fearless and I got home relatively unscathed. Sultan the garagista was supping his early evening coffee when we get there. 'Is it her, is it her?' Sultan said, pointing at Fearless. He meant the bride. Fearless knew he meant the bride.

'Do I look like I've got a beard!' she shouted. Understandably, he was more than a little confused by her reaction so there was nothing for it but to outline the true story. 'No way,' Sultan said. 'Way,' we said. Finally, by way of an explanation, I said that I thought that the Sapphic Snapper had just stopped plucking. He visibly relaxed. 'That happens in Turkey all the time,' he said.

Private Dancers
Dazzling Darren had decided to open a weekly dance academy, a select institution with a strict admissions policy: it would cater only for ladies of a certain age. To the outsider, this rigid criteria might have seemed strange, but years of theatrical training had taught him three things.

One, he knew never to work with children, or their stage-struck mothers. Two, aspiring young professionals were usually a hopeless cause. And three, he needed to make money. Ergo: ladies of a certain age fitted the bill, and paid it, handsomely.

The repertoire was limited, but popular. Polkas, basic ballroom moves, the twist, some country dancing and several reels. Nothing too enthusiastic, and nothing that involved both feet leaving the floor. His 'ladies', as he liked to call them, eschewed dieting, believing instead in the hugely restorative powers of the Playtex all-in-one.

They wanted the earth to move, but they didn't want to end up in traction. And, of course, they wanted to dress up.

Dressing up was why they had come. Every week they arrived with their holdalls packed with purple sateen, red velvet, and gold taffeta ball gowns. As far as style influences went, it was *Strictly Come Dancing* all the way.

Their husbands, relieved of the possibility of being seen in public with these gaudy creations, gladly footed the dressmaker's bills. Dazzling Darren, ever keen to keep the customer happy, encouraged them in their sartorial fantasies.

'You look gorgeous, darleengs,' he would coo as they exited the make shift dressing rooms. 'So Fonteyn, so Ginger Rogers.' At first, things were quite tame. The odd off-the-shoulder number was as risqué as it got.

But it was only a matter of time before barely concealed competition set in. And it soon became obvious who the main culprit was. Mrs Gorge, by name and by nature, was the first to introduce hand-sewn sequins. Within a couple of weeks she had added a pearl-encrusted tiara to her ensemble.

A feather boa and silver stilettos quickly followed. Not wanting to be outdone, the other ladies followed suit. Hairpieces, costume jewellery, and a heavy dependence on pan stick quickly became the norm. Dazzling Darren struggled to keep up. His own velveteen tuxedo looked tame by comparison. Even his regimental Highland kilt barely cut a sway behind their vast expanse of net petticoats.

As their confidence grew, the ladies wanted even

bigger, even brighter, costumes. They wanted specialist hairdressing. Elaborate props and dry ice. In short, his ladies of a certain age wanted cameras, lights and action.

So, in a bid to keep the cash flowing, Dazzling Darren introduced monthly theme evenings. Initially, it was agreed that they would perform show tunes, the whole class lining up to re-enact the chorus line formations of *South Pacific* or *Guys and Dolls*.

The costumes by now had grown enormous. With little or no regard for the original, each week saw Mrs Gorge pile more and more appliqué onto her bodice. Her already substantial 16-stone frame was virtually undetectable through the added layers of organza and lace.

Meanwhile, as the ladies' outfits grew more outrageous, so did their expectations. Not content with just Dazzling Darren's approval, they demanded a bigger audience. They demanded a show.

It was to be a small affair, no publicity, and all proceeds were to be donated to charity. The class would perform a medley of show tunes, a scene from *The Mikado* and two of the more sprightly members were to attempt a tap dance duet. '*A tribute to Gene Kelly (the later years)*,' explained the show programme.

All the class members had their place in the line-up, except Mrs Gorge who was proving difficult to accommodate. Dazzling Darren's refusal to partner her in a romantic duet was causing an impasse in the production schedule. Why, she mused to her classmates, was he playing so hard to get? Her money, his youth, couldn't he see that they would make the perfect couple?

Finally, fortified by the dress rehearsal complimentary sherry, Mrs Gorge cornered him. 'Are you avoiding me,' she purred, laying her hand on his knee. 'I won't bite, you know,' her overloaded corset pressed up against his chest.

Dazzling Darren grew breathless with anxiety. 'You're just playing hard to get,' she cooed, stroking his hand. 'No madam,' he recoiled. 'I'm just not playing straight.'

It Ain't Over Till...

It wasn't that Gay Opera Singer was fat, he explained, more that he wasn't prepared, quite yet, to give in to the seasonal roles usually handed out to jolly thesps with middle-age spread.

'I mean, darleeng, can you see me with a brace of reindeer?' The question, of course, was rhetorical. Besides, as Dazzling Darren pointed out, it would take more than a brace to pull his sleigh. So, a diet was called for. And, in keeping with his theatrical persuasions, the Dr Andrews diet, that year's celebrity regime of choice, had seemed like the perfect solution.

As long as he refused any offers of vegetables, minerals or bread-sticks and ate only calorie-laden fat, Dr Andrews promised Gay Opera Singer the body of a teenage pop idol. His food bill grew. Each morning was greeted with a hearty fry-up: never less than four rashers, three sausages and a liberal helping of black pudding. Lunchtimes stretched into tea as he battled to fit in the endless courses of cream-enriched fine fayre. Restaurants gave up clearing his table – there seemed little point, he never left.

Miraculously, the pounds rolled off. The more Gay Opera Singer consumed, the thinner he got. But professionally things were growing rather more pear-shaped.

He had begun to notice something strange in his audiences' behaviour – a distinct cooling in their affections. Admittedly, he no longer conformed to the operatic stereotype, his barrel chest now more of an adolescent pimple, but somehow he didn't think this was the cause.

Nor could anybody claim that he had dramatically changed his repertoire. Ever the populist, he liked to think he gave the fee-paying public what they wanted – a comforting tour around the easy-listening classics.

No, it was something else, something he couldn't quite put his finger on. Nightly, as he peered out into the auditorium, it seemed there was a problem developing with the sought-after front rows.

No sooner would he reach the peak of his pitch, his throat fully opened to deliver the requisite arias with the highest degree of emotion, than those seated up close and personal would recoil in horror. Gasps of revulsion would rise up as pews of elegantly clad music-lovers frantically scrambled backwards out of the most expensive seats in the house.

Rapidly, word spread, and it became impossible for the box offices to even give away the front row seats. Sniggering comments were rife amongst the other cast members. Finally, Gay Opera Singer could take it no more. 'What is it?' he shouted one evening at the few remaining diehards peering up at him. 'What have I done?' he pleaded, in a radical departure from the usual *Don Giovanni* script.

And so it was, in the vocal unison usually reserved for cries of 'encore', that the fans delivered their reply. 'Halitosis,' they shouted, before heading for sweeter-smelling seats in the Gods. It seemed his lack of audience appeal was a fat thing, or rather an eating-too-much-fat thing. Apparently, the high price to be paid for Dr Andrews's miracle diet was breath so bad it could stop traffic. Luckily for Gay Opera Singer, his new affliction had reached the well-tuned ears of Sven, a man with a mission.

He was waiting for the stricken singer at the end of the performance. 'I have been sent to save you,' Sven announced, evangelically. 'And to let you know that you are not alone,' he added, mysteriously, before handing Gay Opera Singer a leaflet bearing the words, 'AA – Andrews Anonymous'.

'Like you, these people were all victims of that cruel regime,' continued Sven, and produced several snapshots of beautiful, thin, model-like figures. Confused, Gay Opera Singer nodded but didn't open his mouth.

'Now, due to me, they are now back to their normal selves,' Sven crowed triumphantly. 'And soon, you too will be fat again,' he added. Gay Opera Singer's cry could be smelt from five streets away.

Big Girl Power

Hemmed in by the recycling plant and a sprawling Seventies council estate, Les Mums' new home was in the uncharted zone at the borough's edge, far beyond the reach of the baristas and the vegan café on East of Islington high street. Still, it had been almost cheap, and whilst they were apparently the only lesbian couple on the street, little Liam certainly wasn't the only child with an anonymous father.

Two weeks after moving in, Les Mums decided to throw a house-warming party. *'In the spirit of peace and giving,'* the invitation read. *'Bring a bottle.'* Amongst the guests were several women who had formed the core of a once-radical separatist club. Some of them hadn't been seen in years and there had been a few changes. Five had sperm bank babies. Two had 'gone straight' and then gone back again and one, Carla – now Carl – had had a sex change. Although, still dressed in her statutory dungarees with a number two cut, even she had to admit it would have taken an expert to spot the difference.

The guests arrived laden with organic gifts and demanding infants and were soon busying themselves settling down to some co-breastfeeding; the latest nutritional choice among the East of Islington Sapphic set. As the conversation flowed, the infants were seamlessly passed from one breast to another, thereby avoiding what Les Mums believed to be the root problem in heterosexual relationships, 'empty male boob syndrome'.

The party had got into full swing and everyone was about to be seated for dinner when the bell rang and Mum-Mum dashed to open it. As the door swung back, she was confronted not with a shiraz-carrying late arrival but a man in a balaclava holding a gun and sporting an aggressive attitude. Forcing his way in, he pushed Mum-Mum against the wall and held the pistol to her head. 'Jewellery,' he mumbled. 'And don't even think about calling for your husband.' Mum-Mum agreed readily; now clearly wasn't the time to correct his patriarchal prejudices.

Peeling off the Indian silver that she had worn since she was a student, she could sense his disappointment. 'Is that it?' he said incredulously as she handed over the last of it. 'Is that all he's given you?' She sighed. After all he did have a point. When was the last time Dad-Mum had bought her so much as a nose stud?

Dissatisfied with his booty, the disgruntled robber tried to manoeuvre her down the hallway, towards the sound of the other guests and what he presumed would be a greater haul. Mum-Mum hadn't the nerve to tell him he was wasting his time. Protest badges maybe, but pearls definitely not. Still, this way lay help, and help was what she needed.

As they turned the corner towards the dining room, Carl came out of the bathroom, caught sight of what was happening and charged towards them. Waving her once-female arms in the air and shouting, 'OFF OFF OFF,' at their assailant, she presented quite a formidable picture. In the Eighties she had once taken an intensive self-defence course in case she was ever confronted with the Yorkshire Ripper and she had waited 20-odd years to use it. It seemed she had forgotten none of her training.

On seeing Carl's 17-stone bulk looming towards him, the robber visibly shook, dropped his gun and bolted for the door. Carl ran after him – she had also done the course on performing a citizen's arrest. Catching up with him in the street, she rugby-tackled the terrified man to the floor, removed his belt, tied him up and pinned him down with her foot. Several neighbours came out to see what was going on. 'Are you a copper?' the robber squeaked. 'No,' replied Carl. 'I'm a transgender lesbian with anger issues.' The robber grunted. 'Oh yeah,' he said. 'I've seen your lot on Jeremy Kyle.'

Wedding Belles
Never ones to be slow in coming forward, Gay Opera

Singer and his consort Dazzling Darren had booked their big day as soon as the new gay partnership came in. And what they lacked in a bride, they were going to make up for in costume drama.

'Bustles, darleeng, bustles,' Dazzling Darren enthused whenever a bemused guest asked for direction on the Victorian dress code. 'And practice your quadrilles.'

This may have been a gay wedding but there was to be no room for Abba impersonators and mobile-disco queens. Instead, a retinue of classically trained singers and musicians had agreed to perform, for free, on the misunderstanding that this was to be an audition of sorts.

'You never know who's going to be there, sweetie,' Gay Opera Singer had enthused at the vaguest mention of a fee. 'After all, who's to say that Pavarotti wasn't discovered at a wedding.'

To counterbalance the top table, it was agreed that Dazzling Darren's best man was to be a woman, a girl eminently qualified for this dirt-dishing job, not least because they first met after she discovered her then boyfriend actually preferred Dazzling Darren. 'I've waited years to have my say,' she announced upon taking up the task. 'And what I'd like to say is; "It should have been me!"'

The rest of the cast were given walk-on roles. The waiters and waitresses were non-equity stage hands and the scene-setters unemployed actors dressed in booty from the Royal Opera House wardrobe clearance sale.

The catering, however, was to be strictly Gay Opera Singer's domain. Never one to trust the culinary talents of others, he had decided to prepare and cook a

Victorian banquet for his 150 guests aided only by a star-struck drama student.

For four days and three long nights they slavishly followed the recipes entombed in Mrs Beeton's *Modern Household Cookery*, the 1861 edition. Game pies, ribs of beef, hocks of ham, it was a real man-sized feast.

Finally the big day arrived. The groom and groom marzipan figurines were set, the piano finely tuned, the vows well-rehearsed when, halfway through completing the chocolate bombe dessert, disaster struck. With one whirr of the Moulinex, the top of Gay Opera Singer's ring finger was no more.

The star-struck drama student, a keen follower of ER, quickly seized his chance to play a lead role. He fished out the essential marital ingredient, grabbed its owner and drove at break-neck speed to the local casualty department.

'I'm getting married in three hours,' Gay Opera Singer screeched as he lunged through the doors of A&E. 'And he needs this finger,' the star-struck drama student added, brandishing the tin foil-wrapped appendage.

It could have been the attention-grabbing detail of their Victorian dress frocks, or it could simply have been a desire to end the Stanislavski sobbing, but whatever the reason, the triage nurse bumped them to the top of the queue.

'You have saved my marriage,' Gay Opera Singer cooed as the bemused doctor put the finishing touches to his fine stitching. 'I don't know how I can thank you,' he added. 'Just remember to keep it up at all the times,' the doctor advised as he signed the release form. 'I always do, darleeng,' Gay Opera Singer replied as he exited.

With only minutes to spare, he made it to the wedding ceremony. Holding the bandaged finger aloft, he beamed at the assembled party of friends and family, and took his place alongside Dazzling Darren on the specially set podium.

For some of the guests, it was a confusing new detail in an already confusing scenario. Lacking an explanation for the bandage-covered ring finger being held in the air, whispered questions about its significance rippled amongst the more elderly members of the audience.

For one of Dazzling Darren's octogenarian great aunts it could only mean one thing. 'It's a gay symbol, dear,' she murmured to her neighbour. 'I think it's what they wear instead of a wedding dress.'

But her more forthright sister had a clearer measure of the situation. 'Oh no, dear,' she corrected her firmly. 'It's the fickle finger of fate. He's had it removed.'

9

Time Out

Gone Dogging

Dogging wasn't the first thing on the Poetess's mind when she set off for her autumn mini-break, but she had claimed to be open to new experiences, and it was certainly something new. It all started with her desire to get away, to leave behind the rat race of similes and haikus in search of 'getting back to basics'. And it didn't come more basic than a trip to Canvey Island.

Armed with a faded map and a car on its final warning from the AA, she was accompanied by her companion, Friendy. The specifics of their relationship were unknown, but as Friendy was the only person prepared to sit in the passenger seat, it was generally agreed that they were made for each other.

'We should meet the locals,' she told Friendy as they headed off in the wrong gear. 'And get a feel for their world.' Friendy, calmed by Valium bought on the internet and a flask of coffee laced liberally with cheap brandy, nodded.

The journey started off uneventfully enough and in only double the time it should have taken they arrived on the grey shores of the south Essex coast. Save for one café, four youths and two dogs on an eight-bore chain, Canvey Island was closed. 'We don't get the tourists any more,' the café owner sighed, as they looked over the limited menu. 'Not enough excitement for them.'

The Poetess was surprised. True, there was a down-at-heel feel to the place and the caravan park looked like it had seen better days, but she was captivated by what she saw as its 'rawness'. It had 'untapped passion', she told the café man as he handed over the special order scampi butty. The café man smiled. 'Well,' he said. 'If it's passion you're after you should try Two Tree Island.'

After consuming their carbohydrate heavy lunch – they were on holiday after all and Friendy had been feeling a little faint – they took his directions and headed off in search the passionate place. After driving for several miles in the wrong direction, they finally found Two Tree Island, or at least what they thought was it. A half-mile causeway lead out over desolate marshland, marked only by clutches of saplings and abandoned beer cans, eventually bringing them to a large car park and a slip-way leading into a sludge of drenched water. It wasn't exactly what she'd had in mind.

Milling around in the car park were several men dressed in sports jackets and freshly ironed anoraks. 'Excellent,' the Poetess announced to Friendy. 'Locals. We should meet them.' After draining the contents of her flask, Friendy reluctantly followed.

By the time Friendy caught up, the Poetess was deep in conversation with a man who had introduced himself as Donald, a retired bank employee with a good pension. This latter detail was readily offered. He was more than keen to point out the not particularly obvious appeal of Two Tree Island.

'Over there are two very good hides,' he explained, pointing towards a couple of near shattered sheds. 'And you can always get a place in the car park.' The Poetess said that was good to know, but what were the hides for? Donald lent in, conspiratorially. 'The wildlife,' he said, tapping his nose with his forefinger. 'Some of us like to be discreet.' Even by the Poetess's literary standards, this was obscure.

Out of the corner of her eye, the Poetess caught sight of another man circling them and she beckoned him over. 'No need to be shy,' she said. 'We're keen to meet the locals.' The man blushed. 'Roomy car,' he mumbled. There was no denying it. 'Will you be getting in it soon?' he pressed. 'Yes,' the Poetess replied, truthfully. With that the man shuffled off towards the vehicle. 'He likes to get a good view,' Donald smirked as the man pressed his face up to the rear window. 'Of what?' the Poetess asked. 'The dogging of course,' he whispered. 'Oh dear,' she said. 'We didn't bring a dog.' Donald nodded. 'That's okay,' he said. 'At our age we don't expect anything too fancy.'

9-11

It is testament to how little the worlds of opera and the military cross over that Gay Opera Singer agreed in late September 2001 to fly his company to the Middle East on a whirlwind tour of *The Merry Widow*.

Living as he did in a theatrical twilight world, his

grasp of the political stage has always been limited, non-existent even. Besides, as far as he was concerned, the tour was simply a chance to take the pleasures of musical farce to the grand hotels and estates of this hitherto opera-bereft land.

It was also, he felt sure, a chance to clean up. Big money, even bigger limousines, acres of royal palaces, and offers of lucrative ticket sales was music to his ears.

The fact that at this time everyone except the Australian girls' netball squad was refusing to leave the tarmac at Heathrow caused him barely a whimper of alarm. Gay Opera Singer had a booking, and he was off. 'It's a cultural desert out there, darleeng', he memorably declared on packing his pan stick. 'We'll be mobbed.'

Within days he was leaving frantic telephone messages for Dazzling Darren. Clearly his proximity to what the pundits might have called 'the action' had marginally sharpened his awareness of current affairs. Although admittedly not by much.

In case Dazzling Darren and all their friends hadn't heard, he wanted to warn them of some disturbing news gleaned at a drinks soirée the previous evening. He didn't want to be melodramatic, but according to his informant there were some very odd things being sent through the British postal system.

'Be careful darleeng,' boomed his distinctive baritone. 'Don't sign for any parcels if they contain Tampax,' he instructed. Otherwise he couldn't understand what all the fuss was about, everyone seemed very friendly. 'And the service is excellent', he added.

By his account the tour was going well. 'We'll be mobbed,' may have been an exaggeration, but like the actors from *It Ain't Half Hot Mum*, he certainly had a captive audience. By the time his little troupe had reached the desert oasis of Oman, the entertainers were being greeted like liberating heroes. American film stars might have lost their flying nerve, but the theatre-going public of the Middle East still had a singing queen for entertainment.

Everywhere they went the marbled ballrooms and makeshift theatres were crammed with ex-pat Brits clapping for their country, all of them stoically determined not to let 'Johnny Foreigner' get the better of them.

The fact that most of the audience had little interest in the machinations of *The Merry Widow* couldn't have bothered Gay Opera Singer less. Ever keen to please, he saw no problem in speedily incorporating a medley of Last Night of the Proms favourites at the end of each performance – thereby guaranteeing there was never a dry eye in the house.

Naturally the hoteliers and restaurateurs of this tourist-bereft region were ecstatic. If nothing else here was a man who was prepared to help them flog their wildly expensive imported lagers. In return, they were falling over themselves to accommodate him and his merry band of performers. As long as Gay Opera Singer refrained from mentioning their small local difficulty, a subject about which he was woefully ill-informed anyway, it seemed he was welcomed everywhere with open arms.

Free mini-bars, massages, movies, bigger and better rooms and suites. Eventually, hotels were competing on square footage until finally he was given the royal suite, a concession not even made for visiting English prime ministers on diplomatic missions.

So vast was this suite that it took Gay Opera Singer a full ten minutes to complete the guided tour of its myriad chambers and sub chambers. The master bedroom alone boasted two hot tubs and three en suite bathrooms. Taking breakfast one morning on his 100ft marble sun terrace, he knew he had arrived. With a staff ratio of 20 to one, Gay Opera Singer and his troupe seemed to have the entire hotel to themselves, except, that was, for the two Australian backpackers who had just checked in.

'Is this the bar, mate?' they asked, approaching his expansive new quarters. 'Certainly not,' Gay Opera Singer replied. 'Is it your gaff?' they asked, incredulously. 'It certainly is,' Gay Opera Singer crowed, before reaching for the panic alarm. As his was the royal suite, the response time was rapid and the stunned backpackers were handcuffed and removed before they had chance to pose any further threat. The Cultural Attaché apologised in person later that afternoon. As far as Gay Opera Singer was concerned, he had had a good war.

A Little Bit Ratty

For years it had been known as the Susie Round the Bend Rat Story; a tale of bad service and rodent horror on the Indian subcontinent. Whenever anyone ever dared mention the idea of travelling to Asia, The Rat Story would come out.

She had been staying in a posh hotel in New Delhi, using up the last vestiges of her money before heading home. After months of backpacking round the country, this stopover was a special treat and one she fully intended to enjoy to the max. She had had her first hot shower for several weeks and changed into her one and only cocktail dress – backpacking left little room for haute couture. She had then gone down to the hotel bar and spent the evening being attended to by waiters in starched linen and middle-aged men with roving eyes.

After a meal served on the finest white porcelain and eaten with highly decorated silver left over from the Raj, she finally retired to her room, her copy of EM Forster securely tucked under her arm. As indulgences went, it had been excessive, but it was worth it.

Several hours later Susie Round the Bend was woken by a rustling of the perfectly aligned bed clothes. As she was alone and not expecting any guests, she found the noise rather disarming. But not as disarming as the subsequent pain from her foot and the revelation, on throwing back the highly embroidered sateen bed cover, that a rat was hanging off her big toe.

Unsurprisingly she became hysterical, which caused the startled animal to sink his teeth in even deeper. By the time she had managed to knock him off his purchase, with the help of *A Passage To India*, things were not looking good. A call to the concierge didn't improve matters. They had entertained past and future presidents, the hotel had seen banquets in honour of maharajahs and sultans. This was a first, they claimed.

An extensive search of the room revealed nothing. The rat, sated, had left. Susie Round the Bend had no evidence to substantiate her claim except a rather large hole in her toe, for which the concierge admitted he had no reasonable explanation. A doctor was called and she spent the next three days undergoing extremely challenging injections in the subcutaneous fat on her stomach in order to stave off the possibility of developing a foaming mouth. Never a good look, especially in a single woman.

Ten years on the experience was as fresh for her as the day it had happened. And for her friends, the action replay at holiday time had kept their hard-earned salaries away from tours that would otherwise have included a glance at Lutyens's finest. In fact, it had become a reliable standard for after-dinner conversation amongst most of her social circle. People who had never met Susie Round the Bend had heard The Rat Story.

And then one evening she found herself seated next to a woman who had been at school with the Maharajah of Rajasthan's sister. It was a tenuous link to royalty, but the hostess was proud of it nonetheless and insisted on exploiting it on introduction. Susie's ears pricked up.

Perhaps the well-connected woman knew the hotel? After all, it had been incredibly smart, one of the best she had been assured. The walls were lined with the glowing faces of well-fed Indians to prove it.

The woman said that she had indeed heard of it. Had even had the odd early-evening drink on the terrace. Not that she drank of course, she was a devout Hindu and tried her hardest to live a good life. After all, you never know what might be coming next, she explained to her determined inquisitor.

Susie Round the Bend felt she had little alternative but to explain that she knew what came next, at least if the woman ever decided to check into that hotel. The friend of the Maharajah's sister listened politely. She said she could feel Susie's discomfort. Susie said she thought that was unlikely, her toe still bore the scar and in the damp weather it was prone to irritation.

Perhaps she could consider the concept of reincarnation, the woman suggested. Personally she found that this allowed her to attain a different perspective on most things. It was quite possible that the rat had been a handsome king in a previous life and had simply been unable to resist her charms. Susie Round the Bend thought for a moment, she supposed it was possible. But there was no getting away from it, the creature who had nibbled her toe was still a rat. The woman smiled. 'They're all rats, dear,' she sighed.

Was Elvis Pushed?

'He was simply trying to get a better position from which to throw his voice,' explained the entertainments director. 'I think it was the hip twists during *Be-Bop-A-Lula* that did it, one minute he was there, the next minute, he'd vanished.'

Apparently the Elvis impersonator had fallen overboard while attempting to straddle the handrail at the bow of the ship. None of the cruise personnel present seemed to think there was anything wrong with this. He was simply doing his utmost to keep the customers entertained.

His shows had been flagging; the dome-shaped cabaret room, complete with revolving dance-floor, was less than half-full whenever his name appeared on the entertainments bulletin. He was consistently beaten by Marvel the Magician, quite an insult considering Marvel had to resort to using inflatable rabbits due to the 'no livestock' clause on board the ship.

So, in order to climb his way back up the ratings and

ensure his place on the mid-winter Madeira excursion, the Elvis impersonator had added an extra daredevil element to his act. 'Thankfully, someone made a mental note of where the microphone landed, and we were able to turn the ship around and head towards that point,' the entertainments director said.

As a first-time cruiser, I had become obsessed with what would happen if anyone fell overboard. At a special tea given by the chief purser, the captain and his staff, I had posed the question: would they be sucked underneath the engines of the ship, would they live, would they die?

The experiences of the Elvis impersonator had been given as an example of how the cruise was equipped for all eventualities. He had lived. Less than an hour after thrusting his hips 45 degrees too far, he was being hoisted aboard to a rapturous round of applause from the largest audience he had ever seen.

Unfortunately, he was not around to relay the story himself, having long ago been confined to shore on the recommendation of the ship's doctor who feared that he would attempt greater feats of daredevilry in order to sustain the interest in his act.

They had tried to get him to retrain as a children's entertainer, but so far he had shown a great reluctance to hang up his blue suede shoes.

Nothing the captain had to tell about the jolly japes aboard cruise liners came as any surprise to the Quaker sisters. They were into their 36th season now, and old hands. 'Some of them don't bother at all, dear,' they chorused, referring to the standards of dress now acceptable in the new millennium. 'In our day they just wouldn't have got away with it.'

It seemed the biggest shock was the black sateen briefs being sported by the Burt Weedon Appreciation Society members. Like S&M chicken drumsticks, they strutted around the aft deck in search of rich pickings. Or were, as the bar steward put it, out to 'grab a granny'. And there were plenty to choose from.

'We remember one lady,' continued the Quaker sisters, 'who called the ship's doctor to her room late one night complaining of chest pains. When he got there, she was dressed in a negligee, smothered in perfume and insistent that he examine her bosom. Sadly for her, he was more Kenneth Williams than Leslie Phillips.'

The majority of time taken up aboard the cruise seemed to revolve around food, there being meals at every turn. No sooner had the passengers digested the contents of one, than it was time to be seated for another. Then there were the on-deck barbeques, the midnight feasts, the afternoon teas and the self-service breakfasts at which a lottery winner from Solihull regularly consumed more than what was deemed his fair share of the sausage rolls.

Willy's Walker adapted quickly, entering the cricket five-a-side competition, the quoits knockout, and, most alarmingly, the karaoke – fuelled by the cocktail of the day, a dressed, cherry-laden drink with five-star pretensions. His choice of song, *Wonderful Tonight*, a favourite with minor royalty apparently, was narrowly beaten at the clapometer by a Bonnie Tyler universally acknowledged to be, in bar-room parlance, 'a ringer'.

Then there was the ship's photographer, whose job it was to snap the punters at all embarrassing moments.

These pictures, often taken late at night, were then posted on a board on the forward deck for all to see. He did a roaring trade, as the only way to have this blackmail material removed from public display was to hand over the £3.50 per print. Given the amounts of food and drink being consumed every hour, the health and beauty spa was doing a roaring trade. For a mere £40, they would strap you to a high-voltage machine and electrocute your thighs, thereby guaranteeing that you were able to fit back into your dress for dinner that evening.

Desperate not to have to invest in a larger size wardrobe, I succumbed to and signed up for a course of treatment. Still obsessed with the man overboard issue, as I received my 15 volts I interrogated the beautician. Had she been there when the Elvis impersonator had slipped? She looked at me quizzically. 'He didn't slip,' she blurted. 'I think he was pushed,' I was horrified. Was this normal practise? 'Well, after 25 days of *Jailhouse Rock*, it was bound to happen.'

Thai-ed Up

There were very few venues that provided Gay Opera Singer with the kind of Liberace-style inspiration he craved in order to deliver a mesmerising performance; but a five-star hotel in the Far East worked every time. Gold lamé bathrobes, diamond inlay cutlery, ebony toothpicks, bell boys in starched shirts, topless waiters, these were just a few of the main attractions that had long ago convinced him that Thailand, or more specifically Bangkok, was the very epicentre of the creative zeitgeist.

True, he was often required to adapt his repertoire to

the musical tastes of the guests, but no matter. The louder the applause, the bigger the cheque. 'Even Elton does birthdays, darling,' he was fond of telling those who questioned his artistic integrity.

Recently, he had been persuaded to take a small company of singers on an 'medley tour' of Thailand's finest hostelries, with the added bonus of a stopover in neighbouring Vietnam. Admittedly the facilities in this once-besieged land weren't always up to his usual standard, there would be no sprung dance floor, for instance, and a limited mini-bar selection, but these small local difficulties were outweighed by the size of the cash advance.

The performers, chosen for their range and, more crucially, their inability to negotiate a proper fee, were primed on what to expect. The play list would involve a medley of numbers ranging from Puccini to Lloyd Webber, with the emphasis on the latter. For any ambitious young musician, he insisted, it was the opportunity to broaden their oeuvre. Or, as one agent suggested, the chance to never work again.

As far as Gay Opera Singer was concerned, the first stage of the tour went off without a hitch. At each hotel the swimming pools were heated to perfection, the audiences liberally laced with the all-inclusive cocktails and the door takings neatly folded into thousand baht bundles. By the time it came for the troupe to fly to Saigon, he was planning his early retirement and the singers were praying for their early release. Even a cursory glance at CNN might have told them that neither of these things was going to be happening any time soon. Bangkok airport was under siege from the Peoples Alliance for Democracy – all ten thousand of them.

Using the universal language of mime, coupled with a fistful of hard currency, he managed to fight his way through a howling sea of protestors towards the only official left standing. He was a British citizen. A celebrity. 'I'm a VIP!' he shouted over the cries for justice. Time was money and he had a flight to catch. The official was nonplussed, his allegiance having been bought hours before by a bunch of hardnosed Americans determined to scramble onto the last plane out of there. 'Go home,' the man replied without any sense of irony.

Undeterred, Gay Opera Singer turned his attention on the protestors. 'What do you want, darleengs?' he boomed at them in his well-trained baritone. The politicised mob was unmoved. 'What do you need?' he added, for good measure. Still nothing. Then his lead tenor had an idea. He knew the score to *Miss Saigon*. He'd seen the opening sequence. The rescue teams. The helicopters. The true and rightful ones being airlifted to safety in the arms of khaki clad war heroes. True, they weren't actually in Vietnam, but what did it matter? 'If we start singing,' he said dramatically, 'maybe the butch guys in khaki will come.' After all, who could resist the power of song?

Three bars in and it became obvious that there were quite a few people who could resist the power of song and most of them were in the departure lounge of Bangkok International. The protestors grew angrier. The singers sang louder. Finally the protestors forced them into a corner and were just about to squeeze the last aria from their lungs when an official arrived, surrounded by armed guards. 'Take them to the Bangkok Hilton,' the official shouted. 'We've been saved,' the tenor cried. 'I wouldn't be so sure,' the official replied.

Frozen Pussy

Susie Round the Bend had fancied a little trip away. Nothing too fancy, just a few days on the Sicilian Riveria with a good book and an old hat. It meant finding someone to feed her cats Fanny and Johnny, but she could ask the new neighbour. After all, she could only say no.

'I'd be delighted, dear,' the new neighbour replied. 'I love cats.' Susie Round the Bend thanked her profusely and left behind lengthy instructions, strict meal portions, favourite toys and a spare set of keys to the front door. The cats had never met the new neighbour before, but she was a middle-aged woman and they were two clingy moggies. They were made for each other.

It was baking hot when Susie Round the Bend arrived, and her mobile phone had a very poor signal. It wasn't until the next morning that she managed to retrieve a text message from the new neighbour with what looked like a close-up of Johnny, asleep.

How sweet, Susie thought, she's sent me a picture in case I'm missing him. By lunchtime she'd had enough heat and took refuge in a cool bar. She ordered a drink and fell into easy conversation with one of the local men. He wasn't really her type, but she found that holidays made her more flexible. Besides, he seemed keen, and there was something to be said for that.

As they discussed the relative merits of the local wine, she felt her phone vibrate in her pocket. Excusing herself, she went outside to take the call. It was the new neighbour, wondering if she had received her message. Susie said, yes, she had, it was kind, thank you. Although there didn't seem to be a picture of Fanny.

The neighbour paused. 'No,' she replied. 'Fanny looks okay so far.' Susie Round the Bend became alarmed. What did she mean? 'That's why I sent you the picture,' the new neighbour elaborated. 'Because he looked a little peeky to me.' Susie said she would call her straight back and flipped through her messages to retrieve the picture of Johnny.

No matter how she looked at it, he still appeared to be asleep. She called back. 'He looks asleep to me,' she explained. 'Peaceful even.' The new neighbour was silent for a bit before continuing. 'That's what I thought when I first saw him,' she explained. 'But when I went back in a couple of hours later, it was obvious to me that he was dead.'

Susie Round the Bend suffered a sharp intake of breath. 'Dead!' she screeched. 'What do you mean, he's dead?' The new neighbour said it was pretty simple really, he just wasn't moving. Susie was mortified. 'Oh my God,' she continued. 'Did you try shaking him?'

The new neighbour seemed slightly irritated by the suggestion. 'Of course I tried shaking him,' she said. 'In fact, the other cat seemed to get quite upset and bit me.'

Susie Round the Bend was traumatised. One cat appeared to be dead and the other had turned into a man-eater, and not in a good way. She tried to keep calm and asked the new neighbour what was happening now. In short, where was Johnny? 'I put him in the fridge,' the new neighbour replied. 'It was hot and I thought it was best.'

It was at this point that Susie believed she might have fainted, as she woke to find herself under the shade of an umbrella being fanned by her lunchtime suitor. She tried her best to explain to him what had happened. He nodded sagely. 'Frozen pussy is not good,' he sighed.

She said he was right, on many levels, and she would have to go straight home to sort it out. By the time she arrived back in East of Islington, the heat wave had passed. She turned the key in her front door and crept her way into the kitchen. Everything looked quite normal. Perhaps she had suffered a touch of the sun and dreamt it all. And then she opened the fridge and there was Johnny, squashed in next to some ageing celery like a macabre still life.

Susie Round the Bend recoiled in horror. The doorbell went. It was the new neighbour. 'How was your holiday?' she asked gaily. Susie Round the Bend said that the holiday, as she might have suspected, had been a bit overshadowed by what had happened. The new neighbour nodded. They both stared in at Johnny. 'I never want to come home to a dead cat in my fridge ever again,' Susie Round the Bend finally said. 'Yes,' the new neighbour replied. 'They do take up a lot of room.'

The Italian Job

Begging takes many forms, particularly in East of Islington. There was the usual: spare any change; buy me a special brew; pay for my children's education. And the unusual. At the top of this table was a recent plea for arts fans to dig deep and sponsor one of a line of young hopefuls being trained under the artistic body that is Gay Opera Singer. 'So enthusiastic, darleengs,' he explained in the round-robin appeal. 'So pay them,' came one reply.

His plan was to take these naive novices away from

their dull day jobs and off on an intensive week long residential course to Italy: the only thing that stood between them and a glittering career at the ENO. There was also the small matter of talent, but as their would-be tutor had assured them, where there was a will there was a way. Especially if it was gift-aided. There was to be sunshine, artistic bonhomie, creative tension, a finale performance in front of a non-paying public and accommodation in the very best one-star hotel – food and wine extra. All they needed was an injection of hard currency to pay his not inconsiderable fees. 'If only I could work for nothing,' Gay Opera Singer sighed.

Like potential suitors at a dating agency, details of the star-stuck hopefuls were emailed out to any possible benefactors. In a bid to give everyone a chance, and to avoid being left with a pile of the less attractively endowed, Gay Opera Singer offered his needy students packaged into handy investment parcels. 400 Euros would buy a whole singer, 200 a half and a mere 100 Euros would pay for a quarter, although it wasn't clear what quarter that would be. 'Rest assured,' Gay Opera Singer insisted when pressed. 'Every body part will be rammed full of talent.'

Unsurprisingly, there was a rush on Tony, a six-foot-two West Country Adonis who had never been near a stage but whose picture caption confidently declared that he had 'plenty of hidden depths,' with a close-run second going to Bridget, a Welsh computer operator with a very operatic embonpoint. In the end, it was decided that these two would be reserved for the most committed bidders. For Cambridge and Fearless and I, there had been no leaving anything to chance. Years at the base camp of Footlights had taught Cambridge one thing, he told us. Talent is fickle and it pays to be in the front row waving the cheque book.

The community hall on the outskirts of Milan was half-full of anxious relatives and confused locals by the time we arrived from the airport. *The Pirates of Penzance, La Traviata, La Bohème, Don Giovanni,* you name it, the English imports were giving them all a go to rousing encouragement from their 20 or so English supporters. The Italians were more circumspect. For them the most exciting point of the evening came when Lisa, a primary school teacher from Hull, took a nose-dive into the orchestra pit. Her last-minute decision to perform without her glasses had yielded near-fatal consequences. Still, her fellow students soldiered on and afterwards they were rewarded with a first (and almost certainly last) night party.

While the discounted house wine trickled round the bar, Cambridge fought off stiff competition to get a closer look at Bridget's assets and Fearless and I seized our moment. There, slouched against the back wall, was Tony, the object of my cheque book affection. 'You were glorious,' I lied. Tony smiled, demurely. 'In fact, we both bought a part of you,' I said, pointing to an unimpressed Fearless sitting next to me. Tony bowed. 'You must have got a very big part then,' he smirked. 'Thank God,' Fearless replied. 'For a moment there I thought we'd ended up with your voice box.'

Hotel du Lack
When the idea was first suggested to her, the Poetess could barely believe her luck. There are few opportuni-

ties for the impoverished inner-city sonnet-maker to get away from it all and one had just landed in her lap. In return for the minor inconvenience of assuming the role of 'writer in residence' at a remote West Country hotel, she would enjoy an all expenses paid three week holiday complete with a room with a view.

'We're big on Arthurian legend,' the owner had said when pushed for the finer details. 'With a bit of medieval mysticism thrown in,' he had added. True, the contract had included a rather spurious paragraph suggesting there might be assorted other duties, but the lure of the freebie had already taken hold.

And anyway, how difficult could it be? It wasn't as if they hadn't recognised that she had talent. She felt sure that they would want to make the most of her many academic attributes. After all, the hotel owner had described himself as an art lover with a penchant for Blake.

Besides, dishing out stanza starter courses to literary tourists seemed a lot more appealing than another bleak winter in the litter-strewn streets East of Islington. There really was no contest, she was off on the first available coach.

On arrival things looked slightly different, especially if the Guinevere costume laid out in her bedroom was anything to go by. And should she have been in any doubt, there was always the clarity of the accompanying welcome note. *'We do hope we got the right size,'* it read. *'We like all our maidens to be happy.'*

There had clearly been a terrible misunderstanding. The Poetess had a doctorate, she had once publicly insulted Ted Hughes, she was, in short, serious. Dressing up in a Guinevere costume was not.

Unfortunately, by the time she realised her mistake, the last coach had already left and the hotel had taken on a strangely abandoned feel. Where, she wondered, were all the other guests? And, more importantly, where were the staff? Not to mention the self-styled art-loving hotel owner.

A trip to the foyer and all was revealed. There, encased in a suit of faux medieval armour was the man responsible for luring her here. 'Welcome to Camelot, my lady,' he boomed. 'Pray, where is your courtly dress? Our guests arrive for dinner shortly and you have little to offer them.'

The Poetess was almost speechless. 'I'm supposed to be the writer in residence,' she finally managed to mumble. 'I'm the poet from London,' she added, hoping for some small sliver of recognition. 'Ye Gods, we're all poets here, my lady,' her host boomed back at her. 'The scullery is that way.'

A polite refusal didn't seem an option, so, against her better judgement, the Poetess followed the directions for the kitchen, determined to make her getaway as quickly as possible. In the kitchen things became even more confusing. Stirring the evening's soup course were Janice and Daniel from Ipswich. They were 're-enactors', they explained. Their lives were dedicated to the re-enactment of medieval battles and the wearing of chain mall. They had come to the hotel six months ago to organise a re-enactment weekend, and had somehow failed to leave.

Now they spent their time toiling in the hotel kitchen dressed in their chain mail and making soup. They couldn't remember the last time they had worn civvies. 'We don't miss them, you know,' explained Jean as she clinked across the floor. In fact, they preferred it that way, apparently the chain mall allowed for better ventilation. 'Although we do get a few raised eyebrows when we pop down to the local shop.'

At dinner, taken at a round table of course, the Poetess was seated next to a man in an ermine tabard who explained that he worked for the court. 'Just call me Lancelot,' he chortled. 'We are all friends here,' he continued. 'But pray, my lady, why are you not in proper dress, are you not proud to be by your master's side?'

The Poetess whispered that she had no need of a master, she was, in fact, a 21st-century feminist at the end of her tether. 'Nay,' her dinner companion continued. 'There, behold, your master, the man who hold's the key to your heart and bedchamber, my lady,' he insisted, pointing at the armour-clad, art-loving hotel owner.

That night the Guinevere costume finally came into its own. The road back to London was a long one, but, thanks to the extra insulation of a 10ft tapestry train, it wasn't a cold one.

She's Been Tango-ed

Dazzling Darren had become very big in cold countries. Daily, the communal doormat was littered with letters scented with the smell of perfume and pickled herring: *billets doux* sent from earnest Norwegians driven half-mad by unreasonable light conditions and an abnormal desire to learn the tango.

It all started after he had agreed to fly to Oslo and teach a fading (but still fabulous) Hollywood beauty how to manoeuvre her octogenarian legs around a two set dance routine. It was his first sortie into the world of the silver screen and he was determined to make an impression. Besides, the fee was excellent, and he figured the obscene attention from her overly frisky lap dog was a small price to pay for working with such a big name.

The film director was an up-and-coming New York film school graduate with Oscar aspirations and a desire to mix with the great and the good. Although on this occasion he had settled for a female star who refused to leave her trailer and a male romantic lead with Alzheimer's and a gammy knee. It was not, the producer explained, going to be an easy birth. Or even, the director retorted, an easy death.

But being keen and desperate to collect his credit, Dazzling Darren tried his best. Every morning he would approach the red carpeted steps of the Grande Dame's trailer, music sheet and step notations in hand, where he would charm her into putting her best foot forward. She was loathe to do it. After all, as her assistant was ever keen to point out: 'Honey. She already knows how to put her lips together and blow.'

It wasn't that she wasn't charming. Far from it. Each visit he would be invited in and encouraged to sit plumped up on the velvet clad banquettes while the vivid details of her past romantic triumphs were reheated for his entertainment. With the dog determinedly working the small of his leg, the hours would pass in a graceful blur of vodka martinis and Parma violets.

Nothing could have been more pleasant. It was just the small matter of the work, or, more importantly, the lack of it. 'It takes two to tango,' he would plead periodically, but the great one was unmoved. 'I only tango in full costume, darling,' she would reply before demanding to know if she still 'had it'. Ever the professional on the make, he always answered in the affirmative.

Eventually, however, Dazzling Darren had to admit defeat, although not to everyone. It was decided that the male lead would be not be 'in the loop', as the director put it. It was shame, but as he had arrived wearing a lapel badge saying, *'Please tell me my name,'* it was generally agreed that he wouldn't mind too much. Or even notice.

The decision was taken to use a stand-in for the dance sequence, or as they say in film parlance, a 'stunt double'. But this was not without its complications. As part of her contract, the great star had insisted that no female understudy younger than herself be employed, and as this cancelled out most of the adult population, it was a vacancy still waiting to be filled.

And so it was, with the aid of some firm corseting and the make-up department, that Dazzling Darren took his first whirl in front of the camera. Dressed from head to toe in crinoline and a large horsehair wig, it wasn't what his mother might have wanted, but it was a start. And the local film buffs seemed to love him, demanding he pose for photographs and sign their autograph books.

Chocolates, flowers, invitations to candlelit dinners, as word spread, so did his popularity. In short, he had inadvertently become an overnight sensation. He may have been a man in a dress, but as one fan pointed, in a country that is pitch black for half the year, that was never going to be a drawback.

Afghan Hounded
A trip to northern Afghanistan was not on the top of

everyone's holiday hit list but then Fearless wasn't called Fearless for nothing. Years spent roaming the ink black alleys of Glasgow, juggling a pint of 'meths' while chain-smoking unfiltered cigarettes had prepared her for most things. The rest she just frightened into submission. Not that she didn't believe in being forearmed.

A trip to the Middle Eastern stores on the high street had fitted her with a heavyweight burka and a list of questions about garment etiquette. 'Where's the hole for my roll-up?' being the main one. Her travelling companion, a slight, effete, late-middle-aged man who had eked out a living as a 'lifestyle' photographer was assigned as her 'consort'. He had misgivings from the start. 'I have misgivings,' he said, in case she was under any illusion. 'So do I,' she sneered.

The journey was long, arduous, and accompanied by the sound of his crying and her rank boredom. By the time they reached what was once downtown Kabul it was obvious she was on her own. Not that she wasn't used it. The vagaries of male behaviour rarely fazed her; 20 years ago her boyfriend had gone out for pie and chips and still hadn't returned.

Despite the protestations of the effete one, they were checked into the only hotel still standing, a battle-worn building with limited facilities and no windows. The concierge apologised profusely but Fearless was relaxed. 'In Scotland,' she mimed and signed, 'this is luxury.' Her consort took his room key and locked the door, refusing to leave until it was time to catch the flight home. Initially, Fearless had banged, helpfully, on the other side, shouting words of encouragement like 'stop being such a wally'. But her burka-flapping door rages were upsetting the other residents so she decided to abandon him, and custom, in order to go out for an unaccompanied stroll.

Although dressed from head to foot in an outfit that could have been designed for Darth Vader's less attractive sister, she stopped traffic. Cars, tanks, men on bicycles and boys hanging onto their mother's hands, they all stared and pointed. She hadn't had a reception like it since arriving at a memorial service in a leather mini-dress and fishnet stockings. Her initial plan had been to travel into the mountains in search of peace but she could see this might be a problem now. Even in her tented disguise, without a man she was obviously a sex pest.

Undeterred, she decided she would just have to get a man, after all there were clearly plenty around. Back at the hotel, the concierge, although extremely polite, seemed somewhat alarmed at her suggestion that he might 'find her a bloke'. And even more disturbed at her protestations that she didn't want sex, 'just a fake husband for the week'. Fortunately the general manager did have a brother who had once been in England and might be able to help. 'He knows your ways,' he explained, cryptically.

At nightfall the temporary suitor was brought to the hotel so they could discuss tactics. Would he be prepared to take her up into the mountains to help broker peace? No. Would he be prepared to point her in the right direction? No. Would he be prepared to at least take her out for a drink? No. What was he prepared to do then? Apparently he was prepared to her buy her an ice-cream and then marry her. Fearless was a little startled. Even for a fake holiday romance, it seemed to be going a bit too fast. 'I'm not that easy,' she said. 'That's not what I've heard,' he replied.

10

Back with Mum and Dad

Barking

Piano Pete had been keeping me abreast of the urban style crime wave hitting his parent's quiet pocket of the countryside. So far they had escaped intrusion, but it seemed that his father, the Air Commodore, had decided he didn't want to take any chances.

'We're taking no chances, dear,' he announced to his wife one afternoon. 'What we need is a guard dog.' So, true to his word, he set off for the local pet rescue centre and returned home with a new security system. 'Dear, meet Boris,' he beamed.

Boris was a sheepish looking mutt, a cross between a greyhound and an Alsatian who had fallen on hard times and had no intention of going back there. His previous owners, twice removed, had been Boris Karloff fans and the name had stuck. With a blue muzzle and arthritic joints, Boris was an old dog who had learnt a trick or two, and he knew how to use them.

He rolled over and played dead. He wagged his tail and cocked his head angelically to one side. He lifted his paw for treats and he followed his new mistress faithfully from room to room. But, crucially, he never, ever, barked.

Unfortunately this was not what the Air Commodore had ordered. 'Wait till the blighters hear him growl,' he had proudly boasted during Boris's first stroll around the village. 'He'll frighten them into the next county,' he assured his fellow neighbourhood watch participants.

However, two weeks later, when neither the early morning theft of the gazebo furniture nor the smashing of the geranium pots had managed to stir the would-be-man killer from his slumber, the Air Commodore began to suspect they had a problem.

'He needs some forces discipline,' he insisted, dragging the sleeping Boris out of his fleecy lined basket and into the back garden. 'He's probably just a little out of shape.'

Dressed in combat gear and armed with a makeshift swag-bag, the Air Commodore leapt out of the bushes SAS-style and attempted to make Boris earn his keep. But Boris wasn't playing ball. Boris, ever the survivor, rolled over and played dead until it was time for elevenses.

It wasn't the kind of regimented attention to duty that the Air Commodore had come to expect from his troops. 'He's not worth the dog food,' he shouted. 'I might as well bark myself,' he added, before heading off to the 19th hole.

It was then that Piano Pete's mother had what she later described as an epiphany.

Perhaps, she thought, all Boris needed was some guidance. Maybe it was possible, after all, to teach an old dog new tricks, and perhaps she was the woman to do it.

She would take up barking and the dog would follow suit. Nothing could be simpler, she reasoned to herself.

That evening, after laying the table for supper, she readied Boris for his first lesson. Knowing that her husband would be returning soon, she knelt down on all fours and demonstrated pacing up and down the hallway, listening for approaching footsteps.

Occasionally, she would let go an approximation of a low-level growl, encouraging Boris to join in. Boris was having none of it.

Undeterred, Piano Pete's mother was convinced that her reluctant protégé would get the hang of it in the end. 'Grrr, grrr, boy,' she chanted over and over to the bemused mutt. Nothing. Finally, the true test was upon them as the sound of leather soles crisply resonated on the gravel drive outside.

Piano Pete's mother threw herself into the role with serious gusto. Bouncing up and down on all fours, she howled and threw herself at the letterbox.

For Boris, it was a terrifying sight, and not one that had previously fitted in with his halcyon vision of a quiet retirement. Unfortunately, the more he attempted to escape, the louder Piano Pete's mother barked, until finally the key was in the lock and the door swung open.

There, lit by the porch light, was the Air Commodore and his golfing partner, Major Browning. Boris ran for cover, and Piano Pete's mother let out a defeated whine.

The Air Commodore, unsurprisingly, looked slightly taken aback. The Major, on the other hand, simply leant down and patted Piano Pete's mother on the head before strolling off to the drawing room.

Later, over a sedate glass of sherry, the Major turned reassuringly to his friend. 'Don't know why you're worried about the dog not coming up with the goods, old boy,' he said. 'You've already got a wife who barks. That should be enough to scare any man.'

Undercover Pensioners

David and Delia were undercover pensioners. They weren't working undercover this particular evening, David confided to me, but the rest of the time there would be no telling. There was a lot of counter-espionage out there, and he couldn't be too careful. 'You never know who's listening,' he said, mysteriously.

We were a small group gathered in a bar East of Islington to celebrate Gay Opera Singer's 40th birthday. His mother, Queenie, was throwing the bash, and therefore had control of the guest list. As a result, there were a lot of people present who still thought of him as wearing short flannel trousers, and in a way they weren't wrong, it's just that he didn't do it in public anymore.

David and Delia lived in the same street as Queenie, but due to the secret nature of their undercover work, they preferred not to reveal the actual number. 'Just in case, dear,' they said. However, they had to admit it was a difficult secret to keep, especially as she only lived next door. 'None the less, we like to keep things professional,' they added.

David had retired several years ago after a long and honourable service in a high street bank: he didn't want to say which one. 'Just let me say, they like horses,' he said, tapping his nose.

After a couple of years spent reshaping the garden

and babysitting the grandchildren, they had found that retirement just wasn't exciting enough. 'There were no thrills,' Delia said. 'We used to watch *Crimewatch* and think, "if only".'

It was then that a fellow retiree had told them about Makeover Inc, an employment agency specialising in work for active elders prepared to deny their true selves. 'It was just like being back at the bank,' David said.

After an initial training period, they were given code names and sent home to wait by the telephone. By all accounts, the tension was very exhilarating. 'It certainly invigorated our relationship,' Delia said, squeezing her husband's hand.

Their first job didn't appear to be too tricky. Posing as hungry shoppers, they had to order French fries in every branch of a restaurant chain in north London. While acting as naturally as possible, David and Delia had to surreptitiously count the French fries served in up in their portion. Taking care not to miss a single chip, they then had to transfer them to a plastic bag for future evidence. According to the information supplied by Makeover Inc, several complaints had been received from older customers who felt that more chips were given out to the younger, better-looking, diners. The chain were taking it seriously and it was up to David and Delia to get to the bottom of it.

'It doesn't sound like much,' David said, defensively. 'But you'd be surprised how dangerous that kind of work can be.' It transpired that some of the feckless youths employed to serve in these eateries were less dead than they first appeared.

'One young lad come over and demanded to know

what was going on under the tablecloth,' Delia said. 'In fact, he made me so nervous that I dropped the chips and I had to start again. It was harrowing.' Naturally, they could never divulge the result of the count, but suffice to say that Delia does recommend that older ladies 'make a bit more of an effort' if they want a bigger portion.

Mostly they weren't expected to wear different clothes while 'undercover', but both of them did. David usually sported a trilby, and if it was a big job, Delia sometimes wore a Diana Dors wig. 'All my friends say she looks nothing like me,' she explained, gleefully.

In fact, she was wearing the Diana Dors wig the night they were sent to secretly report on a hotel in Stratford-upon-Avon. 'I'd always wanted to go there,' she said. 'Ever since my "am dram" days after the war.'

The hotel's owner was concerned that his older clientele was abandoning them for a rival establishment up the road and so the job of uncovering the truth was handed to David and Delia. After checking into their room and unpacking in the usual manner ('We like to behave normally,' Delia explained), the undercover duo settled into the foyer with a gin and tonic each and a shorthand notebook. No sooner had they set upon the peanut dish than they were approached by a tall man with a military carriage, dressed in a formal black suit. 'Get out,' he whispered. 'While you still can,' he added, and then walked away. Startled, but maintaining their professional demeanour, David and Delia asked the barman if he knew who the gentleman was. 'Oh him, he's the local undertaker,' the barman replied. 'He's always round here.' As far as David and Delia were concerned, the case was closed.

Willpower

'Would you do me a favour,' Piano Pete had pleaded down the end of his recently reconnected telephone early one evening 'and come round to witness me sign my life away? I'll tidy up,' he added, as an afterthought. It was the latter assurance, rather than the former mournful request that made me to agree to watch him put his signature to a recently arrived 35-page tome sitting amidst the detritus of his flat.

It seemed his father, the Air Commodore, having threatened it for many years, had finally followed through. Fearing the march of time, and the state school system, he had decided to bequeath his not insubstantial fortune to the private education of his grandchildren. In short, his two daughters had produced and would now collect. Big time.

The Air Commodore felt sure that his only son would understand. After all, he had been warned many times over the years, and he had still failed to come up with the goods.

Piano Pete said he was down, but not out. Years of trying to persuade a living, breathing, woman to at least date him had taught him one thing. There was still a slim chance of success – after all, there were a lot of women in the world and he hadn't asked him of all them yet.

Pouring me a glass of very bad white wine, he revealed that he had one final plan and that he was going to stave off signing until he had given it a go. 'I thought I might advertise,' he beamed. 'Where?' I muttered as he dug around on the floor looking for his kettle. 'The *NME*', he said, implausibly.

I pointed out that in my humble opinion, the *NME* small ads were usually reserved for people flogging worn-out instruments and somehow I didn't think that would give any woman the right impression. Besides what was he going to say? Oh that was easy, he continued. 'I'll just explain that if they let me impregnate them several times, I'll pay for the school fees.' Did I think it would work, he asked? 'I think you should just sign,' I replied.

Dragged Up

Coming from the frozen north as he did, Little Sparky regarded East of Islington as a hotbed of social and cultural mores. The bars, the cafés, the transgender support groups and the shops selling only the very best Hasidic hair styling products: it was a different world. But then a life lived in the backwaters of Snowdonia hadn't prepared him for much.

He first arrived in London as a geography student sent to observe the adverse effects of global warming on the city and overstayed. As the months passed, the concerned letters from his parents and tutors got longer. What could be taking him so long they wanted to know? What news of the climate shift? How hot was it? And if it was that hot, surely he should come home where it was still nice and cold, even in July. But Little Sparky was oblivious to their pleading. To use the local parlance, he was 'luvin' it'.

His father, Big Sparky, was not. He'd lived in London as a lad, he was fond of telling his pals in the pub. He knew what its dark charms could do to a young man's hormones. He also knew not to tell his wife. Instead, he decided to get the next train down there. 'See what's happening to the boy,' he said, patting his wife's hand. Make sure he hasn't got himself into trouble. Or anyone else for that matter. Mrs Sparky readily agreed and packed him some sandwiches.

By the time Big Sparky arrived at King's Cross, the roast beef on white had been washed down with six cans of pale ale and a whiskey chaser. Little Sparky barely recognised him at the ticket barrier. True, the drunken wobble didn't help, but it was the Seventies suit ensemble that really threw him. 'What d'ya think?' his father said. 'Still fits me after all these years.' Little Sparky was speechless. His 61-year-old dad had transmogrified into John Travolta: The Disco Years. It wasn't a good look. But Little Sparky needn't have worried. As strange outfits went, it barely registered in the metropolis.

By the time they reached their third pub, Big Sparky was hitting his stride. 'Oh yes,' he said, stroking his four-inch lapels. 'I've not forgotten my way round.' Little Sparky was horrified. If this was reverse psychology, it was working. 'Let's go home, Dad,' he called out, as he veered off towards Soho. But his father was having none of it. It had been 35 years and he had a lot of catching up to do.

He used to come down here when he was young, he explained to his horrified offspring. Before he was married of course. Those were the days. Nothing too fancy though, just a bit of slap and tickle. Little Sparky begged him to turn back but he was on a mission. 'It's round here somewhere, lad,' he kept saying as they strayed deeper into the warren of small streets. Finally, they came to a stop outside a gold painted doorway being heavily protected by a man dressed in a silver evening gown.

Big Sparky rummaged around in his pocket before thrusting forward a dog-eared membership card. The overdressed man stared at its ink-stained numerals. 'Life membership, mate,' Big Sparky explained, confidently. 'It used to be really hot in there in my day,' he added gesturing towards the darkened club. The man looked at Little Sparky and then looked back at his father, taking in the full impact of the original Seventies outfit. 'It's got a lot hotter now,' he said, his large manicured frame still blocking the velvet rope. Big Sparky said he wasn't surprised. His son had told him all about climate change. The man nodded, politely. 'Well, when he's taught you about sex change you can come back.'

Travelling Light

The Air Commodore had been loaned an apartment in the Canary Islands by an old pal. 'Apparently there's lots of local colour,' he had explained to his wayward son, Piano Pete. 'So your mother feels there should be something for all of us to look at.'

As a single man, with little or no visible means of support and an expensive self-image to maintain, Piano Pete ignored the sneers of his friends and still took his holidays with his parents. And this year was going to be no exception. The schedule was always the same. They would arrive in time for lunch, stroll down to a local hostelry, and make contact with what the Air Commodore euphemistically called 'like-minded people'.

Bridge fours would be formed, excursions organised and an attempt made to 'interact' with the indigenous population. Unfortunately, this year things weren't quite what they seemed. Without paying proper attention they had landed at a virtual nudist colony. It had been a shock chance meeting with their retired GP that had given the game away. Dressed only in a Panama hat, he had sprinted across the beach to greet them.

'How wonderful to see you,' he boomed, settling his sunburnt buttocks precariously on a spare seat at their table. 'The wife will be so pleased that you have joined our little gang.' In true middle-class style, they all nodded politely, keeping their eyes firmly fixed on the friend's face. Sticking rigidly to the social niceties, the Air Commodore led the conversation towards the weather and the state of British Airways, before safely landing back at the weather again.

Nobody mentioned the nudity. 'We really must meet up for supper,' the retired GP implored. 'I know some delicious little places for squid. And do get out of those clothes and come down for a game of volleyball,' he added, before rising and sprinting off back down the beach. The rest of their lunch was taken in a stunned silence, Piano Pete and his father taking it in turns to fan his mother's flushed features.

It was a further two hours before she finally spoke. In all her 70 years she had never been so mortified. The beach was out of bounds. As was any thought of joining what she witheringly called 'the exhibitionists'. If they bumped into them again, they would be polite, but firm. But there was to be no social intercourse. 'I will not have that kind of thing on my holiday,' she declared, before retiring to her room for the rest of the day. This put Piano Pete in an awkward position. Desperate for a tan, but keen not to incur the wrath of his mother, he decided on a compromise. He would sneak down to the beach and take his clothes off so as to fit in, but he would hide himself out of view. That way, he felt, he could with all good conscience tell his mother he had not actually joined the nudists.

As plans went, it was a reasonable one. The retired GP, his wife, several friends and a group of lithe, tanned Germanic types with bleached blonde hair and sculpted muscles were several hundred yards up the beach from Piano Pete's rocky hideaway and had no idea he was there.

He would be able to tan his hitherto unexposed regions while ensuring that his modesty and his mother's sense of decorum were both preserved. And on his return to East of Islington, who would be able to resist his new bronzed look? It was perfect.

But as the hours passed, it got hotter and hotter and Piano Pete became increasingly desperate for a swim. Could he risk the run down to the surf unnoticed? What would he do if someone saw him streaking down towards the sea? Finally, taking his social life in his hands, he decided to make a dash for it. Seconds later, he was in the water, naked, and struggling against the fast current. Never the strongest of swimmers, Piano Pete was rapidly being sucked out of his depth. His only hope of salvation – the nudists.

It was the retired GP who heard him first. As his cries for help reached a crescendo he was quickly surrounded by heaving naked bodies. With no energy to resist, he was hoisted out of the water and onto the wide shoulders of several well-endowed German bodybuilders. Like a sacrificial offering, his pink, surf-battered English body was carried aloft, out of the waves, and towards the shore. The rescue party had reached the shallows before the gathered crowd parted and he spotted his mother. As local colour went, it wasn't what she had bargained for.

Tina the Tabby Goes to Spain

No one had ever told Tina the Tabby that travelling in the cargo hold of a Boeing 737 might prove to be a less than comfortable experience, and it had clearly left an indelible impression on her sense of self-worth. 'She's not herself,' Gay Opera Singer's mother, Queenie, had wailed, when her wretched pet was finally prised from its high security travel box. 'She's not talking to me,' she sobbed as the uninterested airport vet gave the distraught animal the once-over.

Queenie had agreed to decamp to Spain for a couple of months in order to escape the rain in Ruislip, but only if she could bring her beloved cat. It had seemed a good idea at the time. Gay Opera Singer had taken up residence for the winter in order to play a season of *Don Giovanni* at one of the grander theatrical establishments, and it always helped to have a firm fan in the audience.

'She'll love it, darleeng,' he had assured his mother when booking Tina's passage. 'The neighbourhood strays are very friendly.' But Queenie appeared less than convinced. The last time she had crossed the Spanish border, Franco was still in power and she had been forced to hide her spending money in her knickers. It hadn't seemed that friendly at the time.

These days they welcomed credit cards but Queenie wasn't taking any chances; her undergarments were a treasure chest of hidden currency. And her belief in Spanish social values little changed. 'Mrs Brown says they eat cats,' she said as her son herded her and her charge into the four-wheel-drive. 'And that they shoot the old ladies first.' Mrs Brown had lived next door to Queenie for nearly 40 years and had never held a pass-port, but she knew that bad things happened 'abroad'. Her motto was: if they don't accept sterling, they don't deserve your money.

By the time they reached the rented holiday house, Queenie and Tina were both in a state of heightened anxiety. The red harness specially bought for Tina's inau-gural stroll up the drive had not gone down well and she was refusing to leave the confines of the car. Eventually she had to be carried to her mistress's bedroom, where she crawled under the bed and resisted all attempts at socialisation.

Over the next two weeks the entire household, along with several neighbours, was conscripted into getting Tina out of her self-imposed prison. Every morning, Queenie would lead Tina on her harness around the garden, the pool, the terrace, the rose bed and inevitably back to the bedroom. There, heartbroken, Queenie would sit, pleading with her sulking feline friend to for-give her for dragging her away from the sounds of the suburbs.

As this farce continued, Gay Opera Singer noticed that the local strays sneering at this absurd scene looked like virtual replicas of Tina the Tabby. In fact, there was barely any telling them apart, except, unlike her, they seemed happy enough to do what was expected of them. They would stroll along the fence, sun themselves on the lawn and wrap their tails round any passing legs in the hope of getting titbits. In short, they were perfect pet material.

And then it came to him, an epiphany, a kind of sixth sense. What he needed was a stunt cat. A cat who would perform all the duties of the 'star' cat, but anonymously, and for a small reward. For the assortment of strays, it was an easy job. Three fishy treats and they were anyone's, and as they all looked the same, it really didn't matter if one of them didn't turn up for work one day. He would just hire another one. Simple.

The following morning, while Queenie was bathing, he slipped into her room and hid the immobile, sulking, Tina in the bottom of the wardrobe. His mother, on returning to her room and discovering her beloved pet was missing, came screaming into the garden in search of help. There, sunning itself on Gay Opera Singer's lap, was a very happy tabby. Could it be? Was it possible? She hardly dared ask.

'Tina,' she cried. On cue, the stunt cat purred and leapt into Queenie's waiting arms. 'It's like a miracle,' she said, stroking the grateful animal. 'You're like a different cat,' she added. Gay Opera Singer smiled, benevolently. 'You could have a point, Mother.'

The Dead Parents' Society

By the time anyone realised what was happening, it had become something of an epidemic. It may have been an age thing, many of them had served considerably more than their three score and ten and they just had it coming. In some tragic cases it was a swift yank from the other side: untimed and unwanted. But for a few, it appeared to have been brought on by sheer boredom. They just simply couldn't be bothered anymore, the dog had died, the neighbours had been carted off and the reward points at the supermarket seemed too worthless to contemplate spending. As one of their number confided before leaping off the metaphorical cliff, what was the point of carrying on when you couldn't even sit up in the bath without the aid of a fully paid-up member of staff and an air-filled cushion wedged up your posterior?

For those left behind, it was understandably heartbreaking. And for any offspring, doubly so. Hurtling towards middle age themselves, the notion that they were next in the mortal queue was too grim to contemplate. Added to which, the realisation that dying elders had replaced property values (or lack of them) as an after-dinner conversation made it even more upsetting. Was it just the residents of East of Islington, or had everyone's parents suddenly joined a death cult?

The first to go was Piano Pete's redoubtable mother, the Air Commodore's wife. Hers was a graceful end orchestrated down to the last detail, as befitted a former headmistress. No wailing mess of loose ends and forgotten thank you notes in her exit strategy. The privet hedge trimmed, the carpet steam-cleaned in preparation for the wake. Even the Ocado man received a mention in final despatches – a note berating him for being late with his last delivery. 'She was always firm but fair,' he sighed on receiving his posthumous assessment.

Next was the Culture Kid's mum, once a flower power child, her descent into peaceful insanity marred only by the public's refusal to accept her newly discovered desire to take her clothes off. Weekly, he would be called to remove her, and her ample bosom, from the King's Road Starbucks where she sat unzipped sipping a grande latte surrounded by mortified customers. When she was finally lowered into her eco basket it was with a plentiful supply of 2lbs of Kenyan finest and a couple of underwired C-cups.

Susie Round the Bend's mother and Fearless' father both went in the same week. The fact that Gay Opera Singer's old dear electrocuted herself on her stair lift whilst attempting a champagne fuelled re-enactment of a Ginger Rogers routine struck some as particularly cruel, but he was adamant she would have wanted it that way. 'At least she went out in a blaze of glory,' he explained in a particularly touching eulogy.

My own father left rather quickly, aided no doubt by his desire to be first on the heavenly 19th.

For Rt-on Rev this new trend had produced an unexpected sideline. Not only was he called upon to deliver a variety of different services, the ubiquitous nature of the Unitarian calling helpfully covering everything from Baptist to blasphemers, he had also become a dab hand at bedside visitations. These seemed particularly popular with those desperate to get on with it. And he didn't disappoint. A few well-chosen words and a touch on the hand seemed to be all it took before the mahogany was being ordered. His record was 12 hours and never longer than 24.

Of course, there were a few old folks who were resistant to his helpful interventions, namely those with nothing wrong with them, but so far there had been no complaints. Although, as one recently widowed scientist pointed out: 'In my late wife's case, that can only be a matter of time and technology.'

Acknowledgements

Richard Ingrams, whose idea it was in the first place and without whom this book wouldn't exist. Fearless, who tirelessly and graciously pulled all the material together and came up with most of the best titles. Philip Argent for the beautiful artwork. Deborah Asher and Claire Daly for putting up with me. The team at *Live* magazine for their Friday facts. Cambridge for getting me started with a name. Jane Bown for the supremely flattering portrait. Martin Rynja for keeping the faith.

A special thank you to Gay Opera Singer, Dazzling Darren, Spooky, Piano Pete, Fungus, Rt-On Rev, Alan Angst, Poshy, Glammy, the rabbis, Les Mums, Susie Round the Bend, the Poetess, Matt Boomy, Sultan, Mr and Mrs Fit, Weirdie Woman, Naivety, Professor Lolly, Fang Fatale, Sixties Starlet, Culture Kid, Zorbina, Somerset, Mr Grand, Fey Jay and the Sapphic Snapper. Plus everyone else who was also there – but didn't realise it at the time.

Some of the passages in this book appeared in an earlier form in *The Oldie*, the best magazine in the known universe.